Rethinking Children's Citizenship

Studies in Childhood and Youth

Series Editors: **Allison James**, University of Sheffield, UK, and **Adrian James**, University of Sheffield, UK.

Titles include:

Kate Bacon
TWINS IN SOCIETY
Parents, Bodies, Space and Talk

David Buckingham and Vebjørg Tingstad (*editors*)
CHILDHOOD AND CONSUMER CULTURE

Tom Cockburn
RETHINKING CHILDREN'S CITIZENSHIP

Sam Frankel
CHILDREN, MORALITY AND SOCIETY

Allison James, Anne Trine Kjørholt and Vebjørg Tingstad (*editors*)
CHILDREN, FOOD AND IDENTITY IN EVERYDAY LIFE

Manfred Liebel, Karl Hanson, Iven Saadi and Wouter Vandenhole (*editors*)
CHILDREN'S RIGHTS FROM BELOW
Cross-Cultural Perspectives

Helen Stapleton
SURVIVING TEENAGE MOTHERHOOD
Myths and Realities

Afua Twum-Danso Imoh, Robert Ame
CHILDHOODS AT THE INTERSECTION OF THE LOCAL AND THE GLOBAL

Studies in Childhood and Youth
Series Standing Order ISBN 978-0-230-21686-0 hardback
(*outside North America only*)

You can receive future titles in this series as they are published by placing a standing order. Please contact your bookseller or, in case of difficulty, write to us at the address below with your name and address, the title of the series and the ISBN quoted above.

Customer Services Department, Macmillan Distribution Ltd, Houndmills, Basingstoke, Hampshire RG21 6XS, England

Rethinking Children's Citizenship

Tom Cockburn
University of Bradford, UK

First published 2013 by
PALGRAVE MACMILLAN

Palgrave Macmillan in the UK is an imprint of Macmillan Publishers Limited, registered in England, company number 785998, of Houndmills, Basingstoke, Hampshire RG21 6XS.

Palgrave Macmillan in the US is a division of St Martin's Press LLC, 175 Fifth Avenue, New York, NY 10010.

Palgrave Macmillan is the global academic imprint of the above companies and has companies and representatives throughout the world.

Palgrave® and Macmillan® are registered trademarks in the United States, the United Kingdom, Europe and other countries.

ISBN 978–0–230–27187–6

This book is printed on paper suitable for recycling and made from fully managed and sustained forest sources. Logging, pulping and manufacturing processes are expected to conform to the environmental regulations of the country of origin.

A catalogue record for this book is available from the British Library.

A catalog record for this book is available from the Library of Congress.

10   9   8   7   6   5   4   3   2   1
22 21 20 19 18 17 16 15 14 13

To Lucy, Jack, Alice and Rory

Contents

Introduction

Perhaps, 'children's citizenship' is a misnomer, as children are in some respects 'not citizens': they have not 'come of age' and consequently do not have many of the privileges (such as full voting rights) or the obligations (such as full financial responsibility) that adults hold. The theorisation of children in political and other branches of philosophy is almost non-existent, and when they do appear, as Gordon says, "it ranges from the mildly embarrassing to the downright ridiculous" (2008, p. 165). Aristotle once mused that the term citizen was to be qualified, "as we might apply the term to children who are too young to be on the register, or to old men who have been relieved of their duties". The requirement of a 'rational autonomy' of citizens has a long history, and central to this is the required concept of competence or *capacitaire* that defines who is capable of being a citizen and excludes others who are judged to be merely dependent upon others.

To make matters worse, the age at which citizenship is possible changes radically over time and place, and is rarely agreed upon by commentators. 'Modernity' has contributed a variety of generational concepts: 'childhood', which was supposedly 'discovered' in early modern Europe (Ariés, 1973); adolescence, known at least since Goethe's *Werther*; 'senior citizens' in post-World War II prosperity. Reflecting today's 'postmodern' era, commentators refer to children as a 'special category', with different 'stages', babyhood, preschool, 'middle' childhood, 'youth', and so on. The understanding of childhood depends upon definitions of adulthood (Jenks, 1996); that is, where childhood ends adulthood begins, and *vice versa* – this involves biological, ideological and social criteria. These definitions are never explicitly stated, and often involve elements of all combined. Even in one specific society someone can be both an adult and a child, depending on the

1

circumstances in which one finds oneself. Variations, therefore, consist of biological and ever-shifting social criteria. In the field of psychology, adulthood and maturity of the human brain are supposedly reached at the age of 25 (see Baird and Fugeslang, 2004). The age at which a child will be able to take on a full adult role in society varies according to diet, the complexity of the society, the responsibilities to be borne in adult society, and so on. Today children are given some adult attributes from an early age; they eat the same foods as adults and wear similar clothes, but there are some markers of differentiation, such as education and certain topics of conversation which exclude them.

Unlike in most countries today, children in the past were formally considered to have responsibility for their crimes (*doli incapax*) for their actions in law in the same way as adults. Yet children have long (and possibly always) been considered a special category; before formal recognition of an age of criminal responsibility, children were pardoned or had their sentences commuted by the sovereign. This happened in England in 1249 to a four-year-old girl, and also in 1748 when a boy, aged ten, murdered a child of five and buried her body. The books of pardon noted: "when he was examined, he showed very little concern, and appeared easy and cheerful ... The boy was found guilty and sentenced to death; but he was respited from time to time on account of his tender years, and at length pardoned" (quoted in Bingham, 2009, p. 26). The issue of the age of responsibility partially reflects when a child should be treated as an adult in respect to the law, and the struggles for a definition reflect the social construction of childhood. For instance, in the Anglo-Saxon period in England, 25 law codes related to the responsibility and protection of children. Seven dealt with the juvenile age limit, and only one was concerned with raising the age at which children should be responsible for their actions (Crawford, 1999).

It is often assumed that in the past children reached adult status at an earlier stage than today, and it is true that, among peasants and the lower classes in the medieval period, it was the commencement of independent labour and the acquisition of manual skills that marked the transition to adulthood. This could be as young as ten or eleven. The Romans approached child/adult responsibility as defining children as those who were unable to express themselves; confusingly, the 'ability of speech' was not concerned with utterance but reflected when the speech of children is no longer just an 'imitation of adults'. According to Bracton, an English jurist reflecting the views of Thomas Aquinas, secular legislation deemed that boys under 14 and girls under 12 were not capable of criminal responsibility, as they lacked intention.

However, children under those ages continued to be punished for murder in some cases.

Another exclusion from adulthood in the medieval period was the invalidity of an oath taken by a child up to 14; his (girls' oaths were given even less weight) father could be entrusted to annul it at any time. The importance of the oath and the ability to make contracts, and thus full citizenship, will be discussed later. However, it is worth noting that in some respects children and young people in the past had to wait longer than children today. In Italian towns in the Middle Ages, young men were not allowed to undertake political life until age 25. Dante, in *Convivio*, argued that only at 25 years of age did the rational element in the human reach its development. The right to manage one's assets also varied between the ages of 15 and 25, depending on the level of training or apprenticeship that the child obtained. Later, in the sixteenth and seventeenth centuries, secular governments extended the rights of parents to legal authority over property and the income of progeny. In Protestant countries even matrimony involved parental consent. Thus, childhood dependence was extended.

Furthermore, times change, and evaluations of competencies can change also. Few today would argue that women and black people lack the competencies for full citizenship. Lord Grey, the liberal politician commenting on the 1867 Reform Bill, declared: "Negroes will be unfit to exercise political power" (quoted in Hall, 1994, p. 22).

Children gradually form a sense of perspective of themselves, themselves as a group and the perspectives of others. Children are thus able to generate shared meanings and social understandings from a relatively early age. Thus, if people in the fields of sexuality, gender, disability, ethnicity and religion are able to assert demands and take on an authoritative role and increase their claims to citizenship, then why should children not similarly be viewed as having collective interests? As Roger Smith concludes:

> While development theories are by no means uniform in their assumptions, and have themselves been criticized and revised, there is no doubt that this perspective remains at the centre of our conceptualisation of childhood, its processes and its purported trajectory, towards maturity and adulthood. Children's 'unreadiness' is thus believed to be a common feature of their lives, and one which has certain clear implications for the ways in which they ought to be treated.
>
> (2010, p. 25)

Cities

The story of citizenship is closely connected to the story of cities. It is hard to establish when the first cities developed, and when they became cities, rather than villages; possibly as early as the eighth century BC, and certainly by the third century BC, quite-developed cities existed in Egypt, the Middle East, Northern India and China. Cities really became established with the development of writing, monuments and large structures, and when the societies were subdivided into classes, occupations, priests and warriors, and were organised by kings. There was a change in the economy from agriculture to a more organised division of labour. With cities a different social organisation was required to maintain order, manage waste, provide food, manage water, and so on. By the time of Rome, the city had a clear idea of itself as a city of identification.

Europe consisted of a collection of small villages and hamlets. However, for our purposes, in terms of contemporary citizenship theory, the coming together in the fourth and third centuries BC of hamlets around the Acropolis developed into what we know as Athens. The civilisation and continuity of the Athenian city have lasted through the ages and have been handed down to us through the dramas, visual arts and the organisation of communities and political structures. Unlike the cities of China, India and later Islam, Athenians had a deep, sophisticated and nuanced notion of citizenship (Weber, 1927/1992).

There were two contrary views of the city. First, in ancient Rome you had the development of ideas of the city, such as a view of the city as a civilising experience with opportunities, optimism and sophistication. Thus, through cities civilisation can develop a sense of reason and civilisation. This is contrasted with the ignorance and squalor of the countryside. On the other hand was the view of Horace and Juvenal, of the city as a monster or predator that ate up values. Cities breed greed and corruption, and lose their identities and values, especially in the work of Juvenal. Cities also developed issues such as crime and disease. It is no surprise, then, that the ideal Roman citizen was more likely the sturdy farmer than the urbane, cultured and sophisticated city-dweller of Athens. The development of city cultures is accompanied by the development of ideas of rural ideals. Children become symbolic of the rural ideal. Smith (2007) explores these themes in antiquity; in depictions in classical art children are present as mythical people who populate scenes, along with legendary satyrs. Because of their perceived purity, innocence and liminality they were often significant in religious and ritual beliefs and ceremonies. In Ancient Egypt the infant was regarded as the God Horus and was depicted sitting on the lap of his mother (Isis). We also have the early Madonna and child iconography: Matthew 18: 3–6, 'become as little children'.

The decline of cities in Europe was quite marked after the fall of Rome with its population of a million people. In the East cities remained, especially in the Islamic world, but in the West the population in cities shrank with the decline of Roman power and did not pick up until the age of the advanced nation states in the sixteenth century and beyond. Cities were not required to collect taxes and develop a bureaucracy. With the decline of cities in Western Europe, almost all markers of 'civilising', such as writing, declined. Children during this time of city decline were often presented as 'unclean', as in medieval times. Infants were born into sin. Augustine of Hippo declared: "It is the weakness of the infant's body which is innocent, not his soul" (Wileman, 2005, p. 16).

In the East, especially in China, the city systems developed and remained urbanised; the eastern cities developed a civil service (described in England as the 'Mandarin class') with a group of people selected by competitive examinations running the Empire. From the thirteenth century in Europe the development of 'towns' and small cities expanded around trade. Here we can think of the development of trade cities in the Mediterranean, such as Genoa, Florence, Pisa, Venice and Cordoba. Max Weber (1927/1992) characterised these cities as a fusion of 'fortress and market'.

However, during the sixteenth and seventeenth centuries, cities in Western Europe increased as a site of political influence, along with the notion of the nation state. The cities became centres of influence, patronage and display; thus, Madrid developed in the centre of Spain as a statement of political control and a site of unity. Paris developed out of the discord of the religious wars as a centre of unison for the nation; St Petersburg developed as a wilful political act, and Berlin and Paris were built as architectural expressions of power. However, Antwerp, Amsterdam and London developed out of trade, so they contain fewer architectural statements of power than Berlin, Paris or Washington DC.

The growth of cities brought citizens into contact with others, as colonised people or as trade partners. Thus, citizenship is closely linked to political and national identities. In France, the *ancient regime*, as well as the early Revolution, relied on the territorial conception (*ius soli*) of nationality; whereas after ten years of war Napoleon established descent (*ius sanguinis*) as the foundation of nationality. Usually in cities death rates are higher than birth rates, and hence cities have needed to top up their populations through immigration; therefore, locally born children are the markers of continuity for cities. Historians such as Peter Laslett (1981) describe the noise and images of children running around cities, everywhere running errands, working, selling, walking and playing. With the exception of the modern western city, cities are pervaded with the energy and noise of children. We will return to the recent developments in western cities whereby children (certainly unaccompanied children) have been virtually removed from the public spaces of cities. Today, children on the streets are seen by adults and the state both as a source of concern and as a potential danger. As Udi Butler summarises with the children of Brazil:

> The feelings the category 'street children' tend to provoke in adults oscillate between two poles. On one side, they have encouraged a proliferation of charities, both national and international, that invariably portray the youngsters as helpless victims of hunger and violence... At the other extreme, in places like Brazil and other Latin American countries, for a considerable sector of the population this category is also associated with urban crime, drug taking, lack of morality and disrespect for the social order. Such perceptions have perpetuated discriminatory and abusive practices by the population in general and, more worryingly, by the state.
>
> (2008, p. 13)

This absence of children from public spaces begs the question of what has happened to children's citizenship. However, before this can be addressed it is necessary to reclaim children's right to be considered citizens. To do this it is necessary to challenge previous constructions of children that have served to exclude them from being considered worthy or capable of having responsibilities or laying claim to rights.

Why children should be considered citizens

In the 1960s and 1970s, an offshoot of the civil rights movement focussed on what David Archard (2004, p. 70) has described as the 'children's liberation movement', arguing that children should be afforded the same rights and responsibilities, and freed from oppression and discrimination along lines similar to black adults or women (see Farson, 1974). One proponent, John Holt, declared: "the rights, privileges, duties, responsibilities of adult citizens be made available to any young person, of whatever age, who wants to make use of them" (1974, p. 15). Holt's position was situated in the ferment of "an anarcho-libertarian rejection of established authority" (Archard, 2004, p. 70) that condemned the school, the nuclear family, patriarchy, and so on. In our more realistic, or cynical, times few take this approach seriously, although it is worth reflecting on the way our preconceived ideas of childhood and adulthood can be challenged. However, absolute freedom and complete protection are largely myths for adults and children alike. As we will see in this book, childhood is an ambiguous status, and children require freedom and protection at different times; similarly, adults too require freedom and protection at different times of their lives.

The importance of a focus on children's citizenship today is highly pertinent and timely. Children today, according to the majority of definitions, are citizens in some form or another, although whether they are recognised as such is discussed in only a few commentaries. Through modern times minorities have pushed at the concept of citizenship, from anti-slavery campaigners in eighteenth-century Britain, to women in the late nineteenth century, to Black and ethnic minority people in the twentieth century, to gay activists, the disability movement and now children. In the United Kingdom the concept of citizenship has changed from one of subjects to citizens almost in a seamless manner. Changes can be revolutionary or continuous; as Gramsci (1971) has pointed out with the development of counter-hegemony, even revolutionary change is preceded by a period of incremental change. However, the concept of citizenship, despite its seemingly benign image, is a highly contested concept, as Bryan Turner (1990) has argued; the history of modern citizenship is characterised by the expanding struggle and conflict for equal inclusion into society. All forms of citizenship in their historical realities are established out of conflicts, and, despite the lofty ideals of equality and fraternity, are deeply hierarchical and stratified. Indeed, much of the scholarship in the 1980s and 1990s (Mann, 1987; Turner, 1990; Harrison, 1991) centred on the erosion of the welfare state in connection with monetarist economic policies and subsequent cuts in welfare, health and education, together with the increasingly international division of labour marginalising the role of the nation state. This renewed the interest in 'rights' to welfare, access to educational institutions and health care; the very issues of social participation and social membership that preoccupied earlier sociological writing on citizenship have also led some researchers, such as Bryan Turner (1990), to return to the work of T.H. Marshall (1950/1992). Marshall's work flourished in the context of post-World War II reconstruction and social justification for welfare provision, and his ideas have their roots in the liberal and individualistic ideas of English liberalism. Marshall's essay '*Citizenship and Social Class*', first published in 1949, argued that citizenship was the principal means for resolving the contradiction between the political equality of the franchise, and the persistence of social and market inequalities. Citizenship, for Marshall, is expressed in three dimensions, namely civil, political and social rights. Civil rights are connected with issues such as freedom of speech, rights to a fair trial and equal access to the legal system; political rights apply to access to political institutions for the articulation of interests; social rights are the basis to claims for welfare in periods of unemployment, sickness and distress.

Marshall's ideas provide us with an understanding of the complexity surrounding a citizen's right to welfare, and the intricate natures of the state and the structure of British capital; they are, however, limited as a way of understanding children's relationship to citizenship. Children, as we will see in this book, have very different forms of civil, political and social rights. Conceptions of children's citizenship are shaped, and largely limited, by the belief that it is *as children* that people are defined, trained, prepared, protected and categorised for their *future* roles as citizens. This has developed in a number of complicated and at times contradictory ways.

It was not just in the form of 'future workers' that children's sense of citizenship was invoked. Ideas of what it was to be a child were also developed and they had an enormous impact on children's citizenship and personhood. Throughout history those excluded from citizenship, such as the poor, women, slaves, and so on, were associated with a 'childlike vulnerability'; for instance, historians Davidoff and Hall (1988) show that middle-class ideals of femininity, in their case, in the nineteenth century were associated as childlike, vulnerable, possessing an incomplete and underdeveloped nature and hence femininity was socially dependent and in need of protection. The feminist critique of this ideology argues that such qualities are not specific 'natures' but a socially constructed ideology which served to maintain the patriarchal domination of women by men (Gorham, 1982). But, while women and children were linked in their social dependency, women came to be characterised as inferior as a result of their sexual biology, while Viviana Zelizer (1985) notes that children were de-sexed into a gender-free zone of innocence or 'sacralized'. Sexual identity constitutes an inner core of a person and is central to a young person's notion of who they are. Under

Article 8 of the United Nations Convention on the Rights of the Child (UNCRC), which acknowledges a right to an identity, a young person has a right to a sexual minority identity (Chan, 2006). Yet discussions of children's sexualities are often clouded with anxieties that serve to define this as an issue that is often silenced. As we will see in this book, these silences usually serve to cloud possible abuses of children, while giving children only a partial or limited space to discuss an important aspect of who they are.

When do children begin to be citizens? There are some who have argued that human rights, and thus citizenship, begin at the stage of conception. Indeed, Joseph (2009) has argued that unborn children have, under the UNCRC, "absolute fetal rights"; however, this has been challenged by Penovic (2011). Most commentators accept that citizenship starts at birth, which can occur after 22 or 23 weeks' gestation, as babies have a right to life, residency and services far outweighing those of tourists visiting a country. Thus, newly born children are registered at birth and the state begins its obligations towards them, including the provision of civil and social rights.

Alderson et al. (2005) show that even newborn babies offering "cooperation with or their resistance to adult programmes illustrate the relevance of rights to them, the newest members of society, as sentient, interacting meaning makers" (p. 71). Thus, newly born babies demonstrate the agency that is necessary for citizenship associated with rights, duties and responsibilities. How do newly born babies demonstrate agency? Alderson (2008) argues that newly born babies begin to display the subtle forms of behaviour that can be 'read' as a form of language expressing their views and preference by parents and those working in hospitals. Drawing on the work of Als (1999), Alderson observes that even babies in neonatal intensive care units are able to cooperate with their 'care plans and can demonstrate various competencies'. For one six-day-old in the unit these include:

initiating breathing movements much of the time;

smooth well organised movements to protect himself;

making efforts to open his eyes in response to his mother's voice;

using strategies such as grasping and holding on, taking his hands to his face, putting his feet and hands together to calm himself.

(Alderson, 2008, p. 111)

This is important, and it is small wonder that children's rights activists emphasise the requirement of attention to children's 'evolving capacities' in the maintenance of their rights (Lansdown, 2005, p. 3). Babies and adults can work in partnership to help each other so that babies can sleep more deeply and gain strength to breathe, feed, grow and become well enough to leave the hospital, thereby reduce costs. This is important, as even young babies can contribute to the system of productivity and profit in societies by contributing to their own form of reproduction. Recognising children's contributions to their own reproduction is important. Qvortrup (2005) has shown how children make an enormous contribution to their health, welfare and education that is seldom recognised. This forms part of current opportunities for investment, future productivity and the future redemption of debts. For instance, we can see how schooling involves hard, unpaid work for long hours; this is not 'paid employment' does not mean that this work is not crucial for future economies.

Similarly, in Mayall's (2008) work with children in contemporary Britain helping in families, she notes that children see themselves as active contributors to families, from as young as five years old (p.47). They are aware of the ways in which they are inducted into family norms, and of their roles and responsibilities. Their roles are not entirely dependent upon parents and reactive to those 'with a duty over them' but rather are in actively taking part in discussion and debates about important decisions in families.

Citizenship already assumes a combination of rights, participation, belonging, fulfilment of obligations and responsibilities, and an availability of resources. Children in today's society look after themselves, look after others, are responsible for the learning they achieve at school, contribute to the production of food, and labour in the maintaining of family homes. Responsibilities are not the sole preserve of parents; children, too, have positive responsibilities that are not just the opposite of the negative terms for indigent or errant children. Recognising children's responsibilities is important; if children are caring for others, then this must be recognised and resourcing decisions must be made in the light of the young carer's full participation.

Caring and education can be understood as child labour (Larkin, 2011). Rather than belittle or challenge children's contributions, recognise them and engage children in debate over workers' rights to information, collective bargaining, and protection from unfair dismissal and fairness in working conditions. Few school children today enjoy such rights at school. Few children have a choice about where they go to school, in the political context of parental choice over their children's schooling.

It is, thus, important that a rethinking should be applied to children's citizenship. Discussions of children's citizenship to date have focussed on their 'lacking' or 'deficits' in comparison to adults. Children are either the focus of educationalists in the debates around 'citizenship education' or the topic of debates around their legal subjecthood, the need for children's protection from public harms, and the focus on children's needs for health and welfare. This book argues for a re-evaluation of the representation and self-recognition of children and for recognition that children also have political identities.

Finally, it is important to recognise that children already do participate in many aspects of their lives. Indeed, governments to date have made some acknowledgement of this in facilitating the 'participation' of children in many governance schemes, although, as will be seen towards the end of the book, these usually involve older children and are located in spaces separate from real governance decision-making.

Changes over time

Children's citizenship is shaped by a whole concatenation of factors that are too many to list exhaustively. However, there are some fundamental aspects that shape this book. The first, and arguably the paramount, element is the state; primarily, because the word *citizen* is contrasted with the word *subject*, which was associated with the condition of most in the West until relatively recently. Immanuel Kant utilised the linguistic distinction between 'citoyen', one who enjoys political rights and is able to participate in elections, and 'bourgeois', a private individual who enjoys civil rights and belonging. The term 'full' citizenship refers to those who enjoy a balance of rights and responsibilities towards the community. This can be contrasted with aliens, serfs, women and children, who remained 'passive' subjects of the state.

But also the relationship between children, the state and their families (for most of early history this means fathers) has been subjected to considerable tension, and in the last 200 years or so has been radically transformed. In England the 'Safeguarding Children' agenda, which followed the inquests into the murders of Victoria Climbié and 'Baby Peter', has highlighted the radically different nature of children's citizenship today. As will be explained in the book, ideas of citizenship have traditionally involved the arrangements between the state and adult men in the 'public realm', and the 'private realm', as feminists have long argued, was something that the state would rarely infringe upon. Current government policies and laws are drastically different from the patriarchal *paterfamilias* of, say, the Victorian age.

Citizenship in the western world has also changed considerably following World War II, the 'baby boomer' welfare state and the remodelling of the welfare state. Each country has followed slightly different paths around children's citizenship. For instance, there are different policies around education, welfare and the monitoring of children's rights. In Britain there has been a 'punitive turn' with contemporary fears about children who behave in ways not expected of them, in particular around those who offend; exemplified in the work of Muncie and Goldson (2006) and Squires and Stephens's (2005) work on 'anti-social behaviour'. In contrast, Finland sees child offenders as needing to be addressed by health services and general child welfare, not in penal institutions (Lappi-Seppala, 2006, p. 194). Skevik (2003) also notes that "Norway has a policy towards parents and children; the UK has a policy towards families" (p. 436).

Second, citizenship has been shaped by the changes in the shape, content and ideologies of the family. Most notable here has been the revolution in gender over the last century. Mary O'Brien (1981) described marriage as an institution created by men to ensure the certainty of men's fertility and later the genetic transmission of property. Social life requires some form of political organisation because there is a requirement to *protect the family*, that is, the family as the primary and inevitable form of human association. Additionally, the family as a source of association displays at a macro-level all aspects of political organisation. Aristotle observed: "For every household is ruled by its senior member, as by a king, and the offshoots too, because of their blood relationship, are ruled in the same way" (*Politics*, 1252b15). In addition to protecting families, political organisation is required to protect private property. A theme running through this book is that women and children over time have been placed in distinctly separate spaces in Northern hemisphere countries (Burman, 2008); thus, discussions of patriarchy cannot be separated from citizenship and family.

Third, the nature of citizenship is shaped by ideas of place, nation, race and ethnicity. For citizenship to work, especially the form of citizenship based upon democracy, it is necessary for all to have sufficient trust in other citizens. The notion of trust is something that concerned modern thinkers, such as Hobbes, Locke and Rousseau, who wanted to understand why people formed political communities. It is necessary for all individuals to obey decisions undertaken by majorities;

we need to have trust in government to be a legitimate arbiter between disputes; we need to trust that governments will hold elections and keep promises to the electorate; if there are welfare benefits, then the rich will have to have sufficient trust and commitment in those whom they are 'giving to'. As Richard Bellamy has said: "Democracy assumes a people, or a *demos*, who feel sufficient solidarity with each other to accept collective decisions and enough mutual trust to cooperate" (2008, p. 70). One of the strongest ways of developing trust and feelings of solidarity is the forming of national identity that features the cohesive properties of shared history, culture and nation (Miller, 1995).

It was Raymond Williams (1988) in his *Keywords* who noted that the word 'nation' was not used in English until the thirteenth century, and then it was used to refer to a racial group, rather than a politically organised entity. Even in the eighteenth century it was more common to talk of 'realm', 'country' or 'kingdom' than nation; however, by the nineteenth century group rights to a 'nation' were becoming firmly established across Europe. In the nineteenth century there were continuing links of 'nation' to 'race', although in the twentieth century 'nationalism', of countries like India, contained many 'races'. The development of the French Civil Code in 1803 was a decisive break from the *ancien régime* and its focus on long-term residence as the foundation of rights and duties became that of just of place of birth (Weil, 2002). Thus, for many European countries there was an emphasis on parentage over place of birth. In this way notions of nation are closely interlinked with ideas of the family, parentage and childhood.

Jurgen Habermas (1994) argued that nationalist discourse was important at the time of the French and American revolutions as a way of subverting privilege and introducing egalitarian citizenship, and enabled the consolidation of nation states in the nineteenth century. However, it was only something partial, which becomes a hindrance in developing citizenship. Nationalism is a cultural construct, not necessarily a political one, and could not form the basis of including and binding together people from a variety of cultural backgrounds. Habermas (1994) talks of a post-national notion of 'constitutional patriotism' in which all members of a community need to participate and show loyalty to the government. He argues that it is not healthy to have groups of people outside communities without the opportunity to take part in decision-making about a community's future. Habermas is thinking of migrants, but children, too, are in reality largely left out of these structures. Not all children can take part in processes of decision-making, but the solution is not to prevent *all* from doing so. Today, the nature of multicultural societies, and the changing ethnic and religious compositions of developed nations have brought new tensions and dimensions to how the state regulates childhood. The nature of the state has also changed as it adjusts to a globalised world. Its relationship to supranational organisations, such as the European Union or the United Nations, has altered the relationship between the subject and state, as citizens can lay claim to new 'rights' codified in the European Convention on Human Rights. With the exception of the United States of America and Somalia, all governments are signatories to the UNCRC and other forms of international monitoring that bring into focus the nature of children's citizenship in all modern states today.

Beyond liberal citizenship

This book explores and critiques what I call 'liberal' ideas of citizenship. By that I mean a form of citizenship that is premised upon and assumes an autonomous individual freely operating in the world without constraint. This, of course, caricatures liberalism. However, over the coming chapters I will argue that this precondition is unrealistic, in that all people, including adults, are interlinked, interdependent and reliant on others. It also, as an ideology, excludes others such as children, and places children as an 'other' that is defined entirely as linked, dependent, reliant and constantly under the influences of other people and thus incapable of making contributions to society. There are further problems with the liberal approach as it is used as a form of ideology. Western countries, especially English-speaking societies, underpinned by liberal democratic principles respect the autonomy of individuals contingent upon their ability to be self-sufficient. It is this conception of autonomy and independence that underpins the 'New Conventional Wisdom' in social policy, whereby families and individuals are clustered as 'essential competitive assets' (Buck, 2005, p. 11).

However, this is a caricature, as Stephen Macedo (1990) optimistically declared of liberal citizenship that "the benefits of private citizenship are not to be sneezed at: they place certain basic human goods (security, prosperity and freedom) within the grasp of nearly all, and that is nothing less than a fantastic human achievement" (p. 39). Radical or left-leaning liberals go further and try to theorise a world where social inequalities are ameliorated or overcome; John Rawls (1972), in his influential *A Theory of Justice*, sets out his 'original position' in which he devises a scenario where everyone seeks to determine, through their rationality, how to maximise their utility. Individuals are placed behind the 'veil of ignorance' (Rawls, 1972, p. 118), so that no one knows their status, their talents, their psychological make-up or the economic or political situation that they are in. Faced with this uncertain scenario, individuals would choose two principles of justice. The first is that everyone is entitled to the same extensive range of basic liberties. The second is that social inequalities are arranged through positions in which they are open to all and to the greatest advantage of those who are least advantaged (as anybody could be least advantaged). This would allow, Rawls would argue, a fairer world where all are able to achieve prosperity and success in life, and those with the least advantage would have some form of favour to compensate for their unequal situation. However, as Kymlicka (2002) notes, Rawls maintains the paramount importance of equal liberty over equal opportunity, which in turn, has precedence over equal resources. There is no radical redistribution of wealth and resources in society, and what is permissible are those things that ultimately benefit the well-off (Kymlicka, 2002).

Bojer (2000) notes that, although Rawls does not refer specifically to children, it is possible to treat children potentially as complete human beings and independent subjects of social justice. Rawls (1993) argued that: "we say that a person is someone who can be a citizen, that is, a normal and fully cooperating member of society over a complete life" (p. 18). Bojer (2005) argues that childhood is a necessary stage that all human beings have to go through to reach adulthood, where they can both judge what is good and have powers of 'reason'. The conditions in which children live will have an impact on their lives in adulthood. Under harsh economic circumstances in childhood they will have fewer opportunities to make their own decisions and improve their welfare when they become adults. This cannot be justified, because of the unfairness of the initial position; furthermore, children cannot choose their parents. However, as Olk has noted, pointing out the relevance of a good childhood to later life, "her argumentation is principally future oriented and fails to justify a good childhood as intrinsically valuable" (Olk, 2009, p. 197).

Other critiques of liberal theories of citizenship have come from communitarians. Communitarians argue that the individual does not exist prior to the community in which they live. Liberal forms of citizenship do not consider issues such as loyalty, duties and responsibilities to the community. Indeed, liberal forms of citizenship, communitarians argue, allow individuals to pursue their individual goals at the expense of the wider responsibilities to the community. Communitarians draw on the work of Hegel to question the attempts by liberal writers, such as Locke and Kant, to speak universally about the philosophy and morality of individualism that are not dependent upon social context for their authenticity. Sandel (1984) similarly attacks the liberal view that community is formed through the process of individuals forming associations independent of the community. It is the community that gives individuals the ability to deliberate, choose and reflect, rather than the 'unencumbered self' (Sandel, 1984, p. 85). In this sense, communitarians argue, it is not the community that conflicts with the individual but the community that gives the individual the meaning of the self.

More recently, Amitai Etzioni has taken up the communitarian agenda, influential in the 1990s and feeding into the philosophy of the Clinton administration and the 'Third Way' in the UK. In *The Spirit of Community* (1995) he argues that the balance of individual rights and responsibilities has lost its balance in favour of the former. This, Etzioni argues, is because the connection between rights and responsibilities has been broken, with ideas of the community being lost to individuals claiming their rights with little or no regard for responsibilities. Because of the short-term political and electoral benefit from the granting of rights, there has been a tendency by governments to offer rights, which has resulted in a 'rights inflation'. The western world has been quick to offer rights, which has led to spectacular growth and a concomitant rise in environmental risks and a threat to the safety of the world, through crime and terrorism, due to the enforcing of rights and a weakening of responsibilities.

The problem with the communitarianism that Etzioni and others offer is that the decline in citizenship in liberal societies may have less to do with moral and cultural decline and have more to do with the political failures of a system of participation that relies on distant 'representative' political systems and a narrow, market-driven privacy of individuals. Either way, children have not been able to participate in communities because of the way in which they have been understood and treated, as *not* being part of communities other than as appendages to families. However, as we will see, this is a relatively recent representation of children, and is challenged in this book.

Structure of the book

The book is structured into three parts. Part I presents a historical discussion of the initial theorising of citizenship. It traces the early discussions of political theory, natural rights and democracy and the evolution of modern forms of citizenship. Nevertheless, these theories continued to actively exclude children from these discussions. The chapters discuss these and other forms of exclusion in their historical context. Part II looks at the development of more inclusive notions of 'rights' and the effect this may have on ideas of citizenship. In particular, it looks at the internationalisation of cosmopolitanism and rights leading up to the ratification of the United Nations Convention on the Rights of the Child. However, the discussion notes the persistence of factors excluding children, the resistance to children's rights and the limitations of the rights agenda. Finally, in Part III, the last two chapters discuss recent political and social theory and the implications of this for theorising children's citizenship. They call for a rethinking of citizenship away from liberal individualist notions to one that emphasises social interdependence and calls for a concomitant re-evaluation of our public spaces to enable the intersectionality of children's identities and a safe and constructive way for the dialogue and dialectics of generation to be facilitated.

Chapter 1 sets the ball rolling by discussing the context of Ancient Greek thought and the theorising of citizenship. The main thinkers discussed in this chapter are Aristotle and Plato, and the issues introduced include early ideas of the state and citizenship; the distinction between private and public worlds; the role of wider civil society associations; who was included and excluded from citizenship and why; and the nature and form of education as a form of social preparation. The chapter then looks at the role and development of Roman law and the beginning of natural rights theory and the nascent ideas of cosmopolitanism. It also discusses the way children were presented and protected by the Roman state's legal system. The final part of the chapter covers the period from late antiquity to the end of the medieval period and also the belief in equality of all before God, but within clear patriarchal structures.

Chapter 2 looks at the development of 'modern' political thought from the classic English 'social contract' theories put forward by Thomas Hobbes and John Locke. The 'social contract' is that which citizens make between themselves and government. The crucial argument in this section is the way others are excluded from this contract, such as women, slaves or children, who were presented as passive and irrational. For women and children, overall responsibility lay with husbands and fathers as only they were the writers of the 'social contract'. The next part takes up the theme of challenges to sovereignty and the foundation of human rights thinking. The section explores the work of Rousseau and the 'general will'. For Rousseau, the state of nature consisted of innocent human beings living harmoniously; with the introduction of private property and power, the beginnings of corruption can be discerned. Unlike previous thinkers, Rousseau had thought deeply about children and childhood in his political theory. Indeed, one of his seminal books, *Emile*, focussed on the nature and type of education that should be offered to boys and girls in preparation for their citizenship. The topic of education forms the basis for the next section of the chapter. Following Rousseau, the two great political revolutions of the eighteenth century occurred in France and the USA, where writers such as Thomas Paine advocated a system of 'rights'. However, in the revolutions the 'rights' only applied to propertied men and did not apply to women, slaves or children. The section ends by introducing some of the challenges to the 'social contracts' between men by feminist-influenced thinkers such as Mary Wollstonecraft and John Stuart Mill.

Chapter 3 develops from Chapter 2 under the context of the industrial urbanisation that occurred during the nineteenth century. These rapid changes brought about a radical rethinking of society and culture. The period saw the development of organised feminist and working-class movements. The process of industrialisation had profound implications for the lives of children. First, children moved from being 'workers' and producers to being consumers and the targets of education. There ensued debates around the nature and type of education being developed. On the one hand, children were assumed to be passive, irrational and in need of 'civilisation', as presented in Rousseau's *Emile*. However, in the early nineteenth century European thought was developing a new conception of childhood and education based around a more competent notion of children. The leading writers, such as Pestalozzi and Froebel, became associated with (very small) social movements, such as the *kindergarten* movement in the nineteenth century. However, progressive educational theories remained marginal to British educational policies. The chapter charts the development of contemporary education, employment and family policies that forms the basis of 'social rights' in the twentieth century and the construction of children as passive, vulnerable and in need of wider state protection.

The final chapter of Part I is dominated by the ideas of T.H. Marshall, who divided citizenship into three aspects: possessing civic, political and social rights. Interestingly, Marshall still made virtually no reference to children, other than their requirement of education. The key moment is the post-World War II welfare state, in which the role of children and their welfare was central. The chapter is divided into sections covering the early part of the twentieth century up to World War II, the Beveridge report and the development of the post-war welfare state; the final section looks at theoretical responses to the welfare state by T.H. Marshall. However, a focus on children developed in different ways in Europe with the rise of fascism and communism, as well as social democracies. Interestingly, and pertinently, the period was also characterised by the development of professional power and the conflation of child welfare with maternity and 'maternalism'. The chapter ends with a discussion of the fragmentation of 'social citizenship' after the oil crisis of 1973 and the rise of 'neoliberalism', alongside an introduction of a children's rights agenda.

Part II continues this discussion of 'rights' and their applicability to children. It looks at the limitations of bestowing rights onto children. The individualistic assumptions of human rights and the persistence of representations of children as 'vulnerable', 'in need' and 'incompetent' are all discussed. The relationship between children's rights and their application in families and by the state is examined.

Chapter 6 addresses the internationalisation of rights and citizenship. It does so by marking the development of supranational structures, such as the League of Nations, the United Nations and the European Union. The chapter concludes with a discussion on the limitations of cosmopolitanism in the expression of international rights for children and some important steps that are needed to ensure social justice and fuller citizenship for children across the world.

The final part of the book is divided into two sections. Chapter 7 discusses 'new' perspectives and ideas of citizenship, although these are built upon ideas of feminism, post-colonialism and globalisation discussed in previous chapters. The chapter draws on recent sociological theory that recognises the complexities around social inequalities and everyday lives. Specifically, the chapter looks at ideas of generation, 'group rights' and a movement away from individualistic theories of citizenship. Of particular note is the 'ethic of care' propounded by feminists as an interesting alternative or addition to the individualistic, 'natural rights' approach advanced by liberal political theorists.

The final chapter, Chapter 8, concludes the book with an urgent plea for a re-evaluation of public spaces of citizenship. It begins by questioning adultist assumptions of civil society that actively exclude and belittle the contributions of children. It then goes on to critique current 'citizenship education' approaches in schools to widen out consideration of citizenship to other spheres of children's lives, such as the home, peers and communities. Through the use of recognition theory

(Honneth, 1995), new challenges to public attitudes and discrimination against children need to be confronted so that children's 'voices' can be expressed, listened to and engaged with. This creates a series of opportunities for dialogue and debate to happen within and between generations. A wider recognition of children's contributions is necessary to enable children to practise and live out democratic citizenship in as full a way as possible.

Part I

1
Children and Citizenship in the Classical Period

Greece

In Ancient Greece half the population was under 15, and archaeological digs have unearthed toys that reflect our modern understanding of childhood, such as rattles, tops, dolls and other items, as well as evidence of richer families having pets. On the other hand, many babies died as infants, and the reluctance to name babies attests to the emotional distance that characterises societies that have a high infant mortality rate. Furthermore, most Greek cities adopted the practice of swaddling children up to the age of two. However, Lawrence Stone's (1977) hypothesis of the high infant mortality rate resulting in the unwillingness of parents to give love and attention to infant children is to be treated with suspicion. Louise Pratt (2007), in a strong example of affective relationships, discusses the beautiful scene in *Iliad* 6 in which Hektor says farewell to his wife Andromache and their baby Astyanax as he prepares to return to battle. In the scene Hektor is a loving father and "an individual devoted to the care of others, so deeply invested in others that he sacrifices his own life in their support" (Pratt, 2007, p. 27). Yet ancient Greek parenthood was nevertheless considerably different from that of today. As Gillian Clark observes:

> Arranged marriage, early childbearing, painful and dangerous childbirth, the abandonment of newborn babies, the practices of swaddling and wet-nursing can all be used to argue that parents and children were at best unlikely to form a strong emotional bond.
>
> (1994, p. 7)

A distinction must be made between rich, aristocratic children and those of the peasant classes: the latter were given more free rein and were expected to work in the fields from a young age. For upper-class children, as we will see, the foundation of democratic societies constrained children into the home, and for aristocratic girls the confinement into the home would last into their marriage, which could happen as early as age 13.

The *polis* of Ancient Athens was essentially an adult male association, and the citizen body consisted of men who would join together in making and carrying out decisions. All male citizens who participated were, in principle, equal; however, it was clear that citizenship, in this classical sense, was based upon social class (as it was open only to aristocratic men) and also 'race', as 'foreigners' were excluded from citizenship, even though foreign-born people far outnumbered Athenian citizens. Ironically, political equality in Athens enabled the establishment of an empire that produced tyranny abroad in its vassal states. There are parallels with the European democracies of the late nineteenth and early twentieth centuries, which had defeated Bonapartism, held in check Czarist absolutism, and created a flowering of artistic and intellectual culture, yet cruelly dominated and exploited the 'dominions' throughout the world.

Central to Athenian organisation were the *phrateres*, which designated a non-familial type of 'brotherhood'. These brotherhoods were open to all 'Athenian men'; all male citizens belonged to a phratry, and the phratry dominated social life. It is illustrative to reflect on the way young males were admitted to the phratry, as it forms the germ of the gradual, or staged, introduction of children (specifically boys) to full citizenship. At an early age a boy's father introduced him ceremonially to the *phrateres*; again at adolescence he was presented ritualistically with shorn hair and was then voted by the *phrateres* as a phratry member. The phratry was involved in the main stages of a man's life, including betrothal. There was a gradual absorption of the young male into the 'public sphere'. The *ephebe* was the first time a young man was separated from his family and placed with a company of peers for an extended period of time. The young men were split from the mature fighting men and posted in the second year to outlying borders of the state. They wore black cloaks that marked them apart from other fighting men. On completion of a young man's two-year service he joined the ranks as a reserve *hoplite*, or citizen foot soldier, alongside other adult citizens. As Beaumont (2000) has noted:

> Athenian male youth's development shows quite clearly that no abrupt dividing line existed between childhood and adult

manhood...roughly between the ages of 13 or 14 and 20 – seem to have constituted an adolescent phase of ambiguous, liminal social status when the youth was considered to be neither truly child or man. (p. 47)

This type of brotherhood association was common in the Greek world, such as the militaristic masculine mess groups of the different *syssitia* in Sparta. The Spartan system had similar ritualistic 'stages' at seven, at 12 (when boys were famously taught Spartan self-reliance and survival skills), and at 20 when they joined the *syssitia*, until the age of 30. After that men were still required to eat with the *syssitia*, although beyond their fighting best. These two forms of brotherhood are illustrative of the staged nature of boys' and men's involvement in citizenship, although in the case of Athens the stages were crafted to fit into a 'democratic' citizenship.

In Athens full participative citizenship was made up of a variety of what we would now call civil society associations, such as religious guilds, drinking groups, traders and philosophical schools. The associations created the sense of community and belonging that was deemed essential to the operation of the *polis*, beyond kinship ties. Interestingly, Greek thought understood freedom, not according to the individual, in contrast to the social contract thinkers we will discuss in the next chapter, but as public and linked it to speech and public action. Perhaps resembling the 'positive' forms of liberty discussed by Rousseau, again this theme will be discussed further in the next chapter.[1] For Ancient Greeks, a good society was one in which arguments were settled through consensus (*harmonoia*); they proceeded from tightly knit communities where public good was placed above private advantage.

While the networks of associations were the social glue of public life and formed the basis of participative democracy, the family remained a key institution. Families in Greece tended to be nuclear and monogamous, providing children for the new citizenry. There were strong rules for citizenship based upon marriage between two Athenian citizens and they excluded foreign-born partners and children from other types of liaison. Thus, citizenship was controlled and the transmission of property stabilised through the familial structure.

Another function of the family in Athenian social values was the control of women and children. Indeed, gender, as well as age, defined citizenship. There are many good commentaries on the position of women in Greek thought (see, for instance, Okin, 1980), but few have focussed on children. Aristocratic women in Athens were citizens, in contrast to foreign women, but lacked independent status. Women and children were explicitly proscribed from entering into any transactions (other than personal items) and could not own property. In this context Ada Cohen (2007) reflects: "women's and children's shared 'minority' status is often invoked, as is their shared subjection to discrimination in the majority of known societies, where patriarchal values dominate" (p. 2). At all times women and children were to be under the protection of a *kyrios*, or a guardian, and with few exceptions were under the legal protection of the family head. For aristocratic women and children the coming of democracy meant the locking out from participation in democracy. While in contemporary agrarian societies there may have been some form of mistrust or devaluing of women and children by men, these were held in check at least by the need for labour in the fields that was undertaken by women and children. With the beginning of 'civilized' urban life, women's and young children's lives were confined to the house, and increased wealth 'liberated' women and children from domestic chores (usually at the expense of slaves and later bonded or waged labour). The layout of Athenian houses was segregated into public rooms for men, and women's and children's rooms, which in larger houses were separated from the street entrance, usually around the courtyard, thus instigating an architectural public/private split within the domestic home.

The development of the famous Greek philosophy encouraged the belief that women and children were less endowed with reason than men. As Aristotle states: "the deliberative faculty is not present at all in a slave, in the female it is inoperative, in the child underdeveloped." Thus the confinement of slaves, women and children to the private sphere is 'justified' only through the deployment of the concept of reason as a higher, more mature, Greek and male characteristic. It is interesting to note that the Greek word for child, *pais*, can also mean slave, thereby a similarity of the characteristic is shown. As Cohen has argued: "In Greek antiquity the word *pais* was ambiguous, sometimes used to contrast child with adult and other times child with adolescent" (2007, p. 4).

There was little difference between boys' and girls' lives up until the age of seven; they were confined to the women's quarters of houses; but then boys would commence their education. Their mother and her retinue instructed girls in preparation for marriage, but this education was usually quite rudimentary, as preservation from the world was the primary concern. Sophocles wrote: "young girls, in my opinion have the sweetest existence known to mortals in their fathers' homes, for innocence keeps children safe and happy always" (Sophocles, *Tereus*, fr. 583).

For boys education was vital, as the ability for male citizens to read and write was taken for granted. Derek Heater characterises Greek education into two forms: one "encouraged individual political and forensic skill, notably rhetoric and judgement, the other emphasised training, indoctrination even, of the youth to obedience to the laws, submission of government and a readiness to defend the state by recourse to arms" (1990, p. 6). Thus, the soldier and the deliberator were seen as mutually reinforcing aspects of citizenship, both requiring a system of education. Athenian law regulated the education of boys by specifying the opening hours of schools, the numbers of boys permitted and the ages of pupils, and regulated the supervision of teachers. Although it was probable that formal education only affected a small proportion of adolescents, it seems that there was concern for the moral protection of children from teachers, who were generally disliked. Instruction was provided in the fields of literature, physical education and music to equip aristocratic young people for the *gymnasion* and *symposium*. The importance of the arts and culture in Greece was highly prized; the word *paideia* includes not just the education of children but also their lifelong 'cultivation', whereby the importance of physical prowess and skills in public speaking was established. Towards the end of the fourth century there was a standard and universal (physical) youth training for all young men under 18, not just aristocratic young men. Further developments in education at this stage enabled a flowering of scientific knowledge, especially in the field of medicine and in general culture.

However, for our own debates around citizenship, the Ancient Greeks provided two of the thinkers with the greatest influence on modern western political theory. The work of Aristotle we will discuss soon, but before him was Plato.

Plato

In many respects Plato has a very bad name in political philosophy. Karl Popper (1966), in his *Open Society and its Enemies*, cast Plato as the originator of totalitarianism. Indeed, his advocating for an ascetic and collective life, guided by 'objective' experts, is an anathema to today's material, individualistic and cynical culture in modern democracies, although Platonic thought is perhaps behind the tendency in Western Europe of consolidating democracies in the current economic climate with 'technocrats' gleaned from the banking sectors. Plato's strand of thought is important to understanding his warning of the dangers of hysteria and mass ignorance and the requirement for education. The centrality of the role of education in Plato's writing as 'the first stage' resonates through political theory across the ages. It also places children and children's relationship to citizenship at the heart of understanding broader aspects of citizenship in both theory and practice. In Plato's ideal city (Kallipolis), he advocated for sexual equality, the deprivation of private property and the abolition of private families, to the point where children are produced by couples planned by older guardians and thus will not know who their biological fathers and mothers are and will be raised communally. However, this was no proto-communist and feminist text, for it was restricted to the class of guardians. Indeed, Plato, along with many of his contemporaries, considered children (together with women and slaves) as prone to the tyrannies of their desires. In *The Republic* Plato argues:

> the greatest number and variety of desires and pleasures and pains is generally to be found in children and women and slaves, and in the less respectable majority of so-called free men. (431C)

What we know of Plato's thought in seminal texts on politics and citizenship, such as the *Republic*, is that it is very much shaped by the death of Plato's mentor Socrates. Socrates was convicted, sentenced to execution, imprisoned and put to death by democratic citizen–persecutors on the grounds of, opposite in terms of the subject of this book, corruption of youth. Following Socrates, Plato's highest political goal was the psychological unity, harmony, flourishing or happiness (*eudaimonia*) of each citizen. This was to be achieved by cultivating the main virtues (*arete*) of wisdom, courage, self-discipline and justice. These virtues could not be separated from each other and all depended on wisdom, or knowledge. Knowledge could not be derived from rhetoric or democratic debate but was a matter of genuine expertise.

Plato, then, had a distrust of democracy, and argued that democracy causes the virtues of wisdom, courage, self-discipline and justice to be underdeveloped. There is a tendency for tyranny to lie at its heart, ready to manifest itself in times of crisis. Individuals are capable of tyranny, and Plato presents metaphors of the struggles between human, Lion and Beast to illustrate how these passions are best controlled through reason. Feelings contrary to harmony, such as indignation or appetite, are not to be controlled through force or suppression but, rather, shaped through education. Plato's educational writings were formed by his debates with and opposition to Sophist teachers who simply advocated for the art of rhetoric as a means of raising moral standards, as well as a political device. However, the 'sophistry' that has come to be used to characterise the dangers of 'sleight of hand' oratory became apparent in the Peloponnesian War of 404 BC and the defeat of Athens at the hands of the Spartans. Plato's writings, and later those of Aristotle, established the urgent need for attention to programmes of socialisation in Greek life. Thus, in the *Republic*, the political philosophy is closely linked with that of education. Plato was deeply concerned with the corruption and political instability of the age, and argued for a more effective and direct form of education from the state itself, rather than leaving the education of the young to private duties of families. Later, in the twentieth century, the philosopher R.G. Collingwood, a passionate believer in home schooling, declared that one of Plato's biggest crimes was "to have planted on the European world the crazy idea that education ought to be professionalised" (quoted in Inglis, 2009, p. 18). Thus, the *Republic* provided a distinct blueprint for the education of the ruling class, who were to learn self-sacrifice, and the education of the ruled, who were to learn obedience.

Concern with education was not necessarily new; practices of instilling control of the basic instincts in children must have been widespread, for Plato appeals to this as a principle underlying hierarchical governance and standards to be upheld in adult life. In the *Republic*, Socrates (according to Plato) argues:

> And this is plainly the intention of the law, in the support it gives to all citizens, and the control we exercise over children, not letting them run free till we have established some kind of constitutional government in them, and have educated the best in them to be their guardian and ruler and to take over from the best in us: then we give them their freedom.
>
> (590e–591a)

In this sense the theme of the *Republic* is concerned with cultivating maturity as a normative ideal. Much of the *Republic* details the form of Greek education and culture that will ensure that people behave justly by checking their appetites and do not experience lust, arrogance, greed or indignation.

So, does everybody achieve a full sense of justice? For Plato, the rational element of most people, including most adult men, is beyond them. He states:

> the simple and moderate desires, guided by reason and right judgement and reflection, are to be found in a minority who have the best natural gifts and best education... This feature too you can see in our state, where the desires of the less respectable majority are controlled by the desires and the wisdom of the superior minority.
>
> (*The Republic* 431 C–D)

Thus, Plato provides an exclusive, or even elitist, theory of citizenship and argues against the democratic assumption that all citizens are capable of making political decisions, as ordinary people's reason is too weak and they are liable to give way to their appetites. Political rule is necessary as most people are incapable of, or deficient in, making fully reasoned decisions. Plato's democracy is thus very limited; few adult men make the grade for competent citizenship, as most fall short of the requisite skills and degree of rationality. Few today will advocate for this as the model to spread democratic well-being across all sectors of society.

Aristotle

More influential towards modern theorists of citizenship are the works of Aristotle, who, according to Faulks (2000), "represents the first systematic attempt to develop a theory of citizenship" (p. 14). Aristotle, more than Plato, emphasised the role of participation as an element of citizenship and the good life. Aristotle's own background, his role as a resident alien in Athens, perhaps explains his more inclusive emphasis on more direct political participation. However, people played the roles appropriate to what Aristotle believed to be their natural qualities. Thus, only some qualified as *polites*, or citizens.

The characteristics of being human are an important element in Aristotle's writing. In his *Ethics* he outlines that humans differ from most animals because they are in essence a 'political animal', or, as one of his commentators Jonathan Barnes (1982) puts it, a 'social animal'. The crucial point is that humans are gregarious creatures and differ from other social animals, such as bees, ants and cranes, in that they can distinguish between good and bad, just and unjust, and so on. This defining characteristic of humanity resonates through historical debates around childhood age at which children come to have this function, or even whether children are born with an innate function to tell right from wrong. For Aristotle, the prime determinant of the capacity to determine right from wrong lies with the possession of reason and the power of thought. Our intellect is 'the divine within us' and is our sovereign and best element. It is the use of the intellect that, Aristotle argued, formed the foundation of flourishing for humans.

Aristotle outlined his theory of citizenship most systematically in his *Politics*. For Aristotle, a citizen is "defined by nothing else so well as by participation in judicial functions and in political office". It was this performance of citizenship that rested as the fundamental aspect of being human. The state's affairs are run directly by citizens, who have defined duties: notably, financial, military and to be part of a judiciary. Aristotle produced a taxonomy of political constitutions that boiled down to three types: monarchy, aristocracy and democracy. The former two would be appropriate if they were able to produce individuals or families who possess more excellent qualities. However, the preferred form was democracy, since acting collectively is better than individual action. Furthermore, the best form of political association would be limited to the ideal of a small city-state (*polis*), which would avoid the disadvantage of political factions that could destroy the good life, as Aristotle had witnessed firsthand at the court of Philip of Macedon.

Another crucial element of Aristotle's citizenship was the principle of liberty, which conforms to the principle of living as one wishes and to "rule and be ruled and turn around". The principles around liberty form the basis of his argument for private property; it is important that this should not be owned by the state, although the state is there to ensure that property is properly governed and put to public use. In this sense, Aristotle's notion of liberty could be characterised as 'negative' in the sense advanced by Berlin (1959).

Although the role of the state is limited in economic affairs, in Aristotle's view it has an important and defining role in social affairs. Most fundamentally, the state is to intervene in the lives of children. Like Plato, Aristotle identifies the role of the state as superseding that of families in the best interests of children. Thus, Aristotle advocated that the state should "consider how the children who are reared are to have the best physique, . . . pay attention to sexual union, determining when and between what sort of people marital relations may exist". He did not go as far as Plato in collectivising childcare, but it was, by today's standards, very interventionist. Education must "be a public one, not the private affair which it now is, each man looking after his own children and teaching them privately whatever private curriculum he thinks they ought to study. In matters that belong to the public, training for them must be the public's concern. And it is not right either that any of the citizens should think that he should belong to just himself; he must regard all citizens as belonging to the state, for each is a part of the state; and the responsibility for each part naturally has regard to the responsibility for the whole" (1337a27–33).

Thus, the liberties of individuals are to be curtailed by the state, leading some commentators, as with Plato, to ask questions about Aristotle being a precursor for totalitarianism. It is also clear that such liberties and citizenship are not to be applied to the majority of the population. The moral virtue (*arete*) of slaves is only minimally required to perform the tasks of the master; those virtues in artisans were similarly to operate only at a minimal level. Within households the male head of household is the source of virtue for his wife, children and slaves. Women, in Aristotle's writing, have no liberty, and justifications for the exclusion of slaves and artisans form large chunks of the *Politics*, especially in Book 1; a human who "belongs by nature not to himself but to someone else, is slave by nature". Immaturity and infirmity should bar people from the political class, and artisans have neither the aptitude nor the leisure to possess true citizenship qualities. However, it is the 'natural' capacities, or, more accurately, incapacities that disbar people from citizenship. Aristotle argues:

> For rule of free over slave, male over female, man over boy, are all different, while parts of the soul are present in each case, the distribution is different. Thus the deliberative faculty in the soul is not present at all in a slave; in a female it is present but ineffective, in a child present but undeveloped.
>
> (*Politics*, 1259b32–1260a14)

In the *Physics* Aristotle states: "What then, is growing? Not that from which it arose but that to which it tends" (1931b16–17). He then uses the example of the acorn and the oak tree to argue that the explanation for the acorn is the oak tree it becomes. Thus, applying this to human beings, children are what they are to become and not what they are; a characteristic of childhood that resonates today with our current acceptance of developmental psychology, or in Prout and James's (1990) challenge to children as *beings* rather than *becomings*. For Aristotle, the child is incomplete, has an inability to control his body and lacks the ability to do good deeds. In the *Nicomachean Ethics* Aristotle writes that a child lacks the capacity to choose; he is absorbed in sensual gratification and is incapable of noble action. In short, childhood was the lowest stage in human life.

According to John Rawls (1972), the *Aristotelian principle* is one in which, other things being equal, human beings enjoy the exercise of their real capacities, and this enjoyment increases the more the capacity is realised, or the greater the complexity. The more proficient someone is at something, the better they will enjoy doing it. Also, if someone is good at both chess and draughts, they will enjoy chess more because of the greater skill and capacity. This leads to a contradiction in our views of children; how do they develop capacities of reason or deliberation if they are not able to exercise it?

Roman citizenship and children

Greek ideas formed the fundamental principles and established the parameters of the theoretical debates around citizenship. The influence of Roman ideas on contemporary western citizenship is just as fundamental, but, rather than dealing with abstract ideas, as Greek thought had done, the Romans introduced a system of laws and codes that still hold influence today. Theorists today contrast this with the obligations-centred practice of citizenship performed by Greeks, in which responsibilities of participation were an important element of pride. As Faulks has observed about the Athenian ideal:

> Thus citizenship was obligations-based rather than rights-based, since the close identification individuals felt between their own destinies and that of their community rendered the notion of asserting one's rights against the interests of the wider community as inconceivable. Obligations generally did not take the form of statutory duties. They were perceived by citizens as opportunities to be virtuous and to serve the community.
>
> (2000, p. 17)

Unlike their Athenian counterparts, Romans never had as much influence over political decision-making. One historian of the Roman period has argued that childhood was not seen to be as important as the older years from puberty that affected the type and quality of the Roman citizen; thus there is a neglect of sources for younger children (Dixon, 1992). The theoretical literature thus dismisses Rome as the site of *paterfamilias*, and commentaries tend to look at the legal issues around inheritance, rather than the more interesting political contexts, family relationships and legal ideas that present a far more nuanced view of citizenship. Faulks has noted that "the liberal discourse of natural rights drew inspiration from the universalistic tradition of Roman natural law" (2000, p. 15). The introduction of natural rights is not entirely academic, as children in Roman legal discourse had specific rights under law for reciprocal affections (*pietas*), parents' care and a share of property – they also had responsibility for care of their parents. As more recent historical research, such as that of Rawson (2003), has noted: "there was no sharp distinction between public and private – where slaves, clients, and patrons mingled and often shared domestic and public space" (p. 3).

Children of citizens in the Roman Empire became an important resource, and the importance of marriage, family and an expanding notion of citizenship established important rights. Augustus's legislation illustrates this movement. The *lex Iulia de maritandis ordinibus* (18 BCE) and *lex Papia Poppaea* (9 CE) provided rewards for marriage and having children (the *ius liberorum*, the rights associated with having children) and penalties for not doing so. It was difficult for childless people to benefit from wills; married men with children were given accelerated office, and *tutela* freed women from financial supervision if they had three or more children. The *lex Aelia Sentia* (4 CE) allowed informally freed slaves to get full citizenship if they produced a child that lasted until one year; children were valuable assets. Pliny, perhaps tellingly, commented on the birth of new citizens "as resources for wars, and as ornaments of peace".

It was in the Augustinian Empire period that representations of children appeared in Roman art. Diddle Uzzi's (2007) work shows imperial art presenting children with their fathers and grandfathers. Diddle Uzzi observes of the wall painting in Pompeii:

> no mother figure appears, fathers take primary responsibility for Roman children in the images produced by the Roman ruling elite; mothers are largely absent from such images. Official imperial imagery...defines the Roman *familia* as a father-child unit. Imagery from the same period, on the other hand, defines the non-Roman family primarily as a mother-child unit, with non-Roman fathers either entirely absent or literally fading into the background.
>
> (2007, p. 62)

The Roman elite deploy the language of parenthood throughout their art and literature. Roman children with the male line intact have the greater call to legitimacy. The Roman images of *familia* are tied to the role of Roman men in public and the tradition of *patria potestas* and the legal restrictions on women during the empire; thus men are seen to take responsibility for children in the public world. Furthermore, the presence of children and men attests to the child's legitimacy and entitlement to the father's citizenship status.

The *patria potestas*, although clearly establishing the father's right of inheritance and governance of children under private law, through the Empire period established moderating principles of emancipation and guardianship, as well as rules of inheritance. In Roman law children were represented as having rights and obligations; age differentiations were noted and children's bonds with the mother's family recognised, to some extent replacing priority given to the paternal line. Furthermore, given the high child mortality rate, there was a legal focus on children as vulnerable. There was concern about the role of the *tutor* as a guardian of a child's morals, and even slave children were represented in law and given some rights. Rawson declares:

> In the law, then, children are represented as requiring the affection and care of a parent or a parent-substitute...They are also represented as having a variety of interests which must be protected: financial, emotional, educational, and an interest in maintaining a certain social standing.
>
> (2003, p. 73)

The law took a view on parenting, distinguishing real affection (*iustae affectiones*) from mere indulgence (*luxuria deliciae*). Fathers had the first claim on children after divorce; the child 'belonged' to the father, but where the child was brought up was another matter. In the later Roman period, after the mid-second century, the child could stay with a mother because of the father's 'bad character', although this did not diminish the father's *potestas*.

Puberty was an important legal marker; *infans* (or those who were insane) could not be liable for damage, and children below the age of puberty could not be prosecuted, as they were perceived as not being capable of criminal consent. Thus, children could not be prosecuted for forgery, could not have caused someone's death, and no child below the age of puberty could be tortured. Children past infancy could be responsible for some of their actions, such as theft and vandalism. Thus, like the Greek ideas discussed above, there was an assumption of a developmental line.

The Roman state had an interest in educating some of its citizens, but performed a fairly reluctant role, and schools were largely privately funded. The Roman state did offer state funds for the teaching of some courses. It also offered financial support for *pupilli*, children who became fatherless while still minors. The law also protected the financial and educational interests of children of divorced parents.

Lawrence Stone (1969) advanced a thesis of England in the seventeenth century moving from a 'closed' to an 'open' society, which, he argued, formed an important impetus for literacy and education. He pointed out that all the key positions in society were monopolised by those who had received a classical education. There was an obvious comparison of a minority in England in command of Latin to that minority in Rome versed in Greek who were able to assert their own sense of 'natural superiority'. Stone contrasts the 'trickle' of eighteenth-century France and the 'flood' in the USA in the twentieth century when new members were incorporated into the new elite. It was not a flood in Rome, but there was an opening up of the elite.

Opportunities for education were more numerous and of better quality in urban centres, and especially in Rome itself. There were many cases of boys being sent to Rome for an education; however, as the possibility of Roman citizenship expanded, along with the territorial conquests and rise in population, class status began to be considered more important than citizenship itself. Those with the rank of landowner or who obtained a military commission were treated with more respect than poor citizens. For Bellamy (2008), the Roman republic of class-based interests, in contrast to the Greek 'concord' of putting private interests to one side, was born amid class struggle between plebeians and patricians. Although citizens had the right to sit on civil bodies and were eligible to be tribunes and magistrates, they never had the political influence of their Athenian counterparts. Power rested with the Senate, which was dominated by patricians, especially among the powerful Consuls.

Stories of the active part taken by Roman women in decisions and cultural life attest to the fact that they were likely to have received some liberal education. There are references in Roman literature to girls' schools and to boys and girls being taught in the same classrooms. There is evidence also of girls being educated at home. There is no evidence of the belief that an education was bad for girls, and there were even thinkers, such as Musonius Rufus, a Stoic teacher in the first century, who wrote about the appropriateness of a good education for girls (see Rawson, 2003, p. 201). But this education needed to be tied in to women's virtues in the sphere of the home, house and children. Marriage was usually the end of childhood in the Classical world, although later the rhetoric of virginity provided girls the option of not marrying and living a virginal ascetic life dedicated to Christ. There were life-course words for girls, such as *puella* (girl), *virgo* (virgin) and *femina* (woman), that acknowledged certain socially constructed stages of the female life course. However, the assumption of the superiority of the male citizen was taken for granted. For instance, Galen argued:

> just as mankind is the most perfect of all animals, so within mankind the man is more perfect than the woman, and the reason for his perfection is his excess of heat ... so too the woman is less perfect than the man in respect to the generative parts.
>
> (Alberici and Harlow, 2007, p. 195)

Sometimes it is said that Romans lacked emotional stability due to the turnover of parents and siblings. But Rawson draws on Esther Goody's (1982) anthropology, which identified five roles of parenthood (bearing and begetting, nurturance, training, sponsorship and endowment of birth status) that broadened out the definition of parenting. With this in mind, and the fact that Roman parents undertook a specialised role in parenting and other household members took roles of nurturance or training, it is possible that, rather than splitting the roles of parenthood of weakened emotional feeling, it can actually strengthen personal relationships overall.

In this sense, Romans had a dense network of close people, be they natural son, brother, daughter, sister, another blood relation, cousins, *collactaneus*, *educator*, *pedagogues*, *nutrix*, the son or daughter of these, other women the father intends to marry, financial agents, aunts, uncles, cousins, grandparents. The house of the wealthy Roman citizen is an interface between public and private life, far removed from the modern privatised space of today. As Rawson concludes:

> The parent – child relationship was, then, a core relationship reflected in law, literature and inscriptions. But it was not an exclusive relationship. Most children lived in a network of other relationships.
>
> (2003, p. 268)

Like Athens, Rome consisted of a number of public institutions and a strong civil society. Rome was organised for some purposes, such as the distribution of food and drink after a sacrifice or a public celebration, into localities (*uici*). Rome had over a million inhabitants and a large and diverse population with a number of ethnic, religious and linguistic components. As Rawson comments:

> the city provided important services and was the locus of much material splendour and entertainment and grand occasions. Attending these occasions, being in the theatre or ampitheatre, viewing a triumphal procession, walking through splendid arcades, under triumphal arches, past statues of notable citizens, all extended the range of people whom children saw and met, created a sense of being Roman.
>
> (2003, p. 210)

Children participated as performers and celebrators in religious festivals. Children were constantly exposed to the public spaces, as they worked there and were often in residence above shops. Slave children came and went, running errands through the streets. All Roman children, it would seem, could spend much time "as spectators or participants in public festivals, celebrations, processions, and performances" (Rawson, 2003, p. 275).

Late antiquity and Christianity

The basis of political obligation in the later Roman period began to display a distinct tendency of a theocratic kind. Earlier, in the Republican era of government, a person's obligation to obey the law had been similar to that of the Athenian, that is, obedience to laws corresponded with the city-state's higher moral laws based upon principles of justice. When Rome expanded and transformed itself into an empire, it was the Emperor's alleged divinity that gradually replaced the moral law of justice. Thus, the laws of the Empire deserved obedience, not because they were just, but because they were the will of an authoritative sovereign.

The creation of the Emperor Augustus finished a parallel process of citizenship that moved away from the particularly close and personal citizen participation associated with Athenian Greece towards a form of citizenship that is based on the similarities between people as human beings. Thus, all men are endowed with a sense of reason and are subject to the same laws of nature. The process began with the spread of Aristotelian ideas across the Greek cities, throughout the Mediterranean and consolidated through the development of the Roman conquests.

The process of this humanistic conception that we are all made the same continued into Christianity, in which it was believed that all human beings are God's creatures, formed in His image.

St Paul drew upon Greek Stoicism, which believed that all men were rational beings and that all men, whatever their status, had the common attribute of wisdom and reason, whether they were rich or poor, free or slave. For Stoics, reflected in Roman thinkers such as Cicero or Seneca, the only qualification for citizenship was wisdom, to which all men could potentially aspire. This became not just an ideal but a 'law of nature'; natural law, emanating from divine will or through the common exercise of the faculty of reason, is, according to Cicero, "unchangeable and eternal" and cannot be contravened morally. This Stoicist natural law supported a very fledgling notion of human rights that was taken on and developed by later theorists.

In the fifth century St Augustine consolidated the dilemma of, on the one hand, a universal citizenship, represented in the *City of God*, and, on the other hand, the demands of temporal authorities in the here and now. The universal brotherhood of the 'City of God' would not be realised in the here and now but in the mystical promise of heaven, or realised on earth only through the second coming of Christ. St Augustine asserts that individuals must concern themselves not with worldly pursuits, but with an inward life of contemplation and prayer. Thus, the Church and religion became the focus for individuals in terms of identity and moral guidance (Clarke, 1994).

The second part of Augustine's doctrine is that the era of Christianity is an essential feature of any good society. We could never hope to achieve absolute justice in this life, as people are by nature sinful and, therefore, the 'City of God' is an ideal to which we must strive on earth. However, people could not fully hope to achieve the justice of the City of God in earthly life, only for salvation after death. The job of the state, according to Augustine, was to make people behave in a way that will ensure their future salvation. The state exists because people are sinful and the role of the Church, as an organised social institution, becomes absolutely central. Only the Church could understand God's will; so, in this life, a person's spiritual interest as interpreted by the Church has priority over all other interests. Thus, the Church has a priority over all other institutions and interests in guiding the actions of communities, especially those of the sovereign. Following Constantine's edict of 313, which recognised religious and civic freedoms of Christians, Christian ethics and values were incorporated into judgements of citizens. Therefore, for the next millennium, the Church, not the state, commanded respect, loyalty and moral advantage, shaped politics and crafted education (Heater, 1990).

However, Augustine's view of the sovereign subjected to the guidance of the Church was challenged and contained ambiguities within Christian doctrine. If spiritual interests have priority over all other concerns, how do we define the boundaries where spiritual concerns end and secular concerns begin? Or, where do we "render unto Caesar what is Caesar's, render unto God what is God's"? The secular/spiritual boundary problem persisted, and that, at the end of the sixth century, Pope Gelasius argued to Emperor Anastasius on the doctrine of the 'two swords':

> There are two powers, august Emperor, by which this world is chiefly ruled, namely, the sacred authority of the priests and the royal power. Of these that of the priests is the more weighty, since they have to render an account for even the kings of men in the divine judgment. You are also aware, dear son, that while you are permitted honorably to rule over human kind, yet in things divine you bow your head humbly before the leaders of the clergy and await from their hands the means of your salvation.

Throughout the Medieval period thinkers of the age advocated the universalist basis of Christian natural law and tried to reconcile this with the sovereign state.

But what about children? The intellectual question of children in the thought of late Romans was more profound than originally thought. Paul Clarke notes that Christians "proclaimed a saviour, born as a baby, who taught that the kingdom of heaven belonged to those who were like little children" (Clark, 1994, p. 4). This brought about a vagueness towards children in the period when adults in the Graeco-Roman world were "distinguished from children by their superior reason and self-control, and their affirmation of power over themselves and their lives...whereas in Christian imagery adults could be urged to identify themselves as newborn babes, naked in the rebirth of baptism, wrapped in pure robes, fed on the milk of basic instruction" (Clark, 1994, p. 25). Yet Christianity fostered a contradictory attitude to children by re-evaluating childlessness, elevating celibacy and promoting an ascetic way of life with no room at all for children (or women).

Such ambiguity regarding children enters the thought of Early Christian writers such as St Augustine, St Basil, St Ambrose and St Jerome, who comment on childhood, as well as marriage, childlessness and celibacy. In education a new proposed curriculum was developed to prepare the child for a life devoted to God and the eternal life that would follow. Christian parents were also concerned with their children's salvation, and brought forward the elements of *equality of all*, as God cared for all, including children, slaves, women and barbarians. However, the way in which this was to be achieved was not uniform. Jerome advocated that children should be sent away from home at an early age to be taught by learned religious orders, whereas St John Chrysostom urged that boys should not be sent away to a monastery until the age of at least ten. The souls of girls were also debated; for instance, Jerome's letter to Paula pondered the best approach to bringing up a girl. For Jerome, Paula must be prepared for a joyless life, to guide her to chastity and single-sex life in a convent. Boys were still given a classical education, but St Basil's *Rule* replaced the stories of Greek mythology with biblical characters. John Chrysostom, in a work entitled *An Address on Vainglory and the Right Way for Parents to Bring Up Their Children*, attended to questions on how children learn and utilised storytelling as a way of gaining a child's interest. Furthermore, Chrysostom was also aware of the various stages of childhood and made direct parallels between children and metaphors of governance. As Phyllis Katz argued:

> Chrysostom further organizes his treatise through a sustained metaphor of the father as a king governing the city-child. The child's body is the wall of the city, his five senses the gates, and each sense is the focus of a specific aspect of a child's education. At the first gate of the tongue, for example, Chrysostom considers how the child learns to speak and what his models should be. These gates represent early childhood. The organisation is sequential and flows logically.
>
> (2007, p. 119)

However, Aristotle's notion of the child as incomplete and incapable of noble actions also shaped early Christian belief. The period introduced the belief of children being damned to hellfire or, later, to limbo. Pope Innocent III, characterising perhaps an extreme form of the ambiguity towards children, believed it was all disgusting, as children were "conceived in lasciviousness and filth, brought forth with sorrow and pain, nourished with trouble and labour, watched over with anxiety and fear" (quoted in Wileman, 2005, p. 16). Later, in the twelfth century, Heloise declined Abelard's proposal because children would not suit the life of a scholar. Could they write with the chatter of servant girls, lullabies of wet nurses, the wailing of infants and the constant untidiness and disorder of small children? However, the legacy of Christianity for later periods did establish an opposition to infanticide, including the killing of disabled and illegitimate children as well as abortion (Nonnan, 1971).

Middle Ages

The period that followed the fall of Rome has received a bad press. The nineteenth-century British historian John Thrupp painted a grim picture of childhood in Anglo-Saxon England, where "at first, the child could be exposed as soon as born: when reared, he could be sold into slavery: he was liable to be punished for his father's crimes, and be sold in payment of his debt" (quoted in Crawford, 1999, p. xi). In another example, in Sally Crawford's reappraisal of childhood in the medieval period, she cites Anita Schorsch's comments, as late as 1979, that "medieval communities dealt with their children as they dealt with their animals" (quoted in Crawford, 1999, p. xi). More famously, and at the time more influentially, Neil Postman declared that in the 'Dark Ages' 'childhood disappears'. Much work recently has rescued ideas of childhood in this period, and Crawford notes that early in the medieval period the kin group was at the heart of early Germanic society and was responsible for the safety, protection and good behaviour of its members, including children.

There were, nevertheless, some profound differences from today. In medieval literature it did not necessarily matter what condition children were in, as there was no perceived impact on adult behaviour, no matter what the state of abandonment, fosterage or orphanage. Parzival's noble blood determined his skills, not childhood and training. In Old English poems it was argued that, no matter how carefully and lovingly parents reared their children, they would have no control over them once they left home. So in the medieval world there was little conception of child development, little conception of prerequisites or sequential learning, little conception of schooling as a preparation for an adult world. Up to the twelfth century a literary education was not considered part of the training even for a noble, and children of more humble origins would have had no access to it. King Alfred of Wessex, in what is now known as England, did not educate all his children. The monastic world would have had some schooling, as monasteries had a 'child master' in a minister, but formal schooling did not exist to any great extent, although plenty of elite tutelage took place within families. It is little surprise that ideas of citizenship waned and an engrained hierarchical social structure developed. In some continuity with late antiquity, a subject's loyalty in the feudal system was to the Church and the state; there was a conjoining of identities to *both* lord and Church. Derek Heater (1990) was more precise when he observed: "a subject's loyalty could be diverted by the Church, in everyday terms it was demanded in practice by the local lord" (p. 21). Thus, the geographical proximity to the power that was exercised was key. Through the Middle Ages local identities developed to become regional identities, which, in turn, became national identities. However, even in large and relatively sophisticated countries such as France, Poland-Lithuania Commonwealth, England and Spain, by the sixteenth century an individual subject was just that, tied in to the particular local relationship with their superior. The term *citizen* would have made little sense to most living at the time.

There were, however, still some working ideas of seeing childhood as a separate entity. As Shulamith Shahar (1990) observed: "no society with any awareness of its own essence and aims could endure as a society without ways of transmitting knowledge and cultural traditions during the late stages of childhood, and without an effort on the part of those entrusted with the task of socialization of the young generation" (p. 1).

During the plagues in the fourteenth and fifteenth centuries, fathers were urged to provide love and support to their wives and children. Joseph in the Catholic faith was presented as the ideal father as protector of Mary. Within the writings of Augustine, there is a predilection to sin that increases and reaches its peak during adolescence. Clearly, there is some idea of sequential stages occurring here. Furthermore, within Augustine's work there is the positive idea of the process of baptism that makes children more innocent than their elders. Thus, childhood was also seen as a period of faith, purity and innocence. The passing into adulthood entails the loss of innocence and joy. The thirteenth-century poem *Le Roman de la Rose* featured a 12-year-old girl who knew nothing of evil and innocently lacked any hypocrisy. Some medieval commentators suggested that a child's prayer was stronger than an adult's. There was also plenty of consternation about the nature and extent of 'stages' within debates about legal responsibility.

For Heater (1990), the Middle Ages did, however, include some important forms of bonding that would have profound and important consequences for later notions of citizenship. First, there were firm bonds between the ruler and ruled; this took the form of reciprocal rights, no matter how one-sided. Second, the growth of trading towns, and later cities, enabled contacts with outsiders and differing social relationships around trade and business. These established not only shared rules but also associations; for instance, in towns across Europe tradespeople would merge into 'guilds' and form 'fraternities'. In rich cities, especially those built around trade and commerce, social organisation was centred on city councils. Finally, Thomas Aquinas's resurrection of Aristotle placed the abstract form of citizenship again in intellectual debates. Aquinas uncoupled the direct link to the Christian soul through revelation and determinism, and the active part that reason could take. This had huge implications for later Renaissance scholars who revisited Roman and Greek thinkers.

Notwithstanding the importance of developing reason in children, there was still the necessity of socialisation, which mostly involved some loose or defined form of education. As Shahar argues:

> Every newborn child was burdened with the weight of Original Sin, but baptism bestowed divine mercy and forgiveness, and within the limits of the human condition it was possible to educate the child and develop in him those character traits and patterns of behaviour considered desirable.
>
> (1990, p. 162)

Medieval education was primarily left to the supervision of families or the village priests. Education was to raise the human being into Christian morals, and this knowledge took precedence over worldly knowledge and vocational skills. To be a good Christian meant to observe the rituals of worship and the moral injunctions of scripture, especially the Ten Commandments; to refrain from the seven deadly sins (lust, pride, covetousness, envy, gluttony, anger and sloth); to refrain from cursing and swearing; and to nurture good qualities such as charity. Secondarily, education was to fulfil intellectual predilections and prepare the child for his or her role in society. This included modesty and chastity in girls and discipline in boys. The soldier citizen appeared to supersede the deliberative citizen. Up to the twelfth century, education or schooling did not involve academic study. Then, following Elias's (1994) civilising process, the knight was to become a man of truth, justice, modesty and honour. Young knights in castles were the defence force and formed the nucleus of armies. The age of chivalry soon gave rise to more liberal arts, literacy and the *lingua franca* of Latin used in law across Western Europe. Later, secondary education for the wealthy was centred around cathedrals, but increasingly around city councils. The teaching was still the three disciplines of the Trivium – Grammar, Rhetoric and Logic. Several large cities in Germany and Italy opened up commercial schools. University foundations spread across Italy, Germany and the Low Countries.

The growth and development of urban areas and the concomitant trade gave rise to a new class of burghers, guildsmen and traders. Elementary or Song Schools developed in the first towns in Italy and Flanders, and in Florence by the fourteenth century boasted an attendance of 8,000 to 10,000 children. These were the schools attended by prosperous burghers and bankers; the curriculum included arithmetic, book-keeping, correspondence and sometimes foreign languages. Bankers and merchants had apprenticeships that lasted three years in Florence and ten years in London. Lower down the social order, some craftsmen trained their own children, as the product of their labours became increasingly valuable. Apprenticeship contracts were signed between parents and guardians and were subject to the statutes and supervision of guilds. Education for the lower orders was tied to their expected trades; there was only a partial, if any, interest in their suitability for public life beyond their trades.

Conclusion

A view of the classical and medieval worlds raises a number of important preconditions to children's citizenship that were to shape Renaissance and Enlightenment thinking. First, there was a tension between Aristotelian and Platonic views. In Aristotelian participative citizenship, many deliberative citizens were to make decisions protected from the over-intervention of the state. On the other hand, the Platonic view of the enlightened elite, excluded most from deliberative decisions. The tension between participation and exclusion reverberated through the Roman and medieval periods. Second, it is important to note the use of Roman law as a way of establishing some form of rights, even for those with the least power, such as slaves and children. Third, Christianity planted the idea of equality of all people, including children, slaves and women, in the eyes of God. Fourth, these were shaped by a patriarchal structure that encouraged any form of social movements and actions to be based around 'brotherhoods', excluding women and children. The principal elements of patriarchy included control of property and the deployment of reason as something that was inherently male and adult. Finally, politics and architecture combined to produce a distinction between the public world of men, ideas and decisions, and the private world of domesticity and reproduction. In Britain before the Romans arrived, village life was based around the roundhouse. Romano-British villas succeeded the roundhouse design of settlement, representing an increasing separation of domestic from public life.

2
Renaissance: Prelude to Modern Political Theory

If one takes a widespread view of European history up to the twelfth century and the height of feudalism, the political debates were between the advocates of Papal authority on the one hand and the imperial demands of the Holy Roman Empire on the other. The latter claimed direct divine origin of its authority, unmediated through the Church. The opposition to Papal authority prepared the ground for those who would later argue for the priority of private conscience over the dictates of all kinds of external authority, including the Church. The political landscape was changing from the twelfth century, towards a fragmentation of 'Holy Empires' and the rise of independent European states. Norman Davies (1997) talks of the 'crisis of Christendom' between 1250 and 1493. In Europe:

> People knew that Christendom was sick; they knew that the ideals of the Gospel of Love were far removed from the prevailing reality; but they had little idea of how to cure it. The senior Christian state, the Byzantine Empire, was reduced to a pathetic rump. The Holy Roman Empire could not control its own mighty subjects, let alone exercise leadership over others. The Papacy was falling into the quagmire of political dependence. Feudal particularism reached the point where every city, every princeling, had to fight incessantly for survival. The world was ruled by brigandage, superstition, and the plague.
>
> (1997 p. 383)

This process coincided with a resurgence of natural law theorists in the twelfth century, with the rediscovery of classical Greek and Roman teaching generally and with the work of Aristotle in particular. The Aristotelian view comes out clearly in the works of St Thomas Aquinas, whose theme was that the laws of nature are discoverable through the exercise of reason and do not necessarily require revelation or scriptural interpretation. This, with the proliferation of and consolidation of states, and the challenges to papal moral authority, both internal and external to the Church, gave rise to a transformation of these debates and a radical reinterpretation of natural law.

By the time Hugo Grotius applied the principles of natural law to 'international law' in the early seventeenth century, there were no references to religion as a condition of just law. Also absent from Grotius' theory was the idea that moral law is only obtainable through scriptural revelation or part of God's will. The law of nature is still evident, reflected in the rational nature of the universe and the fact that principles of natural law are self-evident and unchanging, even to God. Thus the secularisation of political theory had begun, and arguments other than those of Christianity were needed for claims of political authority.

By the time of Niccolo Machiavelli, writing in the early sixteenth century, there was a radical break with medieval thought, such as that expressed through St Thomas Aquinas. First, Machiavelli rejected the utility of advantage of pursuing ideals, religious or otherwise, as it was the pursuit of power that was important; effective political action only follows from the raw pursuit of power. Second, it is men who are the measure or currency of history, as it is men who make history, rather than divine providence. Finally, and following on from the recognition of human agency free from God's will, it is men who make or break governments. It is this attention to the will of men that forms such a crucial cornerstone of modern political thought and underlies the basis of citizenship theory. The use of the word 'men' is important, as it defined a specific and narrow view of human nature which excluded not only children but also women and subordinated, propertyless adult men from being capable of citizenship. Concomitant with the theory of human rights and citizenship was the central place of private property within the political order.

The association of property to citizenship is key. It was the ability to make and fulfil contracts that defined citizenship status, and this capability was something that was crucial in the development of what Marshall referred to as 'civil citizenship'. Children were written out of this process, and during the course of writing children were represented as incapable of full personhood and thus excluded from citizenship; an assumption that continues for the youngest children today. Children shifted from being active participants towards a special group requiring little more socially than education. The importance of public education preceded these writings, with Elizabeth 1 of England declaring the importance of national education as a source of national cohesion. Her injunction in November 1558 declared:

> that all teachers of children shall stir and move them to the love and due reverence of God's true religion now set forth by public authority.
> (quoted in Heater, 1990, p. 28)

Thomas Hobbes

A key thinker who decoupled political theory from religion and formulated the theory of the 'social contract' was Thomas Hobbes. Writing in England, Hobbes drew on the burgeoning physical sciences to locate politics as a 'science', adopting a 'scientific methodology' drawn from Copernicus, Galileo and Kepler to undermine the Aristotelian view of the state of nature. Aristotelian writers, such as Aquinas, were wrong because things do not have essences and assigned locations and are not determined by some 'great chain of being'. There was no divine purpose which orchestrates all the diverse parts of the universe. There was no point in looking for a divine purpose to discover why things or people behave, and there was no outside standard by which we could evaluate the conduct of humans or governments. Hobbes's starting point was a rudimentary theory of mind, in which an individual's knowledge is constructed by thoughts. These thoughts come from sensory experience and are made sense of by speech or language. Thus Hobbes originated a psychology of how reasoning occurs in the brain. This has implications for children and women, but first it is necessary to accept the radical nature of a theory of human knowledge derived from individuals. Hobbes constructs from his theory of the mind a theory of human nature which is centred around the 'rationality' of, at first, a sense of one's own survival and, following on from this, a desire for power to ensure one's survival. Rationality is key; however, reasoning for Hobbes is but 'artificial', while passions are natural. Humans have the ability to reason but also "the privilege of absurdity; to which no living creature is subject but man" (quoted in Wayper, 1959, p. 53). And "the ablest, most attentive, and most practiced men may deceive themselves and infer false conclusions" (quoted in Wayper, 1959, p. 53).

Hobbes's individual, while seeking power, is joined by everyone else utilising their rational capacities and arriving at the same conclusion. Thus, everyone wants to have power, so that they can increase their belongings to the greatest possible extent, to maintain their own safety and well-being. Here we have the famous Hobbesian state of nature in which life is "nasty, brutish and short". Everyone has an interest in escaping the state of nature; again, employing their rational capacities, they realise that they can better avoid death and plan for the future. People in the state of nature would want to make peace amongst themselves. For Hobbes, everyone has a natural right to preserve their life; however, it is necessary to limit their exercise of natural rights if other people are prepared to give up some of theirs. The more the renunciations of rights, the more the peace got. These renunciations are the contracts made between people that Hobbes calls covenants. Covenants are like contracts such as buying goods from shops, but it is crucial for individuals to keep to them. Why do people stick to their covenants? As people do not trust each other to stick to their covenants, it is necessary to ensure that political society is in place to ensure that people can afford to keep their contracts. An agency that is sufficiently powerful to enforce the keeping of covenants has to exist, that is, the sovereign; thus, "covenants without swords are but words." This person, or agency, is then authorised to act on behalf of all those doing the transferring.

The key question, then, is: who can be 'authors' of these covenants, or contracts? Interestingly, for Hobbes women are entitled to make contracts, as "there is not always that difference of strength or prudence between man and woman" (Hobbes, 1651/1968, p. 253). However, inanimate things like bridges and buildings cannot be authors: "likewise children, fooles and Mad-men that have no reason ... but can be no authors (during that time) ... longer then (when they recover the use of reason)" (1651/1968, p. 219). Therefore, "because the first instruction of children, dependeth on the care of their parents; it is necessary that they should be obedient to them, whilest they are under their tuition" (Hobbes, 1651/1968, p. 382). Hobbes argued that children owed a debt of gratitude to their parents for having nurtured and protected them. Thus, they should obey parents. However, as Gutman (1980) has argued, this presumes that biological parents do nurture and protect their children; this may or may not be the case, and it cannot therefore be understood as the right of a child to be nurtured. Under this logic of children claiming their rights at adulthood, children cannot claim the right to nurturance in the here and now; this is only an assumption that the child may challenge when they reach adulthood at some stage in the future. The only form of protection of children's 'rights' to nurturance, welfare and well-being will be the Hobbesian legislators' power and right to take the child away from the family as an act of retribution.

John Locke

The starkness of Hobbes's leviathan to act on behalf of children gave virtually no agency to the state of parenthood acting in between government and children. The English philosopher John Locke continued a theory of politics combined with an idea of human development that placed 'parenthood' as an important institution but within specific rights and limits.

The Renaissance, while limiting the power of the church, never dispensed entirely with religious ideas to develop political theory. Later in the seventeenth century Locke used religion in his own notion of the 'social contract' to provide a natural law of individualism and a political society to protect private property. In Locke's second part of *Two Treatises of Government*, entitled *True End of Government*, we are struck by the importance Locke attaches to the freedom of the individual. The treatises were published in 1690 in order to justify the 'English Revolution'[1] of 1688, and we find that personal liberty is the overriding ideal, which political society exists entirely to protect. Locke uses the word 'property' to refer to that which belongs to each person and encompasses each person's life, liberty and possessions. Property, for Locke, is a term referring to the thing a person needs to be free; the sole purpose of political society is the protection of each person's property from invasion or appropriation by others, whether other private individuals or governments. The invasion or appropriation of a person's property is a violation of their rightful freedom. For Locke, the central idea is personal liberty, and the only kind of political arrangement to which people owe obedience is one that protects them in their rightful amount of personal liberty.

In order to justify political society, Locke, like Hobbes, instigates a hypothetical pre-social 'state of nature'. In the state of nature all persons are equal; by this, Locke means that nobody is entitled to exercise absolute power over another. Nobody is born a slave and everyone is equal in the eyes of God. All individuals have an equal right to be free. What form, then, do political power and authority take? In order to answer this question, Locke shows how some writers, notably Hobbes and Robert Filmer, confuse political power with other forms of power that some persons exercise over others. One of the kinds of power which have been mistakenly viewed is the authority fathers exercise over their children. This confusion is the one he directly attributes to Filmer's patriarchal writings in support of the Stuarts. Filmer was not the first writer to mourn the weakening of the patriarchal family.

Jean Bodin, a century before, viewed a father's passing of his authority as *paterfamilias* to a sovereign in order to act as an equal with other heads of households as a weakening of the bonds of society. Locke in his two essays *Two Treatises of Government* used the concept of the social contract as a counter to the vulgar patriarchy outlined by Robert Filmer. Filmer's view of patriarchy argued that the right of kings reflected the patriarchal authority of Adam and his successors over Eve and their children. Locke questioned the extent of women's passivity, the ownership of children and structuring society according to kinship, nevertheless retained women and children in a subordinate position at a societal level.

Locke pointed out, interestingly a point previously made by Hobbes, that any authority of one person over another that is based on biology must be an authority that resides as much in mothers as in fathers. Locke utilises the scriptural writings that make no distinction between mothers and fathers. Locke acknowledges that it is understandable that parental power might be mistaken for absolute power. The authority the parents exercise over their children is very considerable. However, the authority is only temporary and is restricted to the period of a child's life that precedes the 'age of reason'. Locke states:

> Children . . . are not born in this full state of equality, though they are born to it. Their parents have a sort of rule and jurisdiction over them when they come into the world, and for some time after, but it is a temporary one. The bonds of subjection are like the swaddling clothes they are wrapt up in and supported by the weakness of their infancy. Age and reason as they grow up loosen them, till at length they drop quite off, and leave a man at his own free disposal.
>
> (Locke, 1690/1986, pp.142–143)

In *Some Thoughts Concerning Education*, published in 1693, Locke introduced a 'developmental' understanding of a child's nature. The purpose of education was to produce a rational man by controlling the child's environment and the writing of learning on the blank slate of a child's mind. Central to Locke's psychology of children was the distinction between the child without reason and the (educated) adult in possession of reason.

The law of nature is a moral code of conduct which is discoverable by reason, so the conduct of a person who is not yet rational has to be governed by someone who is, in this case the parent. Once one has become a rational person, one becomes formally responsible for one's actions and the authority of parents ceases. One of the problems of absolute power justifying absolutism is the difficulty in which Filmer would find himself in the case of a monarch dying and leaving his throne to an infant son. Would Filmer claim that the infant sovereign cannot be subject to anyone else's authority and may govern according to his own will? Locke argued not. You may be able to outgrow parental power, but not political authority.

Locke turns next to the master–slave relationship, and notes that slaves own neither their lives nor their labour; therefore the relationship is one of absolute power. Locke argues that this is not a model of political authority, because, unlike even parental relationships, it does not arise from within the framework of the law of nature. Parental authority is consistent with the law of nature because it is consistent with the principle of the moral equality of all rational beings, children in Locke's view being without reason. The master–slave relationship arises from a violation of that principle of self-preservation and the injustice of an aggression against another life; thus, you cannot become a slave through contract. Slavery arises from an injustice, and this cannot be an appropriate model for political authority.

How, then, does political power come to exist in a society of equals? Locke argues that in the state of nature everybody has not only property rights to their lives, liberty and estates but also their 'executive right of nature'. This is the right to take any action necessary and appropriate to protect or restore their property from aggression. Since the function of government is to secure individuals' property, it follows that the only authority a government can have or take is whatever is included in individuals' executive rights. Since the executive rights naturally and morally belong to each individual, the only way government can be established is by those individuals transferring their executive rights to the government. As in Hobbes, government is created by the rights transferred to it by individuals and authority comes to exist. However, unlike in Hobbes, individuals do not transfer *all* their rights, only their executive rights, that is, those rights people have to take any action necessary to protect their property. Government is thus created through agreement among a number of people pooling their executive rights. In this case government becomes like an umpire, adjudicating and arbitrating between conflicting claims. The function of government, then, is to protect private property by adjudicating controversies and attaching enforceable penalties to its verdicts. Governments making and executing these judgements must not violate the private rights they are preserving. For this reason absolute monarchy cannot be a genuine source of government because, by definition, it is not bound by any law, including the law of nature. Authority is caused by *consent* of any group of persons to incorporate them into a political society in which, thereafter, a majority vote is sufficient to determine what shall be law. Power is strictly limited by consent. Children here do not, or cannot, hold property and thus have no executive rights to offer in any government of consent and can only have their natural rights protected by either parents or government.

The advantage of a 'civil society' through consent that leads to government has distinct advantages, albeit from the point of view of adults. First, civil society provides laws that can be codified and made more clear and certain for governing people's conduct towards one another. Second, in civil society persons are not required to judge in controversies or conflicts, as third parties are used for judgements. Finally, the overwhelming strength of the whole community can compel perpetrators to be punished and they can be made to compensate their victims, rather than leaving this to be secured by the victims themselves.

It is now worth reflecting on the historical period after the Renaissance had taken its course, and the impact this had on children's lives. The period gave rise to the processes of individualism, private property and politics reflected in Locke's *True End of Government*. At the beginning of the Renaissance there was no sophisticated conception of individualism. As Pinchbeck and Hewitt observed of the fifteenth century:

> the current conception of society in which the family, not the individual, was the essential unit of social organisation. In such a view, children were no different from the adult members of the family in that they were all conceived as component parts of a far larger unit, the extended family, to whose interest those of the interrelated nuclear families of parents and children were subordinated. The promotion of family ambition, the advancement of family interest, not the realisation of private ambition and the achievement of personal success were seen as the common, all-important social task.
>
> (1969, p. 13)

Increasing affluence made it possible for wealthy classes to discriminate domestically between servants and family, with separate servants' quarters being built. Also, the growth of middle-class yeoman farmers, merchants and tradesmen led to smaller homes and a more personal family life. The books of the 1500s were highly moralistic, reflecting the rise of middle-class power and influence. The middle-class conscious-ness was based on moral rectitude that was reconciled with social and economic salvation. The determination to acquire knowledge was the route to the middle-class rise to power. Thus, a considerable number of elementary schools were founded over the period, following the exam-ples of those in France and Germany. The previous elite's requirement for chivalry and military prowess was being replaced by the need for a more subtle art. Thus, the 30 years leading up to 1512 saw the estab-lishment of grammar schools and the admittance to these schools of boys aged seven. John Locke, in *Some Thoughts Concerning Education*, advocated the broadening out of the subjects taught in schools, stressed the importance of French and supported modern textbooks, rather than ancient classic writers. Thus, for Pinchbeck and Hewitt: "utilitarianism had become the watchword for the new age, and to meet this want other kinds of school were instituted" (1969, p. 283). The effect of for-mal education was to extend childhood, previously conceived to end at seven or nine, to a long formative period. As Cunningham has observed, "children came to be subjected to a 'sort of quarantine' before they were allowed to join adult society" (1995, p. 6). For poorer children, schools to the end of the period would provide an important form of social control and an agency of social discipline for the lower social classes. The Charity School movement began in 1699; the Society for the Promotion of Christian Knowledge (SPCK) incorporated many soci-eties and by 1730 had established 132 schools nationwide. These schools had a clearly defined didactic education, they were there to encourage discipline, obedience and conformity.

Erasmus, writing in the early sixteenth century, declared: "The child that nature has given you is nothing but a shapeless lump, but the mate-rial is still pliable, capable of assuming any form, and you must so mould it that it takes on the best possible character" (quoted in Cunningham, 1995, p. 44). Similarly, Locke in his *Essay Concerning Human Under-standing* noted that people are "Nine Parts of Ten are what they are, Good or Evil, useful or not, by their Education", thus popularising the way in which children are born as a blank slate, with no pre-existing tendencies. Cunningham (1995) notes two important implications of this position. First, the implications for "child-rearing were enormous, bestowing colossal power and responsibility on the educator, who must write on the paper or mould the wax" (p. 63). Second, although Locke says children "should be treated as rational Creatures" and thus their curiosity encouraged, this incipient child-centredness was continually blunted by his stress on the overall purpose which was to produce an adult who conformed to the role of someone in her or his rank" (Cunningham, 1995, p. 64). The focus of education, then, was to produce citizens not in the here and now but as the 'complete' adult citizens who would materialise in the future.

The Enlightenment

The Enlightenment was an intellectual movement that existed over a wide span of years, consisting of a number of writers over many countries in Europe and North America. The principle of the light of reason combating the ignorance, mysticism and tradition which characterised orthodox Christianity was perhaps encapsulated by Immanuel Kant's proclamation that "enlightenment is man's emergence from his self-incurred tutelage...Dare to know! Have the courage to use your own reason" (quoted in Beck, 1963, p. 3). Interestingly, the debates around 'tutelage' and its translation from German centre on its similarity with the condition of childhood, as one characterised as a period of ignorance, supervision by others and dependence. The power of reason, *philosophes* argued, would lead to self-determination and a critical enquiry that would be open to doubt and suspended judgement.

The goal of the Enlightenment project was that all knowledge was to be 'useful' and directed towards practical questions. Thus, they attempted to collect and order existing knowledge and transmit this to future generations, encapsulated in Diderot's *Encyclopaedia or Reasoned Dictionary of the Sciences, Arts and Crafts*, published between 1751 and 1772. There was a firm belief that knowledge would not only challenge prevailing religious and moral beliefs but also lead to greater virtue and happiness. Children were to be key in this, as potential harbingers of a new and bright future of reason. The optimism that children presented was taken up by Immanuel Kant, thereby assisted in fashioning the modern construction of childhood as offering hope and progress for the future.

Immanuel Kant

A key notion of Kant's (1788/1967) moral theory was one of 'autonomy', understood as the capacity of the will to choose independently from the desires stemming from our nature as sensuous beings. Humans are unique in having autonomy. Non-human animals act by instinct or nature, or, in Kantian terms, they do not 'will to act' but act according to instinct. By contrast, humans have reason. In following their rational will, they act autonomously, not under the sway of external or natural forces but according to their own conceptions of what they ought to do. However, there are limitations to reason, according to Kant. Human conduct might not be guided by reason; it might be prompted by appetite or emotion rather than rational reflection. Thus, autonomous conduct is something that we human beings are capable of rather than the situation in which we are.

Nevertheless, the ideal, for Kant, is for us to follow a moral law whereby individuals act autonomously according to a law-like reasoning that can be prescribed by themselves, rather than under the tutelage of an external imposition. Kant's famous categorical imperative declared: "Act in such a way that you always treat humanity, whether in your own person or in the person of any other, never simply as a means, but always at the same time as an end" (1785/1998, p. 91). All persons are 'ends in themselves' and each person needs to be respected and to be respectful of all persons. Kant's views of an autonomous individual's ability to be a critical, autonomous being proved influential on later thinkers, such as John Stuart Mill and Ronald Dworkin. Kant rarely referred to children in his philosophical writings, and his ideas have been taken up by later writers to exclude children from the 'categorical imperative'. Kant did, however, discuss education. In his *On Pedagogy* Kant argued, optimistically, that education constantly improves through the generations along the path towards the full realisation of humanity. Kant argued for the social conditions to be put in place to produce a general good. Education has an important role to play in this, he argued:

> Good education is precisely that which produces everything that is good in the world. The seeds which lie within people must be constantly developed. For the basis of evil cannot be found in the natural constitution of people. The only cause of evil is that nature is not brought under control. People contain only the seeds of good.
>
> (1964, p. 704)

Kant stresses that education is to be more than just the handing down of knowledge from one generation to the next; it needs to be more ambitious:

> Children must be raised not towards the current, but the future possible improved state of the human race, that is, the idea of humanity, and everything appropriate to its destiny. This principle is of great

importance. Parents generally raise their children only so they fit into the existing world, even though it may be ruined. They should, however, better raise them so that a future, better state is brought about.

(Kant, 1964, p. 704)

The politics of the Enlightenment, apart from the challenge to hierarchies, introduced new arenas for humanitarian reform, ranging from the spread of toleration to ending slavery and improving medicine, and led to economic wealth. The world of the Enlightenment was the 'perfectibility' of human beings through the medium of improved knowledge. Major thinkers associated with the Enlightenment built upon this premise; next we consider Adam Smith for his economic theories and Jean Jacques Rousseau, who, like Smith, formulated a theory of human 'perfectibility' and a belief in the importance of education.

Adam Smith

A great deal has been written about Adam Smith, sometimes portrayed as an advocate of the 'free market', and his principle of *laissez-faire* is now applied to government policies worldwide. Smith's legacy was not confined to the English-speaking world. His work inspired Prussia and other German states to abolish serfdom and other exclusionary practices (Nathans, 2004). Smith's most famous book, *The Wealth of Nations*, characterises new Enlightenment thinking in the economic and social sphere, as well as in the scientific world. Smith, as an enlightenment *philosophe*, was interested in 'useful' knowledge, and his *Wealth of Nations* was a handbook for the usefulness of 'political economy' in society. Smith took on board enlightenment notions of 'self-love' and transferred this to rational self-interest. However, by way of contrast to the neo-Darwinist principles of an aggressive market today, Smith's market was based upon peaceful competition, and a wealthy nation is one in which all economic classes benefit from economic growth. Our basic self-interest urges us towards preservation and to improve our condition, although not through lust or aggression, characterised in Hobbes's state of nature. The important precondition of realising this self-interest is the liberty to operate in a free market, entailing the liberty to move, work or invest. There is a requirement for a sovereign, but this is to ensure order in the market.

In Smith's other famous work *Theory of Moral Sentiments*, published in 1758, he outlines a moral framework where he finds not only self-interest but a complementary natural disposition to take an interest in the condition of others. The basis of this interest in others is the sympathy we have, naturally derived, towards our fellow humans. Indeed, when people are not able to sympathise, we judge it as improper, indecent or bad. Children have a special 'natural' capacity to engender people's sympathies. Smith says: "The weakness of childhood interests the affections of the most brutal and hard-hearted" (*Theory of Moral Sentiments*, Part IV, Section II, Chapter 1). This sympathy is closest in the family. Smith says:

> With what pleasure do we look upon a family, through the whole of which reign mutual love and esteem, where the parents and children are companions for one another, without any other difference than what is made by respectful affection on the one side, and kind indulgence on the other.
>
> (*Theory of Moral Sentiments*,
> Part I, Section II, Chapter III)

Natural sympathy works in close proximity; it is more difficult to make sympathy work with strangers. Thus Smith argues against the custom of sending children away from parents to be educated, whether in a school or a place of work. He asks:

> Do you wish to educate your children to be dutiful to their parents, to be kind and affectionate to their brothers and sisters? Put them under the necessity of being dutiful children, of being kind and affectionate brothers and sisters: educate them in your own house. From their parent's house they may, with propriety and advantage, go out every day to attend public schools: but let their dwelling be always at home ... Domestic education is the institution of nature; public education, the contrivance of man. It is surely unnecessary to say, which is likely to be the wisest.
>
> (*Theory of Moral Sentiments*,
> Part IV, Section II, Chapter 1)

Smith here draws a contrast between the safe and cosy image of a private sphere and that of a more dangerous public sphere that was the 'contrivance of man'.

Smith's philosophy is mostly associated with the 'minimal state'; he certainly argues against government interventions (or any other institutional interventions) as a violation of natural liberty. Such interventions tend to be inefficient as they lack adequate knowledge, encourage bureaucracies and obstruct incentives. However, there are areas of legitimate intervention around defence, the operation of justice and the provision of some public goods and services. One of these public services is in education, and he devotes two sections of the *Wealth of Nations* to the question. While Smith was scathing about the practice of educating children away from the home, he advocated a system of public day education for all boys.

The free market produces a paradox in commercial society. On the one hand, greater wealth is generated through the expansion of markets, innovations and progressions in the division of labour. A free market society produces more happiness or utility than any other system. However, this growth happens at the same time as growing inequalities. These inequalities do not, according to Smith, derive from inborn qualities but are a product of education and habit. In contrast to the condition of the labouring poor in Britain, where families have four children in the hope of two surviving, the freedom of North America enables an adequate subsistence for labourers, where:

> Labour is there so well rewarded that a numerous family of children, instead of being a burthen, is a source of opulence and prosperity to the parents. The labour of each child, before it can leave their house, is computed to be worth a hundred pounds clear gain to them ... The demand for labourers, the funds destined for maintaining them, increase, it seems, still faster than they can find labourers to employ.
>
> (*Wealth of Nations*)

Smith argued for a public form of education. This has direct relevance to the training of citizens and the maintenance of stable democratic government:

> An instructed and intelligent people, besides, are always more decent and orderly than an ignorant and stupid one. They feel themselves, each individually, more respectable and more likely to obtain the respect of their lawful superiors, and they are therefore more disposed to respect those superiors. They are more disposed to examine, and more capable of seeing through, the interested complaints of faction and sedition, and they are, upon that account, less apt to be misled into any wanton or unnecessary opposition to the measures of government.

Public education is to be one of the public goods and services to be maintained. However, this public education is only to last until the age of 12 or 13, as Smith was highly critical of the university system. He believed that salaried staff would not be encouraged to provide a useful form of knowledge and there were no mechanisms to prevent poor teaching. Furthermore, as a product of the Enlightenment, he believed the influence of a religious foundation in education skewed the curriculum, including Latin, Greek, theology and the arts, to producing clerics, but with only a limited degree of scientific or applied knowledge. In short, universities and boarding schools did not equip young people for the demands of the economy. This, ironically for Smith, is in marked contrast to the education of girls and young women, of whom he states:

> There are no public institutions for the education of women, and there is accordingly nothing useless, absurd, or fantastical in the common course of their education. They are taught what their parents or guardians judge it necessary or useful for them to learn, and they are taught nothing else. Every part of their education tends evidently to some useful purpose; either to improve the natural attractions of their person, or to form their mind to reserve, to modesty, to chastity, and to economy; to render them both likely to become the mistresses of a family, and to behave properly when they have become such.

Jean Jacques Rousseau

Although continuing the interest in perfectibility, education and improvement, and an exclusion of women and children from the public world of citizenship as discussed below, the work of Rousseau can be seen by way of contrast to the English social contract theorists. Rousseau believed in the ultimate changeability of human beings through social action. It is then, perhaps, no surprise that Rousseau devoted a large portion of his writing to education and how this could lead to a better society. While Locke wrote about children as being mouldable, like wax, he never developed the truly transformative potential of new generations that Kant dreamt of. Harry Hendrick recently observed that Rousseau offered a more radical and nuanced understanding of childhood, together with an "opposition to cold Reason, which concluded that childhood, naturally drawn to virtue, should be valued for itself, rather than solely as the precursor to adulthood" (2011, p. 142).

Rousseau believed that everything ultimately depended upon politics. His observations of Italian politics led him to believe that change in government can lead to a change in human nature. Although most of his writings attended to the human corruption that arose out of government and 'civilisation', he observed not progress but the opposite. Before society, people in a state of nature were "wandering up and down the forests, without industry, without speech, and without home, an equal stranger to war and to all ties" (*Origin of Inequality*, p. 79). Rousseau had a pessimistic view of historical achievement. Rousseau was regarded as an Enlightenment *philosophe*, as he was opposed to privilege and superstition. However, he displayed a greater patience for Christian principles than many of his Enlightenment contemporaries, yet he was firmly opposed to the hierarchies associated with the Church. Importantly, Rousseau did maintain that a virtuous constitution would be enabled through good government. Social life, then, had possibilities.

Before discussing the importance of change and how this relates to children and education, it is necessary to discuss his analysis of inequalities. For Rousseau there are two types of inequality: first, there are natural and physical inequalities between people; and, second, there are moral, political and deliberative inequalities. The first is due to nature but the second is within human control. Rousseau argued that our natural inequalities are insignificant, but in society we become morally unequal. Hobbes and Locke were wrong about the states of nature because they transpose qualities that people can only have in society. A state of nature is either conflict or insecurity, and the government is required to ensure peace, through the consent of men that allows "privileges which some men enjoy to the prejudice of others" (*Origin of Inequality*, p. 49). The error the English social contract theorists made was in understanding how they get their nature. For Rousseau, property comes before war; property is the first institution of society. He conjectures:

> The first man who, having enclosed a piece of ground, bethought himself of saying 'This is mine', and found people simple enough to believe him, was the real founder of civil society.
>
> (*Origin of Inequality*, p. 84)

Rousseau argued that private property arose out of an agreement with other people, and with private property you get the growth of numbers and the passing of property to other generations. The earth becomes divided, and rich and poor can gain nothing other than becoming against each other, therefore begetting a state of war. With the state of war the rich contrive legitimacy of classes and move to stop the war and protect property. Thus, Rousseau argues, everyone keeps what he has and drives the poor into further poverty. Governments are thus established on a fraudulent basis whereby the poor only have their lives at risk; the rich have their property and their lives at risk.

Preceding private property was the "habit of living together"; living together in families was not pernicious in itself, as they:

> gave rise to the finest feelings of humanity, conjugal love and paternal affection. Every family became a little society, the more united because liberty and reciprocal attachment were the only bonds of its union.
>
> (*Origin of Inequality*, p. 88)

However, this social institution led to a differentiation of roles in which women concerned themselves with the home and the man "went abroad". When this led to greater human contact it caused rivalry, vanity, envy, shame and contempt for others. Furthermore, with the development of agriculture and metallurgy, people had property they meant to protect from the envious. This newborn society brought about a state of war with "rivalry and competition on one hand, and conflicting interests on the other" (*Origin of Inequality*, p. 96). Thus inequality arises when people identify others in relation to themselves and make comparisons. The significance of natural differences (the strongest, fastest, etc.) becomes moral when we apply values and start to rank people. Private property goes to the dextrous and eloquent, who form a government to legitimate property. He argues:

> the origin of society and law, which bound new fetters on the poor, and gave them new powers to the rich; which irretrievably destroyed natural liberty, eternally fixed the law of property and inequality, converted clever usurpation into unalterable right, and, for the advantage of a few ambitious individuals, subjected all mankind to perpetual labour, slavery, and wretchedness.
>
> (*Origin of Inequality*, p. 99)

In direct reference to Filmer, Rousseau contrasts the patriarchal authority of the father with that of the sovereign: "nothing on earth can be farther from the ferocious spirit of despotism than the mildness of that authority which looks more to the advantage of him who obeys than to him who commands" (*Origin of Inequality*, p. 103) or of the father, who has only the temporary advantage of being obeyed, rather than commanded. When the child reaches adult age, "from that time they are both equal...being perfectly independent of the father, and owing him only respect, and not obedience" (*Origin of Inequality*, p. 103). Rousseau rejected the overall Renaissance view that fathers must take charge in child-rearing; instead, they should lead by 'quiet authority'. Thus Rousseau reinforced the stark and exclusive difference between the 'dangerous' public world and the 'safety' of the private sphere.

Rousseau's text *The Social Contract*, published in 1762, the same year as his book on naturalistic education, *Émile*, discussed below, set out a programme of explaining not why people *should* behave according to the law, but why they *ought*. He establishes an argument for a virtuous constitution where equality is created, rather than reproducing the inequality in the state of nature. As well as equality, it was also necessary that the social contract should create the conditions of 'liberty', in a social way that binds people together. In marked contrast to the individualist liberty of Hobbes, Locke and Smith, Rousseau argued that we needed to have control of and autonomy from our impulses. Our 'natural' liberty is one that we have in a state of nature and enslaves us, similarly to animals, to our impulses. 'Moral' liberty, on the other hand, is our obedience to the laws that we prescribe to ourselves, thus superseding 'natural' liberty.

The *Social Contract* is an account of our entry into society. Running through the assumption of the *Social Contract* is the notion of human perfectibility, our capability for improvement and the possibility of a radical metamorphosis in human nature. With human association we pass from physical to moral possibilities. The *Social Contract* establishes what is needed to create a society where individual liberty is made compatible with social organisation. For Rousseau, there was no going back to the state of nature, but he wants to recapture those elements in natural man that can be saved, or an association that will protect and defend all people: "while uniting himself with all, may still obey himself alone, and remain as free as before" (*Social Contract*, p. 191). If liberty is self-determination, what political system is compatible with this? Rousseau advocates a (rather Aristotelian) republican constitution, similar to the Athenian system, where every citizen is a member of the sovereign assembly and laws are to be passed by the complete citizen body. Self-determination happens in two ways: first, as a citizen voter you have the capacity to make sovereign laws; second, as a subject of those laws you made in the citizen assembly, you have power over others, as you do over yourself. Thus in the civil state a radical change occurs, "substituting justice for instinct in his conduct, and giving his actions the morality they had formerly lacked" (*Social Contract*, p. 195). In short, the civil state provides "moral liberty, which alone makes him truly master of himself; for the mere impulse of appetite is slavery, while obedience to a law which we prescribe ourselves is liberty" (*Social Contract*, p. 196).

The discussion of Rousseau's ideas seems, at first sight, to be rather abstract. Indeed, some commentators have described his ideas as leading to totalitarianism (Berlin, 1959). However, it is important to note the two notions of liberty being discussed here and how they link in with children's liberty. Many liberals and libertarians would prefer negative liberty to Rousseau's positive liberty. However, it is necessary to remember Rousseau's problematisation of inequality. Hobbes, for instance, would have argued that a starving child could eat, as there is no one stopping him or her. However, Rousseau would argue that he or she would have to possess the wherewithal to do so; people are not free if they are under social or economic burdens. They are only free if we educate them, train and employ them so that they can think properly, free of their restraining needs. For 'negative libertarians', who believe in freedom from constraint, restraint can only come from the outside, not from within your own nature. To use another example, negative libertarians would say that if you are prohibited from taking drugs then your liberty has been decreased, even though they may be bad for you. However, positive libertarians advocate a 'forcing to be free', in which prohibition increases liberty by forcing you to be free of dependence.

Given Rousseau's belief in perfectibility, his conviction in the possibilities of human change and positive liberty, it is a small surprise that he thought and wrote a great deal about the education of children. Rousseau's writings were influential at the time. His major treatise on education, *Émile*, sets out his programme and is worth attention. It is very much influenced by, and in reaction to, Locke's *Some Thoughts Concerning Education*. Nevertheless, it is important to bear in mind Rousseau's other works. For instance, in *Origins of Inequality* and his description of the state of nature, Rousseau did not see children, once they left infanthood and the mother's prerogative, as passive, but as active and free. They were:

> active, swift of foot, and vigorous in fight...he learnt to surmount obstacles of nature, to contend in case of necessity with other animals, and to dispute for the means of subsistence even with other

men, or to indemnify himself for what he was forced to give up to a stronger.

(Origin of Inequality, p. 85)

However, in *Émile* he makes clear that: "We are born weak, we need strength; helpless, we need aid; foolish, we need reason. All that we lack at birth, all that we need when we come to man's estate, is the gift of education" *(Émile*, p. 6). Interestingly, Rousseau emphasises the importance of mothers as the optimum carers of young children. He condemns wet nursing as weakening the rights and duties of mothers and infants to each other. In contrast to Locke, the latter believing in the ultimate harm to children caused by women's 'cockering', Rousseau believed that the mother had the 'right' of child-rearing. Rousseau, however, believed in the importance of public education as paramount in making a good society. Private education at home is not desirable: "but how will a man live with others if he is educated for himself alone?" *(Émile*, p. 9). Vocational education, as advocated by Smith, is also limited, as young citizens need to learn to "bear the buffets of fortune, to brave wealth and poverty, to live at need among the snows of Iceland or on the scorching rocks of Malta" *(Émile*, p. 10). For Rousseau the state is the paramount political relation to the child, over and above the father. In the *Origin of Inequality* Rousseau declares:

> From the first moment of life, men ought to begin learning to deserve to live; and, as at the instant of birth we partake of the rights of citizenship, that ought to be the beginning of the exercise of our duty. If there are laws for the age of maturity, there ought to be laws for infancy, teaching obedience to others: and as the reason of each man is not to be the sole arbiter of his duties, government ought the less indiscriminately to abandon to the intelligence and prejudices of fathers the education of their children, as that education is of still greater importance to the State than to the fathers: for, according to the course of nature, the death of the father often deprives him of the final fruits of education; but his country sooner or later perceives its effects. Families dissolve, but the state remains.
>
> (pp. 148–149)

Furthermore, children require the development of reason as it "teaches us to know good or evil...Before the age of reason we do good or ill without knowing it, and there is no morality in our actions" *(Émile*, p. 34). Rousseau here understands children as being 'pre-moral'; unable to make promises, acts or contracts which they do not comprehend. For Rousseau the task of education is to engender in children constraint of their passions and to reduce their dependence on others. He argues:

> The very words *obey* and *command* will be excluded from his vocabulary, still more those of *duty* and *obligation*; but the words strength, necessity, weakness, and constraint must have a large place in it.
>
> (*Émile*, p. 53)

In order to achieve this, Rousseau outlines a radical education that is child-centred and self-directed, from a relatively early age. In *Émile* the tutor should avoid "continually giving him instruction; he acts only at the word of command" (p. 83). In marked contrast to the rote learning of the catechism and 'lessons' of conventional education, Rousseau declares: "I am pretty sure Emile will learn to read and write before he is ten, just because I care very little whether he can do so before he is fifteen" (p. 81).

In the pre-adolescent years, children are not to concentrate on learning archaic languages, such as Latin or Greek (unless they wish to do so), but should be encouraged to re-create the habits of the state of nature. The nearest occupation to the state of nature is that of the artisan, as it is the least dependent upon fortune. The artisan relies on labour alone and is not dependent upon others. The work has mechanical satisfaction and can be of use in any circumstance, for example, for "Robinson on his island" (p. 161).

However, this prepares him for the main task of education that occurs at around 14, when elementary education ends. This is the most important phase of education, as "We are born, so to speak, twice over; born into existence, and born into life; born into a human being, born into a man... As the roaring of the waves precedes the tempest, so the murmur of rising passions announces this tumultuous change... A change of temper, frequent outbreaks of anger, a perpetual stirring of the mind, make the child almost ungovernable. He becomes deaf to the voice he used to obey; he is a lion in a fever; he distrusts his keeper and refuses to be controlled" (p. 172).

The temptations of youth, he argued, can be deterred by protecting children from the harms of society, which compels them to grow up too quickly; preferably by taking them away or withholding them "from great cities, where the flaunting attire and the boldness of women hasten and anticipate the teaching of nature" (p. 192). In the classroom the youth is to learn subjects, sports and 'facts'; however, these are to be taught in a way that encourages equality and eschews hierarchy. He states:

> tutors ... discourage their pupils by always professing to treat them as children, and by emphasising the difference between themselves and their scholars in everything they do. Far from damping their youthful spirits in this fashion, spare no effort to stimulate their courage; that they may become your equals, treat them as such already. (p. 208)

As much of the feminist literature makes clear, this citizenship education, encouraging an autonomous, deep-thinking and humane citizen, is only appropriate for male children. Book 5 of *Émile* focuses on the education of the girl Sophie: "where sex is concerned man and woman are unlike; each is the complement of the other" (*Émile*, p. 321). The female citizen, if she could be referred to as such, has a very different expectation from the autonomous citizen prepared 'for the snows of Iceland or on the scorching rocks of Malta'; rather, she is to be a wife and mother. The education for Sophie consisted of needlework, learning cleanliness and simple religion, but to be "observant and obliging, and all that she does is full of grace" (p. 360). For Émile, he was to "be something, to be himself, and always at one with himself, a man must act as he speaks, must know what course he ought to take, and must follow that course with vigour and persistence" (p. 8). Sophie, on the other hand was:

> to be pleasing in his sight, to win his respect and love, to train him in childhood, to tend him in manhood, to counsel and console, to make his life pleasant and happy, these are the duties of woman for all time, and this is what she should be taught while she is young. (p. 328)

Before we go on to discuss the feminist critique of the social contract theorists, it is worth reflecting on what is happening to ideas of children and childhood in all Enlightenment thinking. First, there has been a sophisticated theorisation of the public sphere as a site of competition and, at times, conflict. This is in contrast to an idealised private sphere of harmony and shelter. It is in the private sphere that children must be located, free from the cares and potential harms of the outside world. Protected by a powerful, rational, autonomous, educated, male (albeit avuncular) citizen/father, children will be 'free' to learn and develop. However, what the Enlightenment also introduced was a narrative of a view of civilisation which held that a person progressed through spheres of increasing education from barbarity or 'innocent savage' to a civilised core. In Enlightenment thinking Others, who were primitive or at an earlier stage of development, were added to the spatial arrangement of the savage being outside the city or in another part of the world (Fraleigh, 2011). In this sense children were always going to be Othered and perceived as lacking.

Women's challenge to citizenship

So far, political theories of citizenship have been restricted to some adult men. Women and ethnic and racial minorities were directly excluded, as they were considered 'incompetent' and were often likened to children in some accounts. However, during the Enlightenment, and later during the French Revolution, women's rights were first voiced, and women's challenge to male political theorists gives some idea of the philosophical obstacles to children today. Given the close connection of women with children, both in women's daily lives and in philosophical theories, it is worthwhile to explore some of the challenges to Enlightenment or male 'liberal' political theories.

Women, like children, were barely mentioned by theorists such as Hobbes, Locke, Smith and Rousseau in their establishment of the rights of men. Women at the time were not considered persons, except for the criminal law. Recent feminist writers (Okin, 1980; Eisenstein, 1984; Coole, 1993) have argued that women are not mentioned because they had no place in the 'public sphere' of law and philosophy. Similar to children, their place was considered to be subject to the will and power of their husbands and subject to patriarchal power. Parallels to children can also be noted in that women's invisibility in this literature was assumed to be natural.

Women's exclusion from citizenship did not comprise just the denial of the vote, property rights, and so on; in England, for instance, exclusion was based on the common law of 'coverture'. Coverture was an institution based on the assumption that the husband covered the wife; thereby on marriage a woman passed on her rights to her husband. Women, like children and infants, required guardianship. In the eighteenth century married women did not have the right to property and could not enter to contracts, and any earnings gained by a married woman belonged to her husband. The law treated adultery, divorce and infidelity differently. Physical assault, such as wife-beating, was considered legal with only some minor limitations. There was more:

married women had no rights over their children, and on the death of the father custody of a child would pass to the nearest male relative. Many forms of employment, and virtually all professions, directly excluded women practitioners. Furthermore, as we have seen in connection with Rousseau's prescription for Sophie, girls' education was primed to the assumption of marriage, not necessarily paid employment.

What justifications were put forward for the exclusion of women? First, exclusion was premised upon the 'natural disabilities' of women; women, it was thought, did not have sufficient physical strength and could not 'reason' appropriately, as they were too prone to their passions. Second, women's social role was so tied to their reproductive capacities that this was viewed as a primary function, rather than one of women's broader capabilities. Third, the 'separate spheres' ideologies placed women, with children, into the privatised space of the home and domestic arena, whereas men were associated with the public world of politics. Indeed, some held that women's 'natural' condition would become 'contaminated' by involvement in the public world and would thus require 'protection' from public issues. From a twenty-first century viewpoint this is anachronistic, and few would suggest that it holds true today. However, the focus on natural disabilities, the connection with social reproduction and 'protection' from public contamination are still powerful current arguments against children's citizenship.

There were, of course, men who challenged this orthodoxy. Condorcet, for instance, in his *Admission of Women to the Rights of Citizenship*, published in 1790, argued that exclusion of women's citizenship was contrary to the logic of natural rights. He declared: "either no individual of the human species has any true rights, or all have the same." He also argued that the oppression of women was customary rather than natural and that this prejudice was firmly embedded in social life. Women's alleged incompetence was due to social convention and not a predetermined natural condition. Besides, this notion of deficit in individuals was not necessary when considering democratic citizenship; citizenship required ordinary, not exceptional, capacities and these are independent of gender. It may be that no women were great scientists or statesmen, but this did not mean that rights were given to great men only. Furthermore, women might be occupied with the begetting and care of infants, but this would also exclude men who worked long hours. In a famous passage Condorcet declares:

> If one admits such arguments against women, it would also be necessary to take away the rights of citizenship from that portion of

the people who, having to work without respite, can neither acquire enlightenment nor exercise its reason, and soon little by little the only men who would be permitted to be citizens would be those who had followed a course in public law.

Rousseau, responding to Condorcet's pamphlet, provided one of the most effective and influential responses to the exclusion of women, arguing that women were defined by their task of reproduction. This was not new – Aristotle had believed women to be misshapen men due to their reproductive capacity – so the idea of inferiority was deep-rooted. It is not so easy to write women into the social contract, as Rousseau's republican theory requires a domestic function that makes women's rights incompatible with the social contract. Theorists to date have written about the state and family as separate entities. One enters citizenship after the family. There is a requirement for a virtuous wife and mother. Despite Rousseau's advocating a non-hierarchical education, children are clearly located within the authority structures of the household. It was believed that each family should present a unity of purpose, and it will fall on one person to make decisions. This comes back to Locke's argument of a husband and father utilising his strength and intelligence to fit the family into citizenship. Despite the vociferous response to writers such as Filmer, who advocated a strong patriarchy, the concern for guaranteed paternity and the apprehension that a bastard might be smuggled into the family were powerful. Thus, it was considered that the law must guarantee the seclusion of women. Rousseau presented the ideology of sexual difference as a potential threat to republican virtue. He believed women to have an insatiable sexual passion that was potentially subversive to male power. Men would lose their virility and strength. Thus women had to be educated into chastity, restraint and obedience.

Women at the time directly challenged these commonly held assumptions; one of the most powerful critiques of Rousseau and the exclusion of women from citizenship came from Mary Wollstonecraft's *Vindication of the Rights of Woman*, published in 1792. In this pamphlet Wollstonecraft utilises Rousseau's egalitarianism to challenge the oppression of women. Her intention was to launch a protest at the exclusion of women in the rights of man specified during the French Revolution. She argued that French Revolutionaries could only justify excluding women if they could *prove* that women have no reason. This would be difficult, as women already display sufficient reason to perform duties. Furthermore, Rousseau's ideas of femininity are not natural, but rather are an artificial construct that is imposed upon by men and accepted by women. Wollstonecraft goes further and argues that there needs to be a revolution in manners and not just equal rights. This transformation requires equal educational opportunities, economic independence and the need to change the relations between genders into a 'rational fellowship'. In short, true emancipation cannot be achieved simply through education and equal rights; more deep-rooted social practices need to be challenged. Today feminist theorists identify the making of the 'social contract' as a key moment in building modern patriarchy.

Patriarchy

Carole Pateman (1988) offers a powerful and succinct critique of social contract theory, so influential in the development of civil citizenship through the eighteenth and nineteenth centuries. Social contract theory, rather than threatening patriarchy, actually reinforced it by replacing the political defeat of the father/king with "modern fraternal patriarchy" through a social contract that "establishes men's political right over women – and also sexual in the sense of establishing orderly access by men to women's bodies" (Pateman, 1988, p. 2). This is achieved through the convention of the marital contract that places women within a 'private' sphere separated from a 'civic' sphere of rationally disposed individuals entering into contracts with one another.

For Pateman, contract theorists have presented a case of individual freedoms whereby equals enter into contracts with one another; however, these contracts generate political rights of domination and subordination. To understand any classic theorist's picture of either the natural condition or the civil state, there must be an understanding of the two theoretical spheres together. The private sphere is part of civil society but is separated from the 'civic' sphere; they are at once in opposition to each other and yet mutually dependent. Women, through the marital contract and the children that follow from this, are incorporated into a sphere that both is and is not civil society.

Modern patriarchy is fraternal, and the original social contract is a brotherly pact against the father. Sex-right is no longer subsumed under the power of the father, in Filmer's fashion, but the masculine right over women is declared non-political. The separation of work from the household and the consolidation of the patriarchal structure of capitalism deprived women of an economic basis for independence. The brothers make a sexual contract and establish laws to ensure an orderly access to women. The marriage contract illustrates how patriarchal political rights are continuously renewed and reaffirmed through actual contracts in everyday life.

Pateman's critique of social contract theory illustrates the complexity of citizenship and campaigns for civil citizenship throughout the nineteenth and twentieth centuries. The sexual contract is not only located in the private sphere but also pervades all aspects of civil society. Feminist campaigns that have been formulated in the language of the ownership of the person, such as the rights to suffrage, abortion, child custody and to civil freedoms as women, render sexual difference as irrelevant. However, it is very hard to be uncontaminated by patriarchal subordination. The story of the sexual contract, for Pateman, throws light on the institution of marriage and how, no matter how hard some try to avoid replicating patriarchal relations, no-one can entirely escape the social and legal consequences of entering the marital contract. Furthermore, patriarchy is not simply about women's familial subjection, as women engage in sexual relations with men before they are mothers and sometimes through the sexual labour market. As Pateman argues:

> The story of the sexual contract is about (hetero)sexual relations and women as embodied sexual beings. The story helps us to understand the mechanisms through which men claim right of sexual access to women's bodies and claim right of command over the use of women's bodies. Moreover, heterosexual relations are not confined to private life. The most dramatic example of the public aspect of patriarchal right is that men demand that women's bodies are for sale as commodities in the capitalist market; prostitution is a major capitalist industry.
>
> (Pateman, 1988, p. 17)

John Stuart Mill

In the nineteenth century significant developments in social thought challenged the view of women as mere appendages to men. As we will see in the next chapter, feminists and others challenged many of the excesses in the laws of coverture over the nineteenth century. In England the ideas of John Stuart Mill, and his partner Harriet Taylor, presented a powerful theory of human nature that began to challenge the social assumptions of those denied citizenship, such as women and working people. Mill took the ideas of natural rights and 'utilitarianism' of the eighteenth century and cultivated them into nineteenth-century concerns. Such concerns included the elevation of self-knowledge, an acknowledgement of the complexity of society and an awareness of human failings.

Mill's conception of human nature, while still fundamentally based on ideas of rationality, was also informed by recognising the diversity of the human condition, including the diversity in physical and biological differences. Individuals have a tendency to cohere around each other and come together to form an overall 'plan of life' in a social manner. Individuals do follow the partial utilitarian principle of seeking to obtain pleasurable experiences, although, for Mill, under the right conditions the self-interest principle will become mutual rather than egoistic. In order to realise their 'plan of life' individuals need to openly discuss their considerations and formulate their own opinions. Thus, there is a requirement for a broader civil society or 'public realm'. People have a unique sense of creativity, although not everyone is equally creative and some by dint of circumstances are unable to imaginatively define and seek an adequate plan of life. If individuals are unable to develop a creative plan of life "there is nothing for them but implicit obedience to an Akbar or a Charlemagne, if they are so fortunate as to find one" (1975, p. 16).

Like Rousseau, Mill believed that the development of men and women came from an essence within themselves, although for this to flourish people require the conditions of liberty that encourages a state of free and open inquiry and discussion. Mill advocated a lively, free and engaging public civil society. It is important for these conditions to be available to all, including those groups of people previously denied the liberty to "create their own sovereignty over himself, over his body and over his mind" (p. 15). Famously, in *The Subjection of Women* Mill and Harriet Taylor forcefully argued that this should apply to women.

Mill, however, like Hobbes and Locke before him, explicitly bracketed out children from the condition of liberty. Mill states:

> It is, perhaps, hardly necessary to say that this doctrine is meant to apply only to human beings in the maturity of their faculties. We are not speaking of children, or of young person below the age which the law may fix as that of manhood or womanhood. Those who are still in a state to require being taken care of by others, must be protected against their own actions as well as against external injury. (p. 15)

Yet Mill's own arguments may lead us to believe that children, and certainly young people, would benefit from his doctrine of liberty in certain circumstances. Mill recognises that the principles of utility could only be learnt "by discussion and experience. Not by experience alone. There must be discussion, to show how experience is to be interpreted. Wrong opinions and practices gradually yield to fact and argument: but facts and arguments, to produce any effect on the mind, must be brought before it" (1975, p. 27).

Thus, there is a requirement for maturation and engagement as social, or political, animals, within civil society for children to fully develop and flourish.

Mill's representation, like the older Greek concerns over children and young people, was that young people are unable to follow their own will, but instead copy or imitate others and are liable to blindly follow bad ideas or customs – the very characteristics he correctly cautioned against in the case of women and working people. Instead, Mill argued that children needed to be trained and taught, but only when "arrived at the maturity of his own faculties, to use and interpret experience in his own way" (1975, p. 72). Where, when and how young people are to learn to interpret experience in their own way, Mill does not say. In a famous passage in his work *On Liberty* Mill hints at an internal and possibly innate awakening and maturity of 'inward forces', utilising the commonly used nineteenth-century metaphor of children and nature:

> Human nature is not a machine to be built after a model, and set to do exactly the work prescribed for it, but a tree, which requires to grow and develop itself on all sides, according to the tendency of the inward forces which make it a living thing.

It is curious that Mill, who argues so vehemently for the real creation of the conditions for utility among adults, expects young people to develop sovereignty of themselves through 'teaching and training'. Passive teaching and training are not likely to challenge mediocrity or to develop the colourful array of 'strong natures' that Mill feels so passionate about. Instead, Mill is more concerned with protecting children "from themselves" and juxtaposes them with people who gamble, drink, are unclean, idle or incontinent (Mill, 1975, p. 99).

However, Mill's ideas are a watershed for children in some respects: he argues for the limitation of parental power and for the state to legitimately intervene on behalf of the child (Mill, 1975, p. 129). By the turn of the twentieth century these ideas were considered self-evident truths. Although he did not regard state education as appropriate, he advocated that the state should provide a voucher system to pay the fees for children to be educated at the school of a parent's choice, and should compel parents to educate their children adequately.

Conclusion

By the end of the eighteenth century the Enlightenment encouraged political theory to develop a form of citizenship in which groups of men would have equal freedom for all persons to pursue their own spiritual, moral and material ends as they judged best. The doctrine of natural rights seemed well suited to that radical task. Modern natural law theorists saw the right to property as being identical with the right of liberty. Hobbes and Locke extended the concept of a property right to include the right to life, which they interpreted as a right to one's body. William Blackstone in his *Commentaries on the Laws of England*, published in the 1760s, took this further in claiming that personal labour is the only natural mode of acquisition and all property is derived from society, with the law assigning possessions to individuals. This can be traced to his fundamental belief, expanding on Edward Coke, that English common law had come to be the perfect embodiment of the principles of natural law. The legal distribution of property, therefore, is in conformity with the natural law. The idea of natural rights gained increasing acceptance through the eighteenth century, but the substance, private property, underwent several shifts in interpretation, culminating in the science of political economy and the development of the labour theory of value. In the work of Adam Smith we find the declaration of property as a natural right, and he attacked any barriers that prevented propertyless people from selling their own labour to the highest bidder. The natural rights doctrine, even in the diluted form of property and labour, continued to function as the primary framework for political argument. It is central to the American Declaration of Independence, in which Jefferson speaks of the inalienable rights of man to life, liberty and the pursuit of happiness – where the pursuit of happiness is arguably substituted by the pursuit of property.

However, during the eighteenth century, natural rights were increasingly associated with the doctrine used to justify the existing system of property rights. This did not include large classes of individuals who were oppressed, not by tyrannical monarchs but through economic inequality. By the mid-nineteenth century few radicals, with the possible exception of Mill and Taylor, turned to natural rights, as they were deemed to encourage inegalitarian societies supported by political institutions that served to justify them. It is also clear, as the above discussion has shown, that natural rights served to exclude women and children, as well as the economically impoverished. Even the children of the property-owning classes were considered 'pre-moral', unable to comprehend or act appropriately in the contract-making public sphere free from dependence upon others. In the following century, with the Industrial Revolution, new ideas that challenged the exclusivity of natural rights and citizenship came to prominence. New, large-scale and more powerful women's and working-class movements challenged many of the assumptions of natural law to lay claims for extending citizenship. These debates affected the lives of children, especially those of the poor. Childhood was a contested category. By the end of the century, children of the poor and working people had been removed from the public world of work and placed within schools, and the bourgeois image of the child as innocent and vulnerable became 'common sense'.

3
The Search for Equality, and the 'Protection' and Education of Children

If we are taking Marshall's phases of citizenship, the period discussed in the previous chapter looked at the first 'phase' of citizenship extension, when 'civil' citizenship was developed. Under the political theories of the time, adult male citizens were recognised under natural rights as individual rights bearers who were recognised in law as worthy of making contracts, owning property and having rights of representation. As we discussed, this excluded as many as it included and, rather than being universal, was quite particular. It excluded children, women, the propertyless and minorities. The gradualist nature of English civil citizenship was soon to be outshone by the two main political revolutions at the time, one in North America and the other in France, which were 'revolutionary' in the sense that the extension of civil citizenship was enshrined in political constitutions. In North America all men were created equal and in France men were born, and always remained, free and equal in their rights. The revolutions enacted the spirit of the Enlightenment: where the fundamental politics were simplified, ordinary people could discern a just from an unjust government. Equality was a simple concept, rights were simplified and these principles could not be given away, whatever the bargain. The declared rights were there to be reclaimed, as they always belonged to people. They were thus *universal* to all citizens.

Closer examination of history, of course, demonstrates that these were not applicable to all human beings within the bounded territories, as they also varied according to sex, race and age. However, the claim to universalism is as powerful today as it was to revolutionary Americans or French. In France, the revolution swept away hereditary rights, the monarchy, and group membership based on the Church or guilds, from which others were excluded. Overnight, a unified state of sovereign citizens was established. The principle of *civil equality*, or the equivalent, recognised through 'natural rights' included equality before the law in France, resulting in the replacement of manorial courts with a unified system of laws, or codes, where rights were protected. Relatedly, the revolutions led to equality of opportunities: access to public offices was no longer reliant upon status at birth, or bought and sold, but depended on ability. In principle, there were no legal impediments to people's interests, and property claims would reflect people's own industry and character.

The principle of civil equality within the revolutions (and gradually in England) introduced *voting* rights equivalent to natural rights, although they illustrate the limitations of civil equality at the time, as they were premised upon the exclusion of the poor, women, slaves and children. Children today still do not have voting rights, as the development of civil rights discussed in the previous chapters was premised on the constructions of children's 'incompleteness', 'incompetence', vulnerability and the 'otherness' to ideas of adult citizenship. This chapter discusses the period after the revolutions in the United States and France, when the franchises of France, the United States and Great Britain, among other countries within the European spheres of influence, were extended. The nineteenth century was a period of distinct development of capitalist social relations, with a concomitant rise of significant radical discourses around social class and gender that shaped the emergence of a distinctly 'modern' concept of childhood. The principal areas discussed in this chapter are the extension of state and other non-state actors' concerns with children's employment, education and sexuality. At the beginning of the nineteenth century most children engaged in paid employment, a minority were educated and the sexuality of children, as Foucault (1976/1998) observed, was rarely discussed publicly. However, by the end of the period a 'universal' child was usually expected not to engage in paid employment, all were to be schooled and children's sexual vulnerability was an object of state surveillance, control and regulation.

This chapter begins with a discussion of the context of the nineteenth century and the development of capitalism during the Industrial Revolution. The Industrial Revolution instigated the counter-discourse of Marxism and feminism as a critique of capitalism and patriarchy. These two discourses, along with traditional conservative discourses of liberalism, religion and economic competitiveness, shaped the construction of the modern child who was vulnerable to sexual and economic exploitation and required a healthy environment conducive to learning. The complex activities of a variety of influences also led to the development of 'child protection' organisations and the local state that were the forerunners of the professional child workers recognisable in the twenty-first century.

Urbanisation, Marxism and children

In the nineteenth century there was another revolution, at least as important to ideas of citizenship for children and others as the French and American revolutions; the *Industrial* Revolution that transformed the relationship between states and households. Given that the idea of citizenship is so closely linked to cities, it is no surprise that the radical development and change of industrial cities in the nineteenth century led to corresponding radical rethinking of citizenship. After industrialisation in England other countries followed: Belgium was perhaps the first, followed by other countries in Northern Europe, such as Germany and, later, France. British economic success, buttressed by military dominance and the development of the Empire, was emulated and eventually eclipsed elsewhere. Not only Europe but also the United States benefited from bountiful resources and a growing population. However, the effects of industrialisation and urbanisation were startling. Manchester, for instance, was described by Charles Dickens in *Hard Times* as the 'shock city' of the nineteenth century; it did indeed shock with its appalling poverty, exploitation and squalor, but also gave rise to radical possibilities in terms of citizenship. The most notable changes, and the subjects of a huge historiography, were the extension of the franchise, the development of a rudimentary welfare state and compulsory education for all children; it is hard to think of this happening without urbanisation.

Historians attribute the pull to the cities to the stagnation of rural wages, the rise of living expenses and the decline in rural occupations for women. The movement of labour to the cities was determined by the decline of opportunities in the countryside. There was an increase in population, and in England much of the population was under 15 – one estimate puts it at over 40 per cent in 1826. Population growth meant a large number of children in families who were dependent upon men's wages, with the stagnation of men's wages leading to the question whether there were work opportunities for married women (Anderson, 1990). However, there was a concomitant collapse in demand for women's rural work; in England this was spinning cloth, which was being replaced by mechanisation.

Children have perhaps always been an important element of labour in pre-industrial societies. What the industrial revolution enabled was an increase in demand and the opportunities for children's labour on a much larger scale. Within cities and factories, children could work for a number of hours, over any day of the week and at any time of the year; they were not restricted to seasonal demands as in previous historical times. The nature, extent and content of children's work changed. The boom in child labour must be understood in terms of the increase in the supply side; there were more children, perhaps due to advances in medicine or hygiene, and the opportunities for women's work (and their contribution to the family economy) had declined significantly, leaving families reliant on a decreasing male wage.

So far the main focus of the book has been on the emergence of 'liberal' notions of citizenship, together with the development of individual 'civil' citizenship. At the time, these very definitions, while bolstering the claims to rising power of the middle classes in Europe and North America, served to directly exclude women and children. However, there were other important processes in the nineteenth century that augured the advent of universal suffrage, education for all and mass citizenship, belonging and shared identity, as well as a view of the state that was the harbinger of good to be embraced, rather than the source of oppression to be avoided or controlled, as the English social contract theorists particularly suggested.

In the early nineteenth century Georg Friedrich Hegel (1942) argued that the state was the best vehicle to initiate the moral betterment of a country's inhabitants. In contrast to the English liberal tradition, Hegel viewed the state as a means to deliver individuals from the slavery of their private egoism. Hegel argued that smaller associations, such as families, guilds, kin and even towns, only existed to serve the needs of their own members. These small associations established local controls on movement and defined a narrow form of self-interest; these traditional rules and customs could only be overcome by a powerful state. It was therefore necessary, Hegel argued, for society's members to be forced into universal citizenship in a way that excluded no one. Karl Marx (1977) built upon Hegel's radical view of the transforming power of the state in his essay *On the Jewish Question*, written in 1843. The essay provided another critique of liberalism's division of the public and private spheres. Marx argued that, according to liberal philosophers, the liberal state provides the conditions for individuals to be free and equal to make contracts in the public sphere. However, in their private lives individuals, whether workers or capitalists, are subject to the market forces considered by commentators like Adam Smith as the most efficient means of distributing resources. Yet, Marx argued, these market forces generated inequalities that subverted those formal rights and citizenship developed by liberal thinkers. After all, those suffering job insecurities, unemployment or low pay are provided little comfort under the false universalism that nineteenth-century liberal ideas offered. Market forces provided differential access to natural rights within the public sphere; it was only by direct state intervention, possibly through the use of violence and force, that inequality and exploitation could be channelled or reversed. Marxist analysis and critique of liberal notions of citizenship bring to the fore what Kirk Mann (1992) later described as the importance of a person's position within a highly stratified paid labour market. Thus, the closely linked connection between citizenship and employment becomes apparent, and we will return to it in the discussion of children below.

However, it is worth reflecting on some caveats to Marxist thinking. Sheila Rowbotham (1979) has argued that women have played a less overt role in Marxist theory. Women were as much a part of the proletariat as men, and, as Engels noted in *The Condition of the English Working Class*, were the majority of workers in nineteenth-century Manchester. One can also point out that children, too, formed a large part of this workforce, one that Rowbotham does not emphasise. Women and children were part of the proletariat as waged workers, but were later confined to the home, which Marx does not see as a part of the production process. In contrast to Marx, who did not see processes of alienation occurring in the home, feminist writers, such as Rowbotham, discuss the private sphere as part of the processes of replenishing the workforce, rearing children and child-bearing as part of production – the 'domestic mode of production'. Later, Jens Qvortrup (1994) would argue that children too were part of the production process, as the work of reproduction replenished the pool of labour available for the capitalist labour market.

Marx did not express any interest in the law of 'coverture', whereby the income of women and children belonged to men. In reality all property and income belonged to the father, and therefore the wife and children were doubly alienated; at least the working-class man possessed his own labour, producing things of value to be exchanged in the market. Feminists argued that there was a gendering of domestic labour relations, and the home was a site of production, not just a private place of consumption. By viewing the home as a site of production and recognising the invisibility of children in the production process a more realistic and nuanced theory can be developed (see O'Neill (1994) for a discussion of how this applied to children). Marx was, in a sense, naive in assuming that, with the removal of private property, the capitalist state would wither away and remove the bases of alienation and exploitation. Marx argued that a communist society would be one of cooperation, and in the *Communist Manifesto* he identified the interdependent nature of human beings, in which the free development of each is the condition for the free development of all, which contrasts with the atomistic liberal view of social and political participation. The mistake Marx made was not realising that the violence used to crush the bourgeoisie would not teleologically wither away but would involve a begetting of violence in itself. Ironically, most so-called 'Marxist' societies to date have tended to use even more force against their citizens than capitalist societies.

However, the contribution of socialists and socialist theorists, not least Marx, is a significant strand of thought that became influential in developing what was known in the twentieth century as 'social citizenship', as well as underlying radical thought up to the present day. Socialists looked to end the deferential class system based on stratification, calling instead for the end of politics of envy and greater mingling between classes. R.H. Tawney (1938), for instance, wrote that something was wrong when "some classes should be excluded from the heritage of civilization which others enjoy, and that the fact of human fellowship, which is ultimate and profound, should be obscured by economic contrasts, which are trivial and superficial" (p. 113).

Marx was right to provide a material analysis of the state, one that had hitherto been avoided, even by radical theorists such as Rousseau and Hegel. Thomas (1984) has observed that Marx condemned liberal notions of citizenship and the state as having uncritical and almost religious overtones. Furthermore, as Faulks (2000) has observed, the *Communist Manifesto* did identify the importance of interdependence for citizens and how this should shape the future of citizenship. In contrast to the liberal view of citizenship rights, which sees individuals as competitors for and limits to freedom, Marx provides a more sustainable view, in which the free development of each is the condition for the free development of all.

Returning to children, it is important to note again how children, within the theories discussed so far, were considered incapable of making responsible decisions, needing an adult male to make choices on their behalf. Children, without the benefit of organised representation for themselves, became subject to determined efforts to 'protect' them from the danger, exploitation and unpleasantness of employment, and an independent life on the streets. Later, Hanson and Vandaele (2003) note that, in the context of today's denial of children's right to work in advanced industrialised countries, children who do work do so without the protection that adult workers receive in terms of pay, hours of work, health and safety, and so on; thus, they do not have rights *at* work. Furthermore, as Liebel (2004) has noted, working children today, denied the full package of labour law rights, are not recognised as equal persons. It is thus necessary to discuss the processes by which this occurred during the nineteenth century.

The nineteenth century witnessed the passing of legislation to protect children from the public realm of the factory, workshop, theatres, mines and the street, thereby consolidated their dependence on both the family and the state. In England this culminated in the 1903 Employment Act, which standardised the piecemeal legislation and byelaws of the nineteenth century. It is worth dwelling on this process a little further and point out the variability, complexity and opposition to the process that occurred in England, and this process is seen reflected slightly later in other European countries and relatively recently in the developing world. Glauser (1997), for instance, has deconstructed usages of 'street children' in today's developing world and uncovers a range of competing interests in the 'cause'; from saving children from the evils of the street, characterised by liberal Western notions, to those who see street children as a criminal problem and a threat to the social order. Placed within the wider historical context, the process of employment control sees a reversal of citizenship for children, away from the employed and autonomous citizen to one of the schooled and 'vulnerable' child that we can recognise in the twentieth century.

Employment of children

In 1851 Henry Mayhew, writing the articles that would form his *London Labour and the London Poor*, described a colourful street life in London, where children undertook an enormous type and variety of jobs; the most visible were children selling a whole range of products. Children were often sent out to work by parents to contribute to the household economy, or were run-aways scratching a living on the streets. Perhaps the liveliness of city life is what Rawson (2003) describes for the city of Rome, and the freedom that this offered children. 'Reformers', on the other hand, feared exploitation of the children by their parents, their possible moral corruption, the lack of education, and the lack of thrift shown by children spending their gains on gambling, attending 'penny gaffs' or on drink. The changes in industrial society led to a new way of thinking about children, what was expected of them, the rights they would have and the changing nature of the relationship between children, the state and families.

What is significant about this period is that the government became involved. It is perhaps easy for us to find it puzzling that the first laws introduced to *protect* children limited the opportunities of employing children before they were eight. However, this is judging the past from the present; it is highly significant that the government, traditionally not interested in the lives of poor children, became interested. Regulating children's employment started a process of other new interventions in the lives of children, notably around their health, education and morals.

From 1802, numerous Factory Acts were passed by Parliament in England with the avowed object of protecting younger workers from injury, overwork and unwholesome conditions. These were more than Acts regulating employment of young persons, as medieval guilds had for a long time regulated the work of children; however, the intention of the guilds had been to prevent not overwork, but rather idleness, among children. The Factory Acts were built upon the existing Poor Laws, whereby parishes were responsible for directing destitute children and orphans into a trade apprenticeship. However, the great objective of the parishes seems to have been the removal of children anywhere and anyhow to keep rates low. Thus, measures by philanthropists and Parliament were concerned with the possible abuses of apprentices in workshops as well as housing orphaned and abandoned children.

The plight of working children was not entirely new to the nineteenth century. In 1784 Manchester, described as the first 'workshop of the world', physician Thomas Percival noted how fever epidemics appeared to spread more noticeably in factories. Following this, Percival influenced magistrates in Manchester to limit the sending of parish apprentices to factories where young workers were expected to labour for more than ten hours each day (Hutchins and Harrison, 1907). The Factory Acts of 1833 and 1844 that followed set a minimum age of eight for employment in a textile factory, a maximum of 30 hours work per week with part-time schooling for three hours each working day. No child could start work in a factory without a doctor's certificate of health approved by one of the newly established factory inspectors.

In 1861 a Royal Commission on the Employment of Children was established in Britain through the pressure of Lord Shaftesbury. The six reports published between 1863 and 1867 were catalogues describing long hours, appalling work conditions, industrial diseases, accidents, dust, fumes, fatigue, bad light and illiteracy experienced by a large proportion of children in the country. The first Report, in 1863, declared that textile workers' hostility to part-time work decreased as improvements in health were perceived to have taken place 20 years after the last Factory Acts; the Commissioners were confident that it was rare to see a child under six working in a factory, and in 1867 these regulations were extended to blast furnaces, rubber and glass factories.

However, this should not give the impression of a pre-industrial 'golden age', as Engels envisaged, where "they did not need to overwork; they did no more than they chose to do, and yet earned what they needed. They had leisure for healthful work in garden and field, work which, in itself, was recreation for them" (1969, p. 38). As Cruickshank (1981) observed, 'child slavery' did not exist so much between child and capitalist as between child and the adult employee who paid the child from his or her own wages. The attention to the 'dark satanic mills' seemed to ignore the miserable conditions experienced by child workers in small workshops and the exploitation often inflicted upon them by their own parents. Indeed, the decline in the demand for children in factories in the second half of the nineteenth century pushed children into the marginal and sweatshop trades, so conditions for children working in workshops may in fact have deteriorated (Nardinelli, 1990).

State action at the time was closely connected with children's citizenship. Robert Walpole, a drafter of the 1867 Factory Extension Act, demanded supervision of workshops and the need for the state to act as "parent of the nation", a term reflecting the state's increasingly important role in the lives of children and an erosion of parental authority. The language of reformers often bordered on racism, as interest in workshops in the 1880s was coupled with the huge influx of Eastern European Jews. Jews were (erroneously) associated with the sweating trades, and it was feared that their competition would drive down wages. The House of Lords Select Committee on the Sweated Trades in 1888 found little substantial change in children's conditions in workshops, despite the passing of Factory and Workshop Acts and also the Education Acts of the 1870s, which forbade the employment of children under ten.

Other trades were also identified as being possibly detrimental to children. The plight of theatrical and fairground children was taken up by Lord Shaftesbury, who campaigned to pass the Children's Dangerous Performances Act in 1879, which made it illegal to employ a child under

14 in any 'public exhibition or performance' which might endanger life and limb. However, the Acts were ineffective, as it was left up to magistrates to define what a *performance* was. It was not until the Prevention of Cruelty to Children Acts of 1889 and 1894 that the police were given the powers to take into custody, without warrant, persons viewed as being in danger. It is also worth noting that the two Acts were passed, according to Lytton Strachey, in the light of feminist work by Millicent Garrett Fawcett and the publication in 1884 of Ellen Barlee's *Pantomime Waifs* (Strachey, 1931).

By the turn of the twentieth century government controls on children's work had increased significantly, and children under ten were totally removed from the formal labour market. However, legislation was often piecemeal, and regulations were only really effective against factories and mines. Much of the enforcement of the Acts was in the hands of police forces, whose enthusiasm varied from county to county. The most effective forces were those pressurised into action by organised feminists, such as those in London, Bristol, Bradford and especially Manchester (Keeling, 1914, p. 38).

A great deal of concern was expressed by inspectors, enquiry commissioners and philanthropists concerning the moral well-being of children in employment. The concerns in the 1860s over agricultural 'gangings' were often articulated around the moral dangers of mixing youths of both sexes in fields away from home and supervision, and males and females performing their private functions in view of each other (Royal Commission on the Employment of Children, 6th Report, 1867). Angela John describes how middle-class commissioners investigating child labour in mines condemned children working under ground in "nurseries for juvenile vice" and sexual corruption, although little clear evidence was produced other than hearsay (John, 1984, p. 41).

There was a considerable double standard as far as the regulation of children's labour was concerned. While scrutiny was applied to public employment in factories, brickyards, theatres, farms and mines, very little attention was given to domestic work, either paid domestic servants or unpaid children working in the home. Lionel Rose reports from census data that, out of the 1,230,000 females in paid 'general domestic service' in 1881, over 98,000 were under 15; and in 1891 there were 107,000 under-15-year-olds out of 1,386,000 (Rose, 1991, p. 36). Although census data are often unreliable, it seems that the census enumerators would underestimate rather than overestimate the number of young workers, as girls would often lie about their age to improve their chances of employment. It also seems unlikely that most of these would have worked for upper-class employers; a great deal of domestic work was for artisans, small farmers and clerks, especially as young girls who lacked experience would begin work, after family commitments, at the social bottom and only later aspire to 'gentlemen work'. Author Flora Thompson, remembering her childhood, referred to such work as " 'petty places' and looked upon as stepping-stones to better things" (Thompson, 1954, pp. 156–157).

It seems unlikely that most domestic servants had fond memories of their 'petty place'. A scan of court reports shows that a 13-year-old girl was repeatedly beaten by her mistress in Manchester in 1886, and this was only discovered when the mistress took to beating the same girl with a red hot poker (*Manchester Guardian*, 12 January 1886)! The novelist Emma Smith's first domestic work ended in her being sexually abused by her master (1954, p. 36). The unpopularity of domestic work is perhaps best illustrated by the number of girls and women who turned their backs on domestic service in the twentieth century when jobs in offices, factories and shops opened up to them.

There were no clear guidelines amid the piecemeal legislation of the nineteenth century. Local authorities, especially in the provinces, lobbied central government to provide them with the powers to regulate child labour in their own districts. It was the campaign by local authorities (supported by philanthropists, some feminists and socialists, religious leaders and children's organisations) that led to the Inter-Departmental Committee on the Employment of Schoolchildren in 1902 and then the passing of the first general Employment of Children Act in 1903, which provided local authorities with powers to issue licences to children in work.

If children were barred from working, then how else would they survive? Reformers were often aware of the consequences of restricting children's work opportunities, and often philanthropic organisations would encourage *regulated* children's street trading, for example establishing shoe-black brigades, messenger running and newspaper selling. Through recollections of working-class people themselves we know that many children made significant financial contributions to the domestic economy through work (see Jamieson, 1986). Many migrants expected their children to contribute to the household economy, and the *padrone* system put Italian migrants at loggerheads with middle-class reformers (Behlmer, 1982). However, by the twentieth century working parents were reluctant to have their children working, and delayed their entry into the labour market until as late as economic circumstances would allow (Hair, 1982). Indeed, a historian of industrial relations Clark

Nardinelli (1990) has argued that it was parents' decision to invest in their children's education, rather than labour, that led to the decline in children's work, not the role of philanthropist reformers. Opposition to protective legislation on children's working conditions was changing too. Socialist and trade union agitation over the use of child labour intensified in the late nineteenth century (Frow and Frow, 1970). In particular, it was feminists within the Independent Labour Party (ILP), such as Emmeline Pankhurst and especially Margaret McMillan, who campaigned most vigorously for the abolition of child labour, so that it became a central part of the party's propaganda well into the twentieth century (Steedman, 1990). The teaching profession also campaigned for further legislation, as did the medical profession (Hendrick, 1997). Interest in the control of children's work was beneficial for both of these professions, and the establishment of School Medical Officers in 1907 began a trend which saw the medical profession become increasingly influential in the passing of protective legislation in the twentieth century (Armstrong, 1995).

The rescue of child workers and street children to give them a more appropriate experience of childhood was believed to form better future parents and future citizens. The child was presented as helpless and passive, and the parents were presented as, at best, ignorant and irresponsible (Dyhouse, 1981). Local authorities and child 'professionals' had the right and duty to impose a model of childhood on the poor. Of course, children were no more passive then than they are now, and evolutionary models of child welfare development must be treated with caution. Corsaro (1997) in the context of the USA emphasised the 'agentic' aspect of child workers at the beginning of the twentieth century. Where children in their early teens were noted for selling evening newspapers, harsh and exploitational entrepreneurs sought to extract profit from children, but were curtailed to some extent after the founding of a trade union by the children to protect themselves. Today, children's trade unions in the developing world form an interesting contrast to many Western campaigning non-governmental organisations (NGOs) (Liebel, 2003).

In 1911 Britain was still wracked by the 'boy labour' problem, in which boys between 10 and 14 years of age were tempted into 'blind alley occupations', such as messengers and newsboys. These jobs, often deemed necessary in working-class households for their income, were viewed, by 'respectable' commentators, as giving boys the income without the responsibility. It was feared that the boys would slip into unruly behaviour and when finished could be thrown into the labour market with no skills or training. This was likened to wider issues around 'race', nationality and the economic health of the nation. As Emsley (2011) has argued: "the miserable, unskilled, untrained and hence unemployed or underemployed men who had followed the boy labour route, were seen as producing still more weak-kneed, narrow chested, noisy and volatile slum-dwellers" (p. 66). Such concerns with the citizenship and behaviour of boys, the economic costs of a low-skilled working class and the supposed slippage into crime continues to shape government concerns in Britain to this day.

Education

Education systems do not grow up by mere chance; they reflect contemporary ideas about social organisation, the nature of knowledge, possibilities of human improvement and notions of citizenship. Nineteenth-century England saw the development of a 'universalised' structure of education for every child: every child, by the end of the century, was legally obliged to attend formal schooling. The exact nature of this formal education was conditioned by a wide range of social factors, including age, class, gender, religion, ethnicity and locality; and each of these was in the process of changing, given the large shift in social understandings and attitudes regarding them over the course of the century, and the complex interrelationship between them. Such shifting complexities affected conceptions of childhood and children, and attitudes and beliefs about the nature of children and childhood affected the types of education available within a society at any one time.

Krishan Kamur (1978) describes the impact of the 'great transformation' perceived by social thinkers in the nineteenth century: the Enlightenment, the French Revolution and the English Industrial Revolution. The French Revolution had a startling effect on the English middle and upper classes; they feared a similar outbreak in England, especially given the appalling conditions much of the working class had to suffer in the large cities as a result of industrialisation. The ideas of the Enlightenment were turned to in order to explain these huge changes, as concepts such as 'reason' and 'progress' replaced the terms 'faith' and 'decay' associated with the religious dogma of the Middle Ages.

Throughout the nineteenth century attitudes to knowledge were changing; traditionally knowledge, especially for working-class people, was transmitted through practice and experience, often from father to son and from mother to daughter in face-to-face interaction. However, the new view that knowledge could be transmitted secondarily through books and teaching, distinct from experience, was gradually being accepted (Musgrave, 1968). There was also a belief, increasingly taken up by industrialists, that scientific and technical education was crucial for competitiveness in the world market. This was reflecting the educational reforms already taking place in Germany and the USA. Since the Industrial Revolution, the system of long apprenticeships into trades was declining, and schooling was seen as a necessary substitute; and it was hoped, by employers, that the people would be schooled into a sober and industrious workforce.

Notions of 'reason' and 'science' were not necessarily replacing religious values; rather, religion itself was becoming more complex. Since the foundation of the Society for Promoting Christian Knowledge in the eighteenth century, evangelical religion played an important role in attempting to provide some schooling for every child. It was felt by a large number of evangelists that education could be used as a rehabilitative way of 'reclaiming' working-class children, and a host of 'Ragged Schools' were established in most towns in England.

These were, of course, changing along with the shifting notion and composition of 'citizenship'. First, the feminist movement, from Mary Wollstonecraft in the eighteenth century onwards, argued for a change in the relationship between men and women, the means for economic independence for women, and an improved educational provision for women and girls, if not on equal terms with boys and men, then superior (Spender, 1987). Educational equality was seen by middle-class feminists to be a first step or a key to other freedoms, such as access to employment opportunities, relief from boredom and an increased ability to fight for other freedoms, and an equivalent right to citizenship with men. Second, it was felt by some working-class leaders that education was a beneficial provision, both as a necessity in itself and as a means to social mobility (Hurt, 1979). Such 'moral force' socialists, such as the Chartist William Lovett, founded adult schools, debating societies and libraries.

Education, of course, is how societies reproduce themselves and their concomitant strata and inequalities. In France, Robert Gildea (2008) remarked of the middle nineteenth century: "what marked out the elite of French society was both education and property. The peasantry had a little, the working class none, and rarely did they have an education past elementary level" (p. 104). For middle and upper-class boys in France there were the Lycées and colleges, and for some the baccalauréat at 18. The class basis of the structure of French education can be illustrated by the fact that in 1855 the sons of landowners, public officials, liberal professions and industrialists made up the Lycées in the North of France (Gildea, 2008, p. 105).

For working-class children, the upper and middle classes gradually warmed to the idea of educational expansion as a means to ensure social discipline. With the urbanisation of cities and the perceived threat of possible unrest, education, it was hoped, could be aimed at the children of the poor, who could be provided with instruction in knowing one's place in the social hierarchy. Against the social contagion of subversive doctrines such as radicalism and anarchism, children would be made into pillars of the establishment. Through the nineteenth century the ideas of liberalism changed from *laissez-faire* arguments to the idealist philosophy associated with T.H. Green in England. Green developed a notion of citizenship based on justice, equality, middle-class values, and a quest for self-help and moral improvement. Green conceived of education as the great social harmoniser and equaliser of both men and women, rich and poor.

Broadly speaking, there were two key nineteenth-century pedagogical beliefs. The first one, 'mechanistic' or 'automatic', informed most educational provision, especially for the working classes. It viewed children acquiring knowledge through repetition and rote learning. It pictured the mind as a kind of machine in which learning could be stripped down to its core 'elements', which formed the basis of a number of combinations, so that, if one element were recalled, the others would be drawn to mind in a continuous column. Complementary to this view was the belief in original sin: where a child's nature was naturally biased towards evil, the task of education was to redeem children and guide them towards the path of righteousness, even if this was 'encouraged' by the use of physical punishment. The saying 'spare the rod and spoil the child' was often taken literally, and children's experiences of schooling were correspondingly often unpleasant and marked by frequent punishment.

The second approach to education, which I shall call the 'progressive' approach, put children at the centre of education, believing that all children have the equivalent potential to absorb knowledge, all children are by their nature good, and the path from birth to adulthood is marked by a series of developmental stages through the state of childhood. Teachers from the eighteenth century onwards found that children, given the opportunity, could show an interest in their work and a degree of responsibility which could not be associated with the belief of a child's innate tendency towards evil. As early as the seventeenth century, Comenius argued for the importance of children being mixed together and influencing each other: "nobody will doubt that a child contributes better than anyone to sharpening the spirit of another child" (quoted in Chalmel, 2003, p. 139). The cooperation of the class could be looked for and the emphasis put upon self-development; the teacher could act in a less domineering manner, assist children in their learning, and offer a broad curriculum.

This approach reflects the broader Romantic Movement that portrayed children in an angelic and innocent light. Building on Locke and Rousseau's view of the child being a *tabula rasa* and capable of both harm and good, Swiss philanthropist Johann Heinrich Pestalozzi and German educationalist Friedrich Froebel were hugely influential on nineteenth-century educational reformers. Both were deeply influenced by Rousseau. They believed that teachers should provide the correct environment, free from restrictions and prohibitions, for children to develop their inherently good characters, and encourage knowledge, peace with nature and union with God.

Pestalozzi, following Comenius, argued that the mother was the most significant mediator of the child to the world. If the mother were absent, the educational relationship would be dull and ineffective and the child would be left to his or her own devices. However, if a mother was possessive or authoritarian, then this left the child with very little chance of initiating learning. Thus, Pestalozzi called for a 'happy medium', although such an important task for developing a balanced and progressive society could not be left to mothers' 'instinct'. Instead, Pestalozzi produced a book in 1801 called *The Book of Mothers*. In it Pestalozzi granted mothers the importance of the child's first years of life: "Let elementary teaching never be the business of reason, let it remain the business of women for a long time before it becomes the business of men" (Pestalozzi, 1801, p. 216). The child should leave the familiar surroundings of the home universe (*Wohnstube*), as these are too narrow for the child to develop and grow, but the school must be able to retain the elements of love, gratitude, confidence and obedience that the child learns from home.

Bringing Froebelian principles to the industrial north of England, W.H. Herford operated a school in 1850 with no merit marking or ranking of pupils according to ability. He attempted to establish a relationship of trust between pupil and teacher, and the provision of pupils with the right to make their own decisions; the school also eschewed mental strain and encouraged the taking of fresh air, did not use punishments or rewards, and provided a non-denominational religious upbringing. Herford established a reputation for teaching women and girls on equal terms with boys, to the point of fielding a cricket team with both boys and girls (Hicks, 1936).

Froebel's ideas had established a much admired system of liberal kindergarten education; however, after the reaction to the 1848 uprisings across Europe, the Prussian state moved to close the schools on the grounds that Froebelian schools trained the youth of the country to 'socialistic atheism' (Heater, 1990, p. 78). The regulation following in 1854 enforced rigid codes in elementary schools for the three Rs and religion. The influence of Froebelian ideals did not completely disappear, but was, rather, crowded out by the debates around the education of the poor. Periodically, men and women, such as Eugenie Schwarzwald in Austria, would push for progressive educational reforms.

These two models are more or less ideal types at opposite ends of a spectrum. Individuals and groups interested in the education of children could usually be plotted somewhere between the two, perhaps leaning one way or the other. The two models above should be considered as simplifications of complexities; however, they are worth discussing, as they represent significant shifts in ideas about teaching through the nineteenth century. The progressive view increasingly gained in influence, although this was by no means a linear or complete process. This was hardly recognisable in working-class elementary schools.

From the beginning of the nineteenth century, teaching in elementary schools was mechanical and relied on rote learning. Discipline was rigid and repressive, and the curriculum restricted to reading and Bible teaching, less frequently included writing and arithmetic (Stone, 1969). The method of teaching in elementary schools was almost totally 'monatorial'. The essence of this method was that the teacher did not direct teaching, but selected certain of the older pupils as 'monitors', although not in the cooperative manner envisaged by Comenius. Monitors instructed small groups of pupils, while the teacher acted as supervisor, examiner and disciplinarian. Although improvements were made to the monatorial system in the nineteenth century, for instance with the introduction of pupil teachers, it remained the norm well into the late 1870s. The type of education for working-class pupils was clear instruction, underpinned by social Darwinism and *laissez-faire* philosophies. For instance, education secretary Robert Lowe declared in 1867: "The lower classes ought to be educated to discharge the duties cast upon them. They should be educated that they appreciate and defer to a higher cultivation when they meet it, and the higher classes ought to be educated in a very different manner, in order that they exhibit to the lower classes that higher education to which, if they were shown to them, they would bow down and defer" (quoted in Wardle, 1970, p. 25).

In 1888 the Royal Commission on the Elementary Acts asked for strict adherence to reading, writing, spelling, needlework for girls and arithmetic, but wished to extend the curriculum to include geography and drawing, with history and singing to cultivate the 'national culture'. They also endorsed "some system of physical instruction such as that recommended by the War Office" (Royal Commission on the Elementary Acts, Final Report, 1888, p. 216). This consisted chiefly of "extension motions, musical drill with wooden dumb-bells and wands, marching, running, hopping, and jumping, a large part of which could be carried on in schoolrooms and in all weathers" (Royal Commission on the Elementary Acts, Final Report, 1888, p. 145). The report stressed the fundamental need for the three Rs to be rigorously applied to the curriculum, which would "secure permanent educational results" (Royal Commission on the Elementary Acts, Final Report, 1888, p. 133).

However, the 1888 Royal Commission on the Elementary Acts produced a 'minority report' that adhered to the more progressive approach, and the reporters stressed the need to educate the child on their 'whole' personality, rather than instruction limited to a future career. The minority reporters tended to be religiously non-conformist and made direct references to Rousseau and Froebel. Henry Roscoe, for instance, writing on behalf of the growing scientific and technical movement, wished "to supplement our present one-sided system of education, which relies on books and on authority, by the introduction of studies which can call into activity mental and physical capabilities which have hitherto lain dormant, or whose growth has, at any rate, been stunted" (Roscoe, 1889, p. 70). The Minority Report concluded: "We think that with very young children the work of the infant school should be mainly formative, and should guide the spontaneous activity of the child's nature. The varied and systematised occupations, so well known in connection with Froebel, are of the greatest value" (Final Report, 1888, p. 305).

Girls' education reflected the idea of 'separate spheres' for men and women (Davidoff and Hall, 1988), and girls were expected to learn to become wives and mothers, care for children and their future husbands. The education of girls in France avoided the huge religious/secularism debates of the 1880s: "as they were not regarded as a political threat and educated not as future citizens but future wives and mothers, for whom piety and virginity were seen as essential even by republican fathers" (Gildea, 2008, p. 342). The education of girls was class segregated. Before the compulsory education acts of the 1870s the state of working-class girls' schooling was similar to that of working-class boys, in that it comprised only reading, religious instruction and a little writing. It tended to be short, lasting only as long as they were not usefully employed. However, the elementary schooling of girls anticipated their domestic roles, centring on sewing and cleaning, with lenience to girls in maths (Dyhouse, 1981). As Carol Dyhouse (1981) points out, there was a strong current of opinion in mid-Victorian society that the poor were responsible for their poverty, and a great many reformers sought to change behaviour rather than conditions. The earlier scepticism over the use of schools to encourage self-help, epitomised by Samuel Smiles' comment "one good mother is worth a thousand school masters", gave way to the belief that future mothers could be trained for motherhood, not only in schools but also through a host of organisations, such as the Ladies Visiting Society, Sanitary Associations and Health Visitors.

Throughout the nineteenth century middle-class girls were mainly taught at home or at fashionable day and boarding schools offering a superficial and non-academic curriculum with emphasis on learning to become a 'lady' (Purvis, 1991). However, given the high cost of middle-class boarding schools, a son's education was given priority at the cost of a daughter's education (Dyhouse, 1981). In France, as late as 1880, 62 per cent of girls were educated by nuns, thereby illustrating the low priority of girls' education (Gildea, 2008). However, from the 1840s a movement began to reform girls' education and to establish schools with a more academic curriculum.

In the nineteenth century the place of religion was also a site of heated debate and contention around 'children's souls'. In England, one of the largest forms of resistance to 'national' education came from religious denominations keen to retain their hold over the education of children, although in England this took the form of debate and compromise. There were similar struggles of 'nations' against religious providers of education. In France there was perhaps the most systematic attempt to provide a coherent programme of citizen education. As early as the revolution there were attempts to make children learn the *Declaration of the Rights of Man and the Citizen*. However, it was not until the 1880s, after the defeat of the Franco-Prussian War, and the concatenation of factors (social, economic and political) that was also leading to the development of state education across Northern Europe, that France developed a curriculum under a Minister of Public Instruction which contained instruction on: "the fatherland: what a man owes his country: obedience to law, military service, discipline, devotion, fidelity to the flag" (quoted in Heater, 1990, p. 84). There was an impassioned debate in which Léon Gambetta, through the 'Belville Manifesto' in 1869, committed himself to free, compulsory, lay education and the abolition of the Concordat, that is, the separation of Church and State. However, this did not succeed, and the struggle of Jules Ferry and the 'Ferry Laws' for free state education and the exclusion of religious instruction "was the beginning of a conflict which was to embitter the politics of the Third Republic almost to the end" (Cobban, 1965, p. 88).

By the twentieth century greater emphasis was being placed on notions of nationality and national unity. In France, instability and the perceived threat of revolution were a backdrop to Durkheim's formulation of his sociology of education, in which teachers were to teach conformity to moral codes (Wilson, 1962). There was a desire for an imagined homogeneous cultural, linguistic, racial and ethnic community within national boundaries. It was these ideals that began to shape citizenship ideals in the twentieth century. Those from different ethnic backgrounds were suspected of disloyalty, leading to, for instance, Bismarck's expulsion of Jews in 1885 and 1886. In the USA, children were seen as a way of integrating the waves of immigrants from Eastern and Southern Europe, and schools were the key institution in this project (Denzin, 1977). In Britain, the lower classes were introduced into a publicly funded school system with a highly instrumental curriculum to mould children into appropriately behaving citizens, a trait that, Robin Alexander (2000) argues, continues to this day.

Children in schools and homes were taught about heroes and glories of the homeland, often to the exclusion of other nations. As Hall (1994) has noted, the Victorian idea of nation, in the British context, "derived its particular and concrete meaning from Empire" (p. 29). Nationality was actively promoted through public education, rituals, flags, anthems and other means of developing an allegiance to the state. Nationalism offset the destabilising effects of class conflict with ideas of nation and nationhood.

The political landscape, then, had changed with the introduction of education. There was a need for a national identification of skills, nationality and citizenship that was based on inclusion and it also defined exclusion. The modern education system used the technique of normalisation by differentiating children and devising different strategies of categorisation and testing. The unified method of writing and communication was used, on the one hand, to homogenise and unify children through the development of language and national identity.

It also had a function of *placing* individual children into an unequal society. Harry Hendrick (1997) draws our attention to the irony that, despite the many and often competing social, economic and political interests around children in the late nineteenth century, by the turn of the twentieth century all children would have a 'proper' and 'normal' experience of childhood through compulsory schooling. Hendrick correctly argues that the control and moral assumptions and practices around 'teaching' produced a dominant image of a "schooled child". By the middle of the twentieth century any experience of childhood, whatever the culture and geographical location, must involve schooling. A 'non-schooled' child thus becomes an aberration and an infringement of a universal right.

This view reflects that of Philippe Meyer, drawing on Ariès' observation that the street of the medieval period was the "seat of business, of professional life, but also of gossip, conversation, entertainment and games" (quoted in Meyer, 1977, pp. 1–2). Before nineteenth-century state interventions children were expected to live their lives and learn in the midst of urban diversity. Children, or more accurately children of the poor, were not separated from the community, but took part in and contributed to the rhythm of social life. In the "undiscriminating sociability of the street" (Meyer, 1977, p. 3) children learned from their parents but also from masters, workshop companions, neighbours and tradesmen. The new process of citizenship established a division between public and private space. There was a "retreat from sociability, this turning in on itself of the family, and its resulting reorganisation around the child" (Meyer, 1977, p. 3).

The process of clearing children from the streets links with the previous discussion about controlling children's employment; it also reflects the ways in which the 'moral danger' of children in the public realm entered social and political discourse, thereby created the ambiguity of children in the public sphere that shapes children's citizenship to this day.

Family, marriage, property, law and the development of 'child protection'

In medieval and early modern Europe and North America, property ownership was a defining characteristic of who was and who was not a full member of society; property allowed a person freedom and power. Also, in peasant societies the family, not the individual, was seen as the essential unit of social cohesion (Pinchbeck and Hewitt,

1969). Children were in this sense no different from adult members in that they were part of a larger unit of the extended family, to which nuclear families of parents and children were subordinate. Family and not personal advancement, it had been argued, was the primary ambition and achievement (Pinchbeck and Hewitt, 1969). However, as Alan MacFarlane (1978) has pointed out, England was an exception to this, with evidence of free contractual relations and inheritance laws from at least the thirteenth century. Furthermore, the English legal system was complicated, as were arguably other legal systems throughout Europe, in that there were numerous branches of the law, such as Common, Ecclesiastical and Statute Law, operating at the same time alongside each other. Holsdworth (1936) argued that Roman law operated under the system of *patria potestas*, which subordinated children to the total control of the father, or, in the case of a father's death, another male guardian. While we saw in Chapter 1 that there were considerable limits to *patria potestas*, nevertheless children could not own property, marry or live anywhere without permission of their guardian.

In the sixteenth and seventeenth centuries, by law, a boy was of age to contract a fully valid marriage at the age of 14 and a girl at 12. But Ecclesiastical courts, which had undisputed jurisdiction in matrimonial cases, had long recognised '*matrimonium per verba de futuro*' or 'espousal' as a legal pre-contract of marriage, and one which could take place above the age of seven. The essential difference is that an espousal was voidable until a child became of 'ripe age' and ratified the espousal (Pinchbeck and Hewitt, 1969, p. 44). Evidence from diaries and literature of the time suggests that child marriage was, at least for the gentry and upper classes, unusual, with at most 5 per cent of marriages below age 15; however, among the poor it seems to have been more prevalent; it was even cited as a cause of poverty by literate commentators of the sixteenth century (Laslett, 1981). However, parental authority over the marriage of children, of most ages, has rarely been doubted. With the decline of feudalism, rights of guardianship passed from the feudal lord to the nearest male relative. It seems that the father from early times could assert his right of custody, inflict 'reasonable chastisement' and prevent marriages which he deemed unreasonable, as could anyone placed in a situation of *in loco parentis*. However, there were certain minor limitations to this authority, such as a child's right to sue in the event of serious injury committed by an adult.

In Prussia the *Untertanengesetz* deemed that a marriage between a Prussian man and a foreign woman meant that she became a Prussian subject. However, if a Prussian woman married a foreign man she ceased to be Prussian. All children of a Prussian couple were Prussian, as were children adopted or legitimated by a Prussian man. The *Untertanengesetz* made the status of females, and male children below military age, entirely a private matter of the family. The Prussian Legal Code, the *Allgemeines Landrecht*, assigned to the husband within these families the ultimate authority on all questions involving marriage, control of the wife's property, whether she traded and how the children were to be raised (Brubaker, 1992).

However, the nineteenth century witnessed a shift in legislation that recognised the child's interest in questions of custody. In England this had to wait until the 1880s, with similar reforms to coverture passed in Scandinavia and North America. Ironically, it was Orthodox Russia that passed the first Married Women's Property Act in Europe, in 1753 (Hunt, 2009). Legislators in the nineteenth century for the first time gave custody of children to the mother, and in some cases did so even if the father was living. Children, then, in the eyes of the law, were seen as having interests of their own, rather than being perceived as entirely in the possession of an adult.

Ironically, the new claiming of rights for women and children came just when legislators were legally defining the exclusion of women. Take the *Code Civil* of 1804 in France: the marriage law declared that "a man owes his wife protection; the wife owes the husband obedience." This remained a statute until 1938. In nineteenth-century France a wife could own property, but she was subjugated to her husband's will. Jean Portalis, commenting on the *Code Civil* in France in 1844, declared the family as the 'nursery of the state', and this was premised on the power of husbands and fathers. The *Code Civil* influenced countries that were occupied by Napoleon, including Spain, Italy, Netherlands, Poland and parts of Germany. In France divorce was impossible until 1884, but here, as in other countries in Europe, challenge and changes were happening.

In English common law, custody of children, in cases of divorce or separation, would usually go to the father, except in cases where the child was at proven risk of serious moral or physical harm due to the father's cruelty or profligacy. From 1839 statutory changes in England began to affect the mother's right to custody, with greater attention being paid to children's welfare. The Matrimonial Causes Act of 1857 allowed the Divorce Court to make custody orders up to the age of 21 on terms as it saw fit to give either parent custody. The Custody of Infants Act of 1873 removed the clause which had prevented women who had committed adultery from having custody of their children who were under seven.

The changes in family law were in part a response to the growing feminist movement. Feminists believed that women deserved legal protection and custody of their children, and that children deserved legal protection, and advocated custody law reform, where they appealed to the needs of children. Custody law depended not only upon the changing perceptions of children's needs and parent–child ties, but also on changing attitudes about women's rights and the relationship between husband and wife.

Feminists such as Barbara Leigh Smith (later Barbara Bodichon) attempted to challenge the doctrine of coverture and establish a separate legal identity apart from their husbands and fathers. Although women were restricted from public positions, except School Boards and Local Government Boards (Hollis, 1987), they developed into an effective social movement. Levine (1987) points out that feminists campaigned, not only for equal statutory provision, but also for a redefinition of the political and legal ideology which disallowed women a public persona. Women's lives, almost in their entirety, were governed by legislation over which they had no control: the property they might own, whom they might marry, the type of education or the form of employment they might take. In addition to married women's property, reforming attention was paid to inequalities in divorce laws, child custody, marital assault and marriage to a deceased wife's sister. The Married Women's Property Acts of 1870 and 1882 were, according to Shanley (1989), "arguably the single most important change in the legal status of women in the nineteenth century" (p. 103). They allowed women to become autonomous economic agents, undermined the notion of coverture, and went some way towards weakening the social, economic and legal stranglehold of adult men on the lives of women and children.

Dependent wives, as well as dependent children, were necessary for the preservation of patriarchy, for this allowed the smooth transfer of property through male primogeniture and preserved order in a society in which dominance and submission were assumed, whether in a household or a state (Stone, 1977). Some writers, such as Lawrence Stone (1990), have belittled the extent to which feminist pressure enacted changes in legislation. Stone suggests that it was changes in the values, morals and behaviour of powerful men that slowly moved the legislature to alter the law. This he links to changes in the social structure, especially the rise of the middling and professional classes. Even if this were true, Stone still makes no attempt to assess the impact of feminist ideas and arguments on the values of these men, nor does he acknowledge the great amount of behind-the-scenes lobbying by women such as Millicent Garrett Fawcett, Josephine Butler, Frances Power Cobbe or Barbara Bodichon. The changes in the social structure that Stone refers to also provided the material conditions for feminist, as well as patriarchal, ideas. The historian Helen Blackburn, who lived through the latter stages of the movement, argued that there was a symbiotic combination of the feminist movement's campaign to challenge family law and equal suffrage that developed in Manchester and mushroomed across the country (Blackburn, 1902).

So how did feminists challenge patriarchal practices? One approach was to directly challenge the violence and abuse perpetrated by men over women and children. Take Frances Power Cobbe's article in *The Contemporary Review* in 1878 on wife torture. The article listed the amount of abuse experienced by women and linked it directly to the principle of coverture:

> The general depreciation of women as a *sex* is bad enough, but in the manner we are considering, the special depreciation of *wives* is more directly responsible for the outrages they endure. The notion that a man's wife is his PROPERTY, in the sense in which a horse is his property ... is the fatal root of incalculable evil and misery. Every brutal-minded man, and many a man who in other relations in life is not brutal, entertains more or less vaguely the notion that his wife is his *thing*, and is ready to ask with indignation ... 'May I not do what I will *with my own*'.
>
> (Cobbe, 1878, p. 64)

Cobbe directly connected the abuse of women with that of children, in declaring that custody of children should automatically be given to a mother in the case of domestic abuse. She says:

> As to the justice and expediency of giving custody of the children (both boys and girls of all ages) to the wife, there can be, I should think, little hesitation. The man who is, *ex hypothesi*, capable of kicking, maiming, and mutilating his wife, is even less fit to be the guardian of the bodies and souls of children than the lord and master of women.
>
> (Cobbe, 1878, p. 86)

Feminism was not acting separately from other social movements. Cobbe's article linked abuse of women and children to the misuse of alcohol, following the temperance movement, which also sought to present children as innocent victims of drink. The temperance tracts by non-conformist Alfred Alsop, among others, portrayed children as idealised models of virtue and purity, with their spirituality overcoming hardships and temptation and bringing out the better natures of adults on the way (Delver, 1870). Reformers saw children as the key to the sober and moral future, and from the 1850s there was a children's temperance journal in existence, the *Band of Hope*. Such groups and individuals saw women and children as harbingers of a future society of sublime moral standards and purity of heart. However, these same characteristics served to confine women and children to the 'private' sphere and deny them any form of citizenship or the ability to partake in public life on the same terms as men.

In the 1880s the host of people and organisations subsumed, for the sake of simplicity, under the banner of the 'social purity movement' campaigned around issues of moral self-control and regulation of men. The movement was noted to have arisen out of the issues surrounding the Contagious Diseases Acts (Jeffries, 1982), although concerns about the state of the nation's morals can be traced back to Ancient Greece. Although not all purists were feminist sympathisers, women's organisations and feminism became a powerful pressure group within the wider movement at the level of public debates. In England, women like Elizabeth Blackwell, Ellice Hopkins, Laura Ormistone-Chant, Millicent Fawcett and Catherine Bramwell Booth became increasingly apparent on public platforms and published journals calling for the protection of the state for those, such as women and children, who suffered from male abuse. Of course, the social purity 'movement' was not just a feminist organisation, it also reflected wider changes in nineteenth-century society, which included: the consolidation of non-conformist involvement in English society after the 1792 Religious Toleration Act; a wider drift towards evangelical methods by established churches; the perceived increase in child prostitution and the so-called 'white slave trade'; Darwinist conceptions of the importance to the species of moral faculties such as self-control, love and altruism (Mort, 1987); and campaigns by socialists against the perceived decadence of the aristocracy. It was ironic that the social problem of sexual disease of young men was tackled by draconian interventions into the lives of girls (Doolittle, 2004).

Purity campaigns for more stringent legislation over public displays of sexuality coincided with alarm in middle-class circles about the immorality of the unrespectable poor, or the 'residuum' (Stedman Jones, 1984). In 1883 Andrew Mearns, a London Congregationalist minister, in his pamphlet *The Bitter Cry of Outcast London*, exposed the perceived moral corruption and absolute godlessness in the centre of London. Mearns argued, to a receptive middle-class audience, that overcrowding in poor districts spread the infection of immorality from the dissolute to honest and upright working-class families. The next year a *Report of the Royal Commission on the Housing of the Working Classes* investigated the appalling overcrowding of working-class housing, which, according to some of the investigators, including Mearns, resulted in incest. The crowded bedrooms supposedly encouraged children to be sexually aware of physical matters from an early age and it was feared that this 'corruption' of children would be detrimental to the long-term morality of the nation.

Prior to this, in 1879, Alfred Dyer, a Quaker, paid several visits to Brussels, where he found evidence of English girls kept as virtual prisoners in licensed brothels. Great publicity surrounded Dyer's allegations in the British press, and Dyer, with the support of Josephine Butler, formed the 'London Committee for the Suppression of the Traffic in British Girls for the purposes of Continental Prostitution': the progenitor of international children's rights movements of the twentieth century discussed in Chapter 6. In 1881 the House of Lords established a Committee to explore the extent of juvenile prostitution and advocated raising the age of sexual consent from 13 to 16 for girls. Stronger police powers, to search and arrest brothel keepers and make street soliciting illegal, were given to the newly professionalised police force. The 1885 Criminal Law Amendment Act passed these recommendations, raising the age of consent and easing the searches of brothels; in addition, it enabled the removal of young girls from 'immoral parents' and singled out all 'idiot' and 'imbecile' females for particular protection (Hansard, August 1885, p. 1553). The Act also slipped in an amendment making illegal all procurement or attempts at procurement of males for public or private indecency, thus "sharpening the definition of and hostility towards homosexuality both in Britain and abroad" (Weeks, 1977, p. 15).

Deborah Gorham (1978) saw the passing of the Criminal Law Amendment Act as an extension of control of young women's sexuality and an evasion of the 'real' cause of juvenile prostitution, which was restricted career opportunities for young working-class women. She also saw the 1885 Act as part of the legislative mood which gave rise to the 1861 Offences Against the Person Act, which was designed to protect a guardian's right to control a girl's sexuality. It reiterated the measures outlawing intercourse with a child under ten, but also contained restrictions designed to protect parental, and especially the father's, control over daughters under 21 years old. For instance, if a man entered a relationship with a girl under 16, the girl's father could charge her 'abductor' with depriving her parents of the services of their daughter; or, if a young woman had property, her marriage could be prevented if the suitor had used 'false allurements', up to the age of 21.

Gorham (1978) continued her criticism of the reformers by pointing out that the social purists extended the domestic control of middle-class girls to a society-wide surveillance of working-class girls. It was no accident that the consent legislation applied only to girls. It has been pointed out before that the socialisation of girls and boys, as outlined by writers such as Rousseau, was quite different; where boys were given priority in education and freedom of play and expression, girls were to be constrained in their play and kept within limited confines. Gorham notes that in the Victorian period middle-class girls' sexuality in particular was morally surveyed, and the reformers wished to enforce this surveillance on the seemingly uncontrolled children of the poor. Due to the noted overcrowding of houses, working-class girls spent a large proportion of their lives on the streets, which were considered by bourgeois sentimentality as 'corrupting' and 'dangerous'. Working-class girls were expected to contribute to the domestic running of the household from an early age, and any restrictions on their employment had broader ramifications. In short, legislation around the issue of the age of consent and family law was tied up with notions of gender, class, majority and citizenship. Women could not become full citizens; their sexuality was seen as needing to be both protected and controlled. Among the middle class and 'respectable' working class of a society there was a sense that they are under threat from 'outcast' groups of people, such as criminals, paupers, immigrants, delinquents, the demoralised and the prostitute. This encouraged muted feelings of both fear and genuine pity and concern.

The contradictions in the need to protect and control children can be seen in the prevailing and totally opposite images of children in the late nineteenth century. The first is what Peter Coveney (1968) has referred to as the 'post-Wordsworthian child' in literature from the 1830s onwards, where the child is endowed with romantic, pristine and angelic qualities. Hugh Cunningham notes that Wordsworthian naturism did not limit childhood to a 'preparatory phase', but would provide metaphors of nature for adults. Cunningham states: "life could be seen, not as an ascent to maturity, but as a decline from the freshness of childhood" (1995, p. 73). The Romantic Movement, in general, fiercely criticised both Puritan attitudes to children and the Enlightenment's adherence to 'Reason' at the expense of 'feeling', otherwise known as the 'cult of sensibility'. Following on from this, Romanticism "embedded in the European and American mind a sense of the importance of childhood, a belief that childhood should be happy, and a hope that the qualities of childhood, if they could be preserved into adulthood, might help redeem the adult world" (Cunningham, 1995, pp. 77–78).

By way of contrast, Cunningham (1995) describes the 'non-child' of the East End gutters, the northern mills and the child worker, which conflicted with the bourgeois ideal of childhood as a separate and delicate stage in a person's life. The campaigns around child protection can be seen as the appropriation of the working-class child to conformity to middle-class ideals. The construction of 'innocent' working-class children appearing alongside 'corrupted' white slaves is remarkable. The state intervened in more vigorous ways to protect working-class children and extended the official legal category for sexual innocence. From the 1880s, the work of the 'professionalising' agencies, such as the National Society for the Prevention of Cruelty to Children and Barnardo's, among others, became increasingly involved in policies relating to children, in terms of the 'expertise' regarding (in)appropriate childish behaviour and behaviour towards children. Recently, writing about sexually abused children, Jenny Kitzinger (1997) has argued that abused children are constructed as innocent victims with adult abusers constructed as all-powerful and predatory. This construction of the passivity of victims generates a powerful protectionist reaction from the state and society. Thus, control of children is tightened further and their estrangement from adults, other than their abusers, is exacerbated.

In 1881, philanthropic activist Lord Shaftesbury still contended that child abuse was "of so private, internal, and domestic a character as to be beyond the reach of legislation" (quoted in Behlmer, 1982, p. 52). Yet, less than five years later, the Criminal Law Amendment Act of 1885 and the Prevention of Cruelty to Children Act of 1889 placed the interests of the child as prime, overriding the traditional deference to familial and fatherly privacy. Parents were the natural protectors of their offspring, but, if they violated that trust, it was legitimate for the state to step in on the child's behalf. As Mary Lyndon Shanley suggests:

> Rather than treating fathers as enjoying a near-proprietary right to their children stemming from procreation, the legislation of the 1880s suggested that by the act of procreation parents had entered

into implicit agreements with one another, their children, and the state to nurture and care for their offspring. Parents who fulfilled their obligations would not suffer state interference, but those who violated the terms of their 'contract' could be forced to fulfil it – for example, by paying maintenance or sending their child to school. If the violation was so gross as to sever the contract, parents might forfeit custody altogether, and if the covenant between parent and child was broken by the natural parent, it might later 'be removed' by another willing to accept the responsibilities of parenthood.

(1989, p. 153)

Thus, there was a severing of legal relations based on biological ties, regarding these relations as voluntaristic or contractual as well as biological.

The introduction of protective legislation created a profound shift in the way adults interacted with children, in particular girls. As Kitzinger (1997) has noted, there are some ironies in the regulation and 'protection' of children's sexuality: first, bolstering the protection of children to ever closer relations and dependency on those who care for them may actually increase the harm to children, as most abuse occurs within normal adult/child 'caring' relationships. Second, by enhancing a sense of denial about children's sexual knowledge and over-emphasising innocence, a full and frank sex education that will protect them is obstructed. In short, Kitzinger argues, protectionist measures can reinforce the passivity of children and unintentionally make it difficult to deal with abuse. It is perhaps no surprise that, after the explosion of discourses and the competing 'regimes of truth' (Foucault, 1976/1998) around children's sexuality at the end of the nineteenth century, the issue of child abuse did not arise again until the relaxation of discussions about sex and the second wave of feminism in the 1960s.

Conclusion

By the twentieth century children's citizenship appeared in the form it has today. There was an ambiguity over children's natural rights, and they were considered citizens in the making, rather than citizens now. Women were at the dawn of receiving voting and other rights equivalent to men's, yet children were as far away from 'political citizenship' and decision-making as ever.

There were a number of professionals monitoring and controlling the spaces of the family/child compact; if there was failure, the state was ready to step in. Teachers, social workers, paediatricians and an array of allied professions monitored and controlled individual children in their families and on the streets. The relationship between the state and fathers would have been barely recognisable to the patriarchy of the eighteenth century. This is not to say that patriarchy had been replaced (indeed, mothers are more likely to be the targets of official interventions into families), but that intervening agencies and people complicated the public–private separation.

People had changed their relationship with the state. One element was Hegelian idealism, which recognised the importance and transformative potential of the state. Hegel's view of the relationship between the individual and the state emphasised the importance, in the state's own self-interest, of developing the civic function in education. Other 'idealists', such as T.H. Green in England, developed a form of liberalism quite distinct from the *laissez-faire* philosophy of Adam Smith. For idealists, the state could be a focus for citizen solidarity and loyalty. The state could promote the good life of all citizens, including those of the working class, by providing basic social welfare and fostering the moral nature of human beings. Green believed that human beings would develop to be responsible and have self-fulfilment only in the right material circumstances. It was clear to Green that human beings would not achieve well-being and social responsibility if all their energies were thrown into subsistence. It was this liberalism that influenced architects of the British twentieth-century welfare state, such as Lloyd George, Churchill, H.H. Asquith and William Beveridge.

Underlying these reforms was the growth of socialist politics and trade unionism. The history of socialism in the nineteenth century, however, was very patchy. In the USA, despite good trade union membership and often violent strikes, there was a failure to establish a socialist or workers' party. Working people's interests had to be passed through sympathetic members of the legislature. On the whole, nineteenth-century legal and political structures remained relatively hostile to working people's interests and in favour of the needs of capital. However, in Europe, despite the divisions between Marxist revolutionaries and social democrats, representation was achieved, up to a point. In Germany, by 1890 the Social Democrats were the largest parliamentary party. Other socialist-leaning parties were established in Britain, Austria, Italy, Spain, Scandinavia and the Low Countries. However, by the twentieth century only Germany had made some advances towards social state welfarism, and these were only introduced under Bismarck's reactionary aims to 'spike the guns' of the left. Nevertheless, the influence of socialism on citizenship was key to the twentieth century as an underlying force; or, in the case of Russia and the Soviet Union, as a specific state. The nature of the relationship between capital and labour formed the bedrock of Marshall's analysis of social citizenship in Britain and forms the overview of the next chapter.

4
Social Citizens

The twentieth century provided the major welling up of ideas on citizenship, and also the development of new ideas on children, childhood and that 'in-between stage' of youth. T.H. Marshall, writing after the turmoil of World War II, identified citizenship as developing through a series of consolidations of national consciousness, democracy and class struggles within a capitalist market economy. As Richard Bellamy (2008) has commented, the twentieth century witnessed the development of "the socialization of the masses into a national consciousness suited to a market and industrial economy by means of compulsory education, linguistic standardization, a popular press, and conscript armies" (p. 46). As a key aspect of this 'socialization', it was clear that children would be educated and provided with an acceptable degree of welfare. However, in return children would accept the discipline of the schooling system and develop appropriate national standards of citizenship 'behaviour'. The visions of national citizenship had earlier origins. The Victorian commentator Alfred Marshall (no relation to T.H. Marshall), writing in 1873, argued for a

> more liberal preparation in youth; steadily learning to value time and leisure for themselves, learning to care more for this than a mere increase of wages and material comforts; steadily developing independence and a manly respect for themselves, and therefore, a courteous respect for others; they are steadily accepting the private and public duties of a citizen.
>
> (quoted in Dwyer, 2004, p. 32)

As Peter Dwyer (2004) correctly observed, Alfred Marshall argued that the social right of education was a key factor in raising the level of 'civilising' those children and young people unexposed to 'respectable' pursuits. What Alfred Marshall encapsulated was a striving for an attempt to form a national character. This he understood through the term 'gentleman citizen' as something that was national, shared, constructive and 'civilised'. It was also something male, corresponding to the age-old concern of producing soldiers and citizens. This construction of 'national citizens' formed part of the twentieth-century concern with citizenship. This 'nationalisation' of citizenship arguably led to the two major bloodbaths in twentieth-century Europe and the horrific moulding of children in organisations such as the Hitler Youth in Germany.

This chapter looks at the British state's increasing involvement in the lives of children, and in particular the 'social citizenship' of providing for those citizens going through hard times. While the provisions of the welfare state must be seen as an advance and a progressive element of citizenship, there were distinct disadvantages and ambiguities to these gifts. The provision of social protection was undertaken with other objectives, notably the construction of a national consciousness and a 'national citizen'. It also became clear that there would be a price to pay; the provision became a tool to discipline elements of the population. The new propensity for greater state and outside involvement in the lives of children coincided with an ideology of childhood that represented children as passive and 'easily influenced by others', making children appear to be unworthy of citizenship.

Social citizenship

However, before this could be achieved there was still a tension in the twentieth century over exactly what form 'social citizenship' would take. The term 'social citizenship' was developed by T.H. Marshall (1950/1992), who identified three phases in the development of citizenship. In the first 'phase', from the Renaissance to the mid-nineteenth century, as discussed in Chapter 2, a sense of 'civil citizenship' was developed alongside natural rights theories. These 'civil rights' included the freedom to own property and to make contracts. This enabled the exchange of goods, services and labour to participate in a market economy, and also involved the freeing of conscience and thought necessary to express dissent and innovate. By the twentieth century sophisticated statistical categories had been developed as a method of counting citizens, such as birth registrations that served to both include and exclude national citizens. Children within this 'civil citizenship' had the 'right' of being legal citizens, residency entitlements and recognition as persons, although as 'minors' they were excluded from most other citizenship powers of decision.

In the second 'phase', discussed in the previous chapter, from the end of the eighteenth century up until the twentieth century, there was a widespread gaining of 'political rights' to association, to vote and stand for election and representation. By the 1920s adult women, rich and poor, had gained political rights in most Western countries. One must emphasise, though, that this did not include children, or others such as prisoners, the mentally ill or impaired adults. Being a 'denizen' of a nation does not lead to voting rights or, in the case of children, the ability or right to make contracts, marry, or participate in jury service or trade union membership.

In the final 'phase', discussed in this chapter, from the middle of the nineteenth century to the mid-twentieth century, citizens with civil and political rights also obtained 'social rights' to "a modicum of economic welfare and security", as Marshall argued. These included the rights to social insurance against unemployment and illness, health care, pensions and free education. All of these, and in particular the right to education, gave rise to the right, according to Marshall, to "live the life of a civilised being according to the standards prevailing in society". Social citizenship arguably extended the ability to practise citizenship to those previously excluded, such as the very poor and destitute. What was important for Marshall was that the claiming of these 'social rights' would not, like the Poor Laws of the past, divorce them from the other aspects of citizenship. Marshall argued that the Poor Law:

> treated the claims of the poor, not as an integral part of the rights of the citizen, but as an alternative to them – as claims which could be met only if the claimants ceased to be citizens in any true sense of the word. For paupers forfeited in practice the civil right of personal liberty, by internment in the workhouse, and they forfeited by law any political rights they might possess.
>
> (Marshall, 1950/1992, p. 15)

The exclusion of the very poor was something contested in the nineteenth century by radicals, socialists and those from the progressive centre to which Marshall belonged. Marshall's essay (1950/1992) outlined ideas of a 'hyphenated society' as a means of analysing the inevitable tensions between a capitalist economy and the welfare state requirements of the modern state. For Marshall there is a constant clash between claims for rights to welfare provision and the need for economic profitability. Subsequently Marshall has been criticised for understanding citizenship as an evolutionary progression and failing to see citizenship as a constantly contested concept (Turner, 1990, p. 192). By looking at the specific example of the emergence of social insurance in Britain, Joseph Melling (1991) argued that social policies of the state came into existence as part of wider movements of political and economic settlements. He demonstrates the complexity of political processes as he traces the emergence and development of discursive struggles, as well as economic structures and state initiatives. This reflects my argument offered in the last chapter over the discursive construction of children, their education, employment and sexuality. Melling correctly notes that the organisation of the British state through the mid-nineteenth century was largely local and limited in nature, rather than centralised and bureaucratic (Melling, 1991, p. 229). In the organising of poor relief there were five agencies involved: trade unions, friendly societies, employers' benefit schemes, philanthropic provision, and the Poor Law itself. From the 1880s citizen rights were contested in the shape of the legal and civil status of labour, and employers fought for control over the local labour markets against increasingly organised labour representation. The consequent welfare provision was dependent on the assumption that the private employer's normal authority was not to be challenged and the employer retained the prerogative to manage workers. There was also a second assumption, that the right to welfare citizenship was conditional rather than absolute; claims to welfare were dependent upon the respectable behaviour of the claimant. Suspicion of malingering, criminality, pauperism, the refusal of employment or the provocation of dismissal meant losing the right to unemployment relief. National Insurance provided the framework for a particular kind of social citizenship bounded by clear moral imperatives of respectability and conformity.

Prior to World War I, the Liberal governments acted to introduce some measures against poverty. This action was partly a reaction to the 'shocking' conditions of the poor, demonstrated by studies of poverty, such as those of Seebohm Rowntree (1901/2000), and the enquiry into 'physical deterioration' that was conducted in the light of the ill health of military conscripts during the Boer War (Harris, 2009). Also, perhaps pressure was applied by the threat of the Labour Party and the influence of idealists – politicians and civil servants taught by T.H. Green. However, it was apparent that rights to welfare, in this context, were given to those considered 'deserving' of assistance (Vincent, 1991). The state was not alone in this; members of the skilled working class were keen to exclude those considered low-skilled, or non-unionised, from collective state provision (Mann, 1992). The term citizenship has always had exclusive characteristics, and throughout history the granting of what became known as social rights has been resisted due to the fear of draining local resources. All towns and cities have struggled to rid themselves of those likely to be a burden. One dramatic example was the town of Erlangen, now Germany; in the eighteenth century it had a population of 9,000, yet some 400–500 beggars each month came to the gates for free meals (Nathans, 2004). This gave rise to periodic purges of beggars.

The formulation of 'social citizenship' also developed alongside other social exclusions. First, social provisions are aimed at indigenous populations, often considered to be racially homogeneous. However, it is estimated that there are up to 9,000 ethnic–cultural groups in the world today, yet there are only 200 states. At the turn of the twentieth century, as still remains the case today, no European nation state consisted of a homogeneous ethnic–cultural group. It was clear from the passing of the Aliens Act in England in 1905 and 1914 that immigration controls and differential access to social welfare had become enshrined in British law. Brubaker (1992) has noted how disadvantaged minority ethnic groups continue to be excluded, not only from the citizenship rights to welfare and the means to be an effective member of the community, but also from *formal* legal membership of European nation states. There has been considerable commentary on how the construction of French citizenship sees the social pluralism associated with ethnic minorities as "permeated by a fear of pluralism, of particularism and of fragmentation" (Laborde, 2004, p. 55). This reflects the Durkheimian preoccupation in the Third Republic that contrasted the advanced, institutionalised, 'evolved' and 'organic' democratic nation based around a bounded culture, a united national territory, as intrinsically modern, with ethnic, hierarchical and 'mechanical' forms of solidarity that were considered regressive. French citizens were expected to privatise their cultural affiliations in favour of an atomised and individualistic structuring of their public life. Such tensions persist today.

Second, the ambiguity of social citizenship can be demonstrated when looking at gender. Much of the legislation in the early twentieth century in Britain aiming to support mothers and their children partially met some women's needs, but served to place recipient women in the private sphere of the home and enabled the state and professionals to define and regulate women's lives. As Fiona Williams says, the services offered functioned to "consolidate women in the home and to tie women's role in the family to the development of the 'race' and nation" (2003, p. 150). Children were the embodiment of the 'race' and it was important for them to be fit and healthy for their future roles as workers, soldiers or mothers. Thus the attention to children and the mothers caring for them, according to Williams, was as much to do with the state of the nation as it was to serve the needs of women and children. Williams points out, furthermore, that women and children were not included in early social insurance legislation, as the object of insurance was the health of adult men. Britain was not unique in this; in the 1930s, Aid for Families with Dependent Children (AFDC) was developed in the United States to provide a safety net to those identified as 'needy'. The 'needy' were defined as those perceived to be from lower and working classes, premised upon a working father and a mother at home with children.

Social rights were regulated in other ways. The problem of high infant mortality rates in France and England at the turn of the twentieth century (Hendrick, 2005, p. 34) brought a medical 'gaze' to the way mothers were bringing up children. Medical knowledge centred on the feeding of infants and also mothering skills, which Jane Lewis (1980) has referred to as 'mothercraft', and medical concern with the infant mortality rate allowed a range of services to be provided to mothers. While on one level this would have offered some form of help and support to hard-pressed mothers, it replaced traditional realms of knowledge and support that women occupied within communities, thereby replacing community support with externally defined medical care. In any case, the contribution of medical knowledge to the improvement in infant mortality rates in the 1920s has been questioned as being too 'limited and late' to have had any effect (Ross, 1993); the explanation is more likely to be social factors, such as improved diet, breastfeeding and environmental improvements. As Lewis notes, infant welfare assumed mothers to be ignorant, careless and indifferent to their children, and policies "ran counter to the demands of women's groups for direct economic assistance" (1980, p. 17). Characteristic of this was George Newman, Chief Medical Officer to the Ministry of Health in 1920, who explained weak and sickly children by blaming women who did not possess the required degree of maternal obligation, intelligence or ability to manage their households (Hendrick, 1994). Assistance and help can be two-faced.

'Discovering' children

The twentieth-century state continued the process begun in the nineteenth century, as discussed in the previous chapter, of increasing interest in employment and education in the lives of children. New forms of knowledge were also being applied to children, with new categorisations and theories of children and childhood. This can be demonstrated by looking at the ways child offending was understood: on the one hand reforming and humane, but also containing elements of fear and control.

The 1908 Children Act established a separate legal system for children. A central feature of the Act established what Pinchbeck and Hewitt (1969) refer to as reflecting "a revolutionary change of attitude from the days when the young offender was regarded as a small adult, fully responsible for his crime" (p. 494). Since the mid-nineteenth century the state had introduced legislation that established Reformatory and Industrial schools for child offenders aged between seven and 15. These early interventions by the state demonstrated a commitment to take the state's *in loco parentis* responsibilities seriously. Although grafted on to a justice system with punishment at its heart, the emerging legislation from 1900 until World War II constructed a model of youth justice that had reform, treatment and welfare at its heart but combined this with elements of control and punishment (Davis, 1990). The principle of *doli incapax* had been, in the European context, quite elastic, and decisions on whether a child was criminally responsible depended upon whether or not the child brought before the courts was perceived by magistrates as 'hardened'. The 1908 formation of Juvenile Courts for offenders between the ages of seven and 16 years effectively defined the years of criminal responsibility, although a child's level of immaturity was still taken into consideration.

The causes of child offending were explained in terms of poor integration, problematic socialisation and poor parenting rather than any innate evil within a child. In 1933 The Children and Young Persons Act forged a firm link of care to both delinquent and neglected children, removed poor children from the auspices of the Poor Law and broadened the definition of those children in need of assistance. Criminologist Hermann Mannheim, writing in the 1930s, considered poverty as the key cause of crime, along with "educational backwardness as well as family quarrels, or the premature death of a parent, or bad housing conditions or unsuitable employment" (1940, pp. 229–300). Mannheim was also shocked at the petty nature of the crimes that resulted in heavy penalties for young people, the most common offences being theft of coal, defacement of buildings and other criminal damage. On the face of it, he argued, none of these offences should result in imprisonment for a child.

However, the period also witnessed retrogressive theories for under-standing children; influential in this process was the work of G. Stanley Hall, who likened children's development to that of the human race, following the trajectory from primitive behaviour to rational civilisa-tion. The child was the embodiment of primitiveness and the adult in a civilised state; however, the adolescent was pulled in different directions, and therefore the storm of emotions was likely to set off behaviours that were difficult to control. While this enabled some form of leniency when dealing with adolescent offenders, it placed children firmly along with the animals and 'pre-historical' adults, thus reinforc-ing the belief in the innate vulnerability, dangerousness and incom-petence of children. Later, in the 1920s, Cyril Burt's influential *The Young Delinquent*, while being sympathetic to working-class life and the appalling conditions in which they lived, utilised eugenic explanations of youth offending based on biological defects. Thus those children accused of crimes were separated from those who were deemed 'normal'.

Further efforts were made by government and other 'professionals' to exert pressures on families perceived as 'special' and 'in need'. The voluntaristic and piecemeal patchwork of charity visitors over the inter-war years developed into a coordinated system of clinics and networks of health visitors. In Britain the number of health visitors rose from 600 in 1914 to 2,500 in 1918, and the number of maternity centres increased from 650 to 1,278 in the same period (Foley, 2001, p. 11). The clinics, Nikolas Rose has argued, introduced diagnoses of norms of adjustment and maladjustments that would become "the centre of a web of preventative and therapeutic child welfare embracing the nurs-ery, the home, the school, the playground, and the courts" (Rose, 1985, p. 154). This, combined with the development of the School Medical Service, encouraged an attitude of measuring, weighing, examining and testing. The data collected provided a collection of mass records against which individual children could be judged against a 'normal' median. As Armstrong (1995) has noted, the growth of these measurements enabled children to become identified with the clinical descriptions of their bodies. The collection of the data and the subsequent 'normalisa-tion' (Foucault, 1973) of children's bodies facilitated the revelation of habit disorders, such as speech, eating and sleep difficulties. In Britain treatment involved 'common sense conversations' rather than psycho-analysis, an approach treated with scepticism in the British medical fraternity (Hendrick, 2005).

Andre Turmel (2008) notes that child observation and some under-standing of developmental thinking existed prior to the nineteenth century. But from the nineteenth century onwards a new emphasis developed, focussing on statistical and social understandings of children as an aggregated mass. Children were subjected to measurements and the data plotted onto weight–height–age charts and graphs which illustrated 'normal' mental and physical progress. This, Turmel notes, augmented a preoccupation with principles of 'normalcy' and deviance, meaning that an 'average', 'healthy' and 'acceptable' child, who progressed sequentially along an age-graded developmental pathway to adulthood, was to be expected and assumed 'natural'; however, digressions from that path required further explanation or 'treatment'. Turmel shows that by the 1930s the developmental paradigm, especially under the influence of Piaget, dominated childhood studies and educational theory, and the new professions of children, such as teachers, paediatricians and so on, came to *see* childhood in a *universalist* form. It was in this period, Erica Burman (1994) has noted, that the statistical average became the 'natural' and 'universal' criteria for identifying children becoming adults. As physical 'maladjustments' were observed within medical centres and by school medicals, the newly established psychological clinics identified deeper psychological problems in children. Explanations for the 'growing problem' of psychological ill health in children were seen to reside in the family and relationships within it, rather than in external conditions, such as poverty, inadequate housing, overcrowding and other social pressures (Hendrick, 1994). Children became drawn into a world defined not by religious and 'moral' reformers but by a medical–psychological 'gaze' that mapped the child's mind into a series of 'natural' developmental stages, just as had been done with the body. Over a relatively short period of time these observations and measurements became normative rather than descriptive. They also fed into a basic level of understanding children as being 'vulnerable', 'incomplete' and bereft of agency. Children were presented as beings who were 'open' to any outside social influence, good or ill; therefore listening to children's views was seen as futile or pointless, for they would only mirror what others had told them.

Piaget (1929/1951), whose ideas were so influential in the post-war education project, although outlining a theory of an evolving competence and capacity for children, did acknowledge the active role of children in making sense of their words, concepts and the world around them. Vygotsky (1978), too, identified 'stages' in a child's development and life, but, unlike Piaget, saw cognitive development as being equally due to social processes and mutual learning. For Vygotsky, learning occurs within social settings, and knowledge and skills are gained through interaction and engagement with others. However, as Berry Mayall notes, "one might expect psychology's discovery of the child as active participant in learning to have infiltrated Western socialization agendas . . . A large-scale structural aim reinforces the construction of children as relatively passive socialization objects" (2009, p. 176). The conception of development gave rise to what Jenks (1996) refers to as the 'deficit model' of children, and filtered into ideas and practices that have led to the exclusion of children from the capability of being worthy citizens.

Golden age of welfare

Against this background of improving health, greater medical provision for children, and the rapid development and advancement of 'knowledge' of children, it is ironic that, as Lorraine Fox Harding (1997) argued, children were not a major focus of government policy in the 1920s and 1930s. Other than legislation primarily aimed at youth offending, there was very little legislation on education or children's welfare, especially when considering the reforms to education and welfare in the period prior to World War I. It is also apparent when compared with the legislative programme after World War II. The images of refugee children were a powerful push on social consciences, and concerns were expressed over undernourished children and those suffering from ill health. There is a difference of opinion about the extent to which the evacuation of nearly one and a half million children during World War II affected British public opinion. Bob Holman (1995) argues for a new sense of compassion among the middle classes, confronted with the realities of poverty made apparent after the bridging of segregated class communities of Britain during the war. John Macnicol (1986), on the other hand, tends to emphasise the ambiguities of the coming together of the social classes. Instead of wholesale guilt in the better-off classes following this 'discovery' of poverty, there was a sense that families were to blame for poverty, ignorance and ill health. This gave impetus to further social work intervention into the lives of 'problem families'. Whatever the sentiments, there was certainly a change in attitude towards the health and welfare of children, and a new willingness for an extension of statutory services.

   The post-war period famously saw the development of the welfare state, which Eric Hobsbawm has referred to as "the golden age" of welfare. Although this should not be over-emphasised, the overall direction of capitalist societies after the war was an inclusive one that emphasised the re-bonding of society. It involved the conciliation and incorporation referred to by T.H. Marshall as a capitalism in which both militant trade unions and capitalist profitability could coexist. It also involved a complex and sophisticated government machinery to provide a welfare state. The Nordic states – Denmark, Finland, Iceland, Norway and Sweden – developed what was called the 'social democratic' form of citizenship based on the "principles of equality, universalism, and de-commodification of social rights" (Epsing-Anderson, 1990, p. 27). In West Germany the 'Basic Law' of 1949 guaranteed basic rights as a binding norm across all institutions of the state, including those of social rights. The social democratic model, to which T.H. Marshall's view is close, places greater emphasis on relations between citizens, rather than between individual and state. Broadly, with less distance between the state and civil society, there was less suspicion of the state as a hostile force. However, the post-war 'social democratic consensus' was not a homogeneous Europe-wide process. In the Netherlands, for instance, a form of communitarianism dominated the debate about citizenship, where moral behaviour and civic spirit were central notions. This emphasised duties, moral obligations, common values, and a restoration of families and communities within the communitarian framework. Thus, citizenship in the Netherlands was located more in civil society rather than the state, but Dutch civil society could still rely upon the nation state's policies of redistribution and social security. Morgan (2002) characterised the post-war expansion of 'social citizenship' in many Western European countries (France, Germany, Italy, Spain and Portugal) as being "minimally concerned with either market efficiency or levelling social divisions" but, rather, "associated with conservative clericalism, a history of corporatist guild traditions, and/or reflected authoritarian bureaucrats, dictators, or conservative religious political party ideologies" (p. 145) and this is a viewpoint different from the one offered by Marshall's consensus-driven and evolutionary drift to a harmonious coexistence of labour and capital.

Alongside this image of a giving and inclusive state was a state that was highly interventionist in the lives of families. Within this framework children were major beneficiaries, for it was they who could bring forward a new and optimistic equality of opportunities and outcomes, as well as deliver the more sophisticated demands of capital. However, this was at the cost of the deficit model of childhood, discussed by Jenks (1996); being constructed as innocent, naïve and passive to their surroundings, children were given less choice in their lives compared to the choices given to adults.

The post-war period did, nevertheless, place social citizenship firmly on the agenda. Children and young people became a metaphor and rationale for the social change of a 'new' Britain. For instance, the 1948 Children Act established local authority Children's Departments that tended to see 'deprived children' and 'failing parents' as one and the same problem; the task of local authorities was to keep children with their parents, unlike with the Poor Law policies in previous centuries. The 1948 Children Act, Hendrick (2005) has declared, was "a significant piece of child welfare legislation, which has been unjustly neglected in standard histories of the welfare state" (p. 44). The Act enabled a child taken into care by the state "to be treated as an individual, with access to the same facilities as any other child in the community, thereby removing the last shred of 'less eligibility' which had survived since the Poor Law Amendment Act of 1834" (Hendrick, 2005, p. 44). The Act was part of an overall package of legislation that established the post-World War II 'welfare state', heralding free health care and a desire to break down class barriers and transform political differences. This is not to say that the Act, as has been observed by nearly all commentators on the period (see, for instance, Fox Harding, 1997; Pinchbeck and Hewitt, 1969), was an unashamed imposition of middle-class standards and values onto those of the poor. The school leaving age was raised to 16, creating an economic drain on households as more children were removed from the labour market; if we remember that the school leaving age was 11 at the beginning of the century, the extra cost of social reproduction put an enormous weight on family finances. One survey by an insurance company in the UK estimates the costs of supporting each child from the age of 11 to 18 at £167,000 (Smithers, 2011). This would be a significant drain on any household.

There was some acknowledgement of these costs; the Family Allowances Act in 1945 introduced a weekly allowance for each dependent school-aged child, although this was not necessarily part of a child-centred policy and the allowances arguably had more to do with maintaining gender relations by keeping mothers at home and alleviating wage pressures at a time of full employment (Daniel and Ivatts, 1998). Nevertheless, children in the post-war period up until the 1970s broadly benefited, along with their parents, from the economic boom.

The late 1940s and early 1950s led to the redefinition and universalisation of the category 'youth' across social policy (Mizen, 2004). The Ingleby Report of 1960 into youth justice reflected the perspective of practitioners in the *treatment* of offenders, as opposed to the punishment model of youth justice, and was concerned with their welfare. Following the 1969 Children and Young Person's Act a new family-oriented approach was adopted, with 'treatments' offered through the home wherever possible, rather than through the courts. Children's and young people's offending in this climate was explained not as a result of 'depraved individuals' but more as the result of social inadequacies or not being able to 'fit in'. Young people's offending was placed in a wider discourse of social welfare.

The establishment of a national and professional childcare service by the 1948 Children Act was another watershed in terms of the relationships between children, their parents and the state. This shifted the state's focus of attention beyond those in the care system and towards 'preventing' children coming into 'the system'. By focussing on the welfare of families, the state changed its focus from meeting the needs of children in its care to providing "support for families in order to avert the need for care and to prepare children for 'citizenship'" (Hendrick, 2005, p. 46). Preventative work continued in a piecemeal manner, and, with the 1963 Children and Young Persons Act, local authorities were given the duty of promoting the welfare of children through a preventative approach. However, the extension of the preventative approach had other consequences too. The policies towards abused or neglected children were placed within a medicalised discourse to explain physical child abuse as a result of individual pathologies of parents and adults within the family. Child abuse was tackled through technical procedures of 'identification', 'prevention' and 'treatment', as if it were a disease. These technical procedures could only, as Parton (1985) observes, at best form a partial solution to child abuse. Social scientific explanations of the phenomenon, largely in terms of structural and political factors, have a more powerful explanatory value. Rather than child abuse being a technical or medical issue, it can be explained in terms of the social and political position of the family, and 'abuses' of children through poverty, poor housing and pollution are as important as abuse from 'psychotic' or 'ill' parents.

Prevention agendas were not singularly used to tackle neglected and abused children *per se*, but they had the consequence of reaching into families in more fundamental ways. Jaques Donzelot (1980), for instance, sees the prevention initiatives as a form of state encroachment into families, under the guise of a benign form of 'welfare'. A collaboration of judicial processes and social services extended the judicial domain into the lives of more children and their families. Even the youth justice approach of welfare over justice cannot be separated from class politics and broader concerns with productivity and conformity, as much as any real extension of the feeling of citizenship (Pitts, 2001).

Education

The nature of schooling is the key way in which the state is able to shape the lives of the young. Children are separated from families, parents, communities and associations for the bulk of a day and are constructed as political and economic subjects. Indeed, during the post-war period critiques of schools as the site of economic reproduction were established (Bowles and Gintis, 1977), leading some, such as Ivan Illich (1971), to demand a 'de-schooling' of society to enable children to be freed from the competitive ideas of capitalism and, in a way reminiscent of eighteenth-century 'negative' libertarians, to be freed from the corrupting influence of state schooling.

Educational opportunities in the post-war period reflected the social welfare model of policy. As noted above, the school leaving age was extended to 16, the divisive and selective 11 plus examination (selective examination at the age of 11) system was toned down and opportunities for further and higher education were funded in the belief that working-class people would access them based upon 'merit' rather than birth. Opportunities for schooling and tertiary education were free at the point of demand. Education, for T.H. Marshall, had a key bearing on citizenship and the making of future citizens. Education was:

> trying to stimulate the growth of citizens in the making. The right to education is a genuine social right of citizenship, because the aim of education during childhood is to shape the future adult. Fundamentally it should be regarded, not as the right of the child to go to school, but as the right of the adult citizen to have been educated.
> (Marshall, 1950/1992, p. 16)

However, the 1944 Education Act continued the aspects of social reproduction; it consisted of a 'tripartite' system of grammar schools (entry to which was gained on passing the selective examination at the age of 11, thus called the 11 plus), secondary modern schools (for those who did not pass the 11 plus) and secondary technical schools (for those adept in mechanical and scientific subjects). The reality was that the tripartite system "condemned large numbers of working class young people to a lower quality education and a life of manual labour" (Mizen, 2004,

p. 26). It never really satisfied the middle classes, who were concerned that the 11 plus was not elitist enough.

Given the complex and differentiated education system in the UK, the implementation of any system was never complete. Indeed, at the time of the 1965 Act, which introduced comprehensive schools and ended selection, there were already a number of comprehensive schools in existence in England, and up to a third of schools in Wales were comprehensive. The belief of the incoming Labour Government was that talent, previously untapped through the selection process, would come forward through the establishment of comprehensive schools. Local education authorities would plan for comprehensive schools locally, with a curriculum more tailored to pupils' needs. The students would benefit from new progressive pedagogical techniques, including 'child-centred' teaching practices and independent learning. Children in most need would have extra resources to make up the 'educational deficit', including smaller classes, new equipment and additional teaching support. Poorer areas identified as Education Priority Areas (EPAs) were provided with further resources to place in local schools. Expenditure on schooling increased from 3.2% of Gross Domestic Product in 1951 to 6.5% in 1975 (Tomlinson, 2001).

With the abolition of the 11 plus, students would enjoy a common learning experience, and greater equality of outcome was hoped for. The comprehensive reforms were aimed at ending the previous historical task of education: to reproduce social inequalities. Comprehensive schools were never going to reform society to perfect equality or meritocracy; as Finn (1987) has argued, they continued to divide the young through 'streaming' classes according to 'ability', maintained separate curricula for 'non-academic' boys or girls, continued selection through examinations and allowed the creaming of resources by private schools. Furthermore, as Halsey (2000) noted, despite the expansion of universities in the 1960s, it was the middle class, not the working class, that benefited. Nevertheless, in this period there was an assumption that investment in education would lift children, and the adult workers they would become, out of poverty. There was a belief in raising everyone from degrading manual work to the new white collar, professional and managerial classes (Halsey et al., 1961).

This focus on the welfare state reflected Marshall's ideas of establishing a universal, state-guaranteed social provision as part of being a citizen of the country. The new rights to welfare would erode the inequalities that were inevitable in the essentially capitalist market system. However, Marshall was very much aware of the tension involved

in his "hyphenated society" (1950/1992, p. 123) of the progressive egalitarian operation of rights to social citizenship, while the economic
system based upon inequality and differential property ownership continued. Indeed, the progressive right to social citizenship was part of a
tradition which emphasised an equality of opportunity while tolerat-
ing an inequality of outcome. This tradition believed that an 'equality
of status' was necessary in order to reduce some of the inequalities
between individuals. He argued: "there is a general enrichment of the
concrete substance of civilised life, a general reduction of risk and insecurity, an equalisation between the more and less fortunate at all levels"
(1950/1992, p. 33), while tellingly maintaining that "equality of status
is more important than equality of income" (1950/1992, p. 33). Thus,
social citizenship relies on a guaranteed minimum income, such as
that offered through child benefit, but this would not necessarily affect
income differentials. Marshall's view consolidated market-generated
inequalities, differential incomes and a stratified occupational hierarchy based around social class that would be held in check by stabilising
certain inequalities through education, training and achievement. Furthermore, the promotion of citizenship would enable an acceptance and
toleration of market inequalities as legitimate by a universal system of
values that regarded a certain level of inequality as fair, as long as there
was an open level of social mobility.

The education system was founded on the assumption of developmental theories of childhood that took as 'natural' the incompetence
and inabilities of children. This image of children as incompetent
has been challenged by the sociological studies of childhood (James
and James, 2004); even the youngest of children are rarely completely incompetent. The conception of children's incompetence leads
to assumptions of children's natural dependence upon adults and, as
another corollary, of children's 'natural' vulnerability. Another side of
the state intervention in families around 'protecting' children was the
application of a perception of children as inherently 'vulnerable' and in
need of protection, and an efficient policing of families to ensure protection. This is not new: the wicked step-parent has a long tradition in
European literature, folk tales and popular culture. Throughout a large
tranche of history the excuse for ill-treating children was that they were
in some form 'wicked' or 'uncontrollable' and corporal punishment was
exacted upon them. Corporal punishment in Britain remained a sanction to the courts until after World War II, although discomfort over its
use grew in the interwar period. There was still a belief among employers that they could punish servants with violence. During the twentieth

century there was an increasing unease about the use of corporal punishment against children, but it remained a sanction available to Church schools until its abolition in 1982.

While it should be recognised that some children are indeed vulnerable and in need of protection, this should not be seen as an overarching or 'natural' condition of childhood. Indeed, many adults have significant levels of vulnerability, but this is not considered the default position for adults. Marshall, too, realised that protection was a two-edged sword. Protection was not given to adult men, as full citizens. For instance, the Factory Acts only protected women and children, as they did not enjoy full citizenship as responsible and competent people. He argued:

> Protection was confined to women and children, and champions of women's rights were quick to detect the implied insult. Women were protected because they were not citizens. If they wished to enjoy full and responsible citizenship, they must forego protection.
>
> (Marshall, 1950/1992, p. 15)

Girls

So far this chapter has looked at children in general. However, while there have been important caveats in the discussion about social class, the twentieth century continued to define citizenship as different for girls and for boys.

As Williams (2003) has argued, it is hard to separate gender from 'race' and nation. From the beginning of the twentieth century there were questions over girls' education, their work and their attitudes. Up to 1920, as with boys, there was a massive expansion in the numbers of girls' societies and clubs, concerned with educating girls about their roles and future responsibilities (Dyhouse, 1981). Although there was genuine concern to protect young women, continuing the trend of the nineteenth-century social purity movement, this was combined with an aim to improve the quality of mothering and housewifery. Foley (2001) notes that policy-makers "repeatedly recommended the education of working class women to raise the standard of domestic competence and to install the proper ideals of motherhood and home life in British girls and women" (Foley, 2001, p. 10). As Yuval-Davis (1997) has argued, women have a very different relationship to national discourse than men; men are seen as defenders of the race, while women are seen as reproducers of the nation as mothers and carers. Thus, the nationalistic discourses targeted at girls looked to police 'proper' behaviour, dress and manners.

Again continuing nineteenth-century concerns over girls' sexuality, Cox (2002) has shown how fears of miscegenation throughout the first half of the twentieth century prompted investigations into mixed-race communities in the seaports of London, Liverpool and Cardiff. The belief among researchers (drawn from local universities) was that local girls who 'consorted' with 'coloured' men tended to be prostitutes, those who already had an illegitimate baby or were mentally weak. The children from these mixed-race liaisons were also considered to be prone to delinquency. The law was used against girls or young women unable to protect themselves sexually. In 1926 the Plymouth Watch Committee urged Local Educational Authorities not to allow back into schools girls who had been 'contaminated' by being sexually assaulted (Emsley, 2011). Indeed, Brown and Barratt (2002) have shown that even children's charities at the time were concerned with the 'contamination' of girls who had been sexually abused before receiving them into their care.

The period after the war brought about profound changes in society in relation to gender. The successful entry of women into the workforce, including heavy engineering, during the war showed that the 'natural' domestic roles and responsibilities of young women were erroneous. However, gender-segregated work continues; by 1968 approximately 40 per cent of girls between 15 and 17 were entering clerical industries, far surpassing domestic service (Osgerby, 1998). Thus, girls were, in numbers, leaving the private sphere and clearly moving into public spaces of economic life. Much of this work, however, reflected and was structured around girls' core responsibilities in the home (Abbott et al., 2005). With the movement of girls and women into the world of employment there was a concomitant rise in consumer goods targeted at girls and young women; notably clothes, records, fashion, cosmetics, magazines and so on. The new economic opportunities for girls and women perhaps led to the 'second wave' of feminism and to fresh challenges to existing gender relations. Feminism served as a liberating force to girls and women that challenged domestic responsibilities and, with the pill, gave new forms of sexual freedom and more control over their bodies. Thus, "girls were at the forefront of social change" (France, 2007, p. 21) and brought about changes in legislation and attitudes, including equal opportunities laws and the further liberalisation of marriage and divorce laws.

The response from British governments to these changes varied, although most tried to maintain existing messages and continue inequality. For instance, as Tomlinson (2005) notes, girls were required to get a higher score than boys to secure a place in a grammar school. Employment segmentation and wage differentials remain, and the female domination of caring professions, such as teaching and nursing, may contribute to the 'semi-professional' nature of these occupations (Abbott and Wallace, 1990). In France, family policies continued to be highly gendered, retaining a vestige of the *citoyenneté des femmes*, in which mothers were considered good women, giving birth to new French citizens. Family policies retained elements of pro-natalism, with preference being given to families with more than three children, and against the European norm France retained restrictions on abortions for under-age girls.

The sexual behaviour of girls remained a social problem, and shaped the criminal justice system, where there was a constant worry about girls' sexual promiscuity. One analysis of sexual crime reporting in the 1970s notes how the issue of 'consent' was rarely discussed when involving under-age heterosexual sex; the girls were either innocent virgins or dangerous temptresses and a threat to powerless men (Soothill and Walby, 1991). In continuity with the earlier twentieth-century concerns over girls, under the guise of their welfare and protection, new powers of intervention were introduced under the Children and Young Persons Act 1969 to allow magistrates and social workers to intervene when girls were suspected of being in 'moral danger'. Furthermore, given the ambiguity of social workers' interpretation of 'moral danger', more girls were placed into care for being defined as 'troubled' or 'troublesome' up until the 1980s (Thorpe et al., 1980).

Crisis and the assertion of children's rights

By the 1970s a semblance of social citizenship had been established in Britain and throughout Europe, and, to a lesser extent, the USA. Children were beneficiaries of this citizenship and there accrued a number of significant 'social rights', to welfare, protection, schooling and so on. However, as discussed above, children were also defined in ways that emphasised their vulnerabilities and deficiencies, and became increasingly dependent upon adults. There were other social changes occurring during this period. First, the state was entering the worlds of citizens, old and young, and claiming many of the responsibilities previously considered a matter of private concern. These commitments became associated with citizen rights. Second, there was a shift to a service-based economy replacing the traditional 'heavy' industries, such as mining, shipbuilding, engineering and so on, traditionally associated with working-class men. Caring and education were areas of growth, with women moving into the labour market. Third, there was a demographic shift to an older population; children became a minority as people lived longer, and with democratic representation power shifted to the older generations, away from young adults and totally away from children, other than the representation of parents and adult carers (Olk, 2009). Finally, there were changes to household structures, including the increase in single-person households, often as a consequence of divorce and separation, and, much later, recognition of same-sex parents.

Regarding aspects of social citizenship in Britain, there was a change of direction in the 1980s. This was a time when the optimistic post-war policies unravelled. The Keynesian economic approach was replaced by monetarism; the societal shame of poverty was replaced by the enthrallment of money, the rich and celebrity; children under 18 who offended were not viewed as victims of circumstances or weakness of personality, but were seen to some extent as conscious and competent people in need of 'justice'; the shared nature of the comprehensive was replaced by 'parental choice'. Under the Conservative governments of Margaret Thatcher and John Major the term citizenship was deployed in a depoliticised way through a narrow construction of 'active citizenship', devoid of political participation and decision-making, where giving money and time was an act of citizenship as well as of charity. Illustrative of this was the consumerist 'Citizen's Charter' that aimed to model the provision of public goods and services on those of the private citizen, such as compensation for delays in services or mistakes by public servants.

Hendrick (2005) also refers to the 1980s as "a decade during which long-established tensions between child care policy, parental responsibility and rights, and the jurisdiction of the state finally snapped" (p. 47). On the one hand, the state came to rely more and more on intervention and coercion within some families (Freeman, 1992); at the same time, the state wished to step back from its responsibilities for families and children's welfare, with erosion of social rights (Dwyer, 2004). State interventions into families in the 1980s were shaped by the eclipse of child neglect and physical abuse, and the domination of images of child sexual abuse. The child abuse scandals would swing from suggestions of too little social work intervention in the case of Maria Colwell, among others, to the actions of over-zealous practitioners in the Cleveland and Orkney scandals.

The decade ended with the 1989 Children Act, which Lorraine Fox Harding (1997) characterised as being paternalistic, *laissez-faire* and supportive of family and children's rights. It was paternalistic in that the Act was concerned with issues of 'parental responsibility' and an aim for a 'partnership' between parents and the state. The paternalism was reinforced through a series of orders on family assistance and education, as well as emergency protection procedures. Legal definition of a 'child in need' was used to provide (or force) a series of support mechanisms to families. Arguably, the most interesting aspect of the Act was the recognition by the law of a child as a 'person in their own right', not a chattel or appendage to a parent. Furthermore, it was legally recognised that the child was more than an object of concern and that children "become more prominent participants in child-care matters and are intimately involved in decision-making processes that directly affect their welfare" (Wyness, 2000, p. 49). Fox Harding argued that it was this recognition of children's rights and the value placed upon paternalism that was the most important element of the Act; although one must recognise the continuation of *laissez-faire* principles (Freeman, 1992).

Looking back at the post-war welfare state, exaggerated claims of halcyon days must not be made. Class-based inequalities pervaded the 'settlement'. To take family allowances, the rate in 1945 was set below the level recommended by Beveridge and was only increased twice, in 1948 and 1967. Thus, the economic well-being of children was closely allied to that of their parents. This was fine in the context of full employment and rising wages. However, the 'rediscovery' of child poverty in the UK by Townsend and Abel Smith (1965) noted that inequalities were actually increasing, as those 2.5 million children from families with unemployed or lone parents were not sharing in the 'long boom'. In 1975 the Labour government transformed family allowances into the new child benefit; this was a universal payment to the parents of *all* children up to the age of 16 (or 19 if they were in full-time education). The universal coverage of child benefit testified to the attempt to tackle children in low-income families, so that all families could enjoy a certain degree of support, and Labour and Conservative governments maintained the commitment to child benefit for the 'building blocks' of the future. However, this did not stop consecutive governments freezing the rate of child benefit. It also occurred alongside a retreat from universal welfare provision (or social citizenship) towards one of targeting and means testing.

The Thatcherism of the 1980s saw rising unemployment and low pay that accelerated the widening gap between those children whose families became increasingly well off and those in deepening poverty. The proportion of children living in households with less than half the average net income rose from one-in-ten in 1979 to one-in-three in 1992. The number of children living in workless households in 1968 was 4 per cent; by 1979 this had risen to 7 per cent and by 1996 to 20 per cent. This was a time period when the richest 20 per cent of households saw their overall wealth and income rise by 24 per cent.

With the introduction of 'neoliberal' programmes under Conservative, New Labour and Coalition governments, education strategies abandoned ideas of consensus and put ideas of the market, individual action and responsibility at the heart of policy. This manifested itself in a number of changes. First, 'market forces' were seen to have the solution to the continuing inequalities and failures in education. The mechanism was to utilise a system of 'choice' and diversity in the school system whereby parents can 'choose' the school best suited to their children. Second, schools were given more control and freedom from local government and given more autonomy in relationship to elected local authorities. Third, at the same time as a loosening of local authority control over schools, there was a massive centralisation of national government power that took control over the curriculum and setting of key targets. Monitoring and auditing of schools were also established. Fourth, selection was maintained and expanded. Schools were able to pick the children who entered their school according to a variety of different criteria, the vast majority based upon notions of 'ability'. Today, in England and Wales, over 36 of the 174 local education authorities still retain an 11 plus system of selection. Indeed, under New Labour the construction of learner support units for 'failing students' and the gifted and talented programmes for the 'high achievers' had in effect mainstreamed selection *within* schools. Finally, the school curriculum was restructured to allow 'vocationalism' into the curriculum. New policies introducing 'skills training' were introduced, replacing the previous emphasis on academic teaching (Tomlinson, 2001). The structures established did not challenge inequalities in the education system. Schools in poor areas could not compete with schools in better-off districts, given the resources required to tackle underlying issues that impact upon learning. Thus, the education system maintained class and ethnic inequalities (Tomlinson, 2005). Importantly, the blame for failure was not put upon the school system, but upon teachers, parents or the culture of the 'underclass'.

The youth justice system has become very much exposed to populist reactions to perceived levels of crime and criminality. The most extreme crime committed by children is murder. Between 1946 and 1968, 28 children under the age of 14 were found guilty of killing. In 1968 11-year-old Mary Bell was found guilty of manslaughter, through diminished responsibility, after strangling two boys aged three and four years. Mary had been psychologically damaged and sexually abused by her mother and her mother's clients. The general discussion and concern in the Home Office and the press was what to do with the girl, as there were no psychiatric hospitals for treating such offenders. However, a quarter of a century later, another news story of a murder of a two-year-old boy by two 10-year-old boys attracted national attention. The two killers had, like Mary Bell, experienced a troubled background; however, the hostility towards the two child killers reflected a collapse of faith in the criminal justice system. It also, perhaps, illustrated a more sinister distrust towards particular children. The number of children under 14 who kill remained constant, at 12 children between 1979 and 1984; however, the controversy led to the review of *doli incapax*.

The toughening approach to young offenders reflected a broader New Labour agenda on citizenship. This drew on the consumerism of the previous governments, its own social democratic traditions and the communitarianism that stressed citizenship obligation and responsibility. This resulted in a number of initiatives seeking to expand active citizenship (including political participation) such as the Centre for Active Citizenship, a biennial Citizenship Survey and the placing of 'citizenship' on the national curriculum. Public services were to be delivered in partnership with other agencies, in particular the private and voluntary sectors. Central to welfare policies was an emphasis on responsibility, particularly through paid employment. Responsibility was at the heart of the criminal justice policy, which was designed to tackle antisocial behaviour and promote a new form of civility. Investment in children, education and childcare was part of a new social investment state that placed children as "citizen-worker of the future" (Lister, 2004). New Labour's family policy placed the moral importance of economic independence through paid work on both mothers and fathers. Thus, the citizenship responsibilities of mothers and fathers were universalised into what Jane Lewis has referred to as an "adult worker" model (Lewis, 1992).

In common with most European countries, both left and right, asylum and immigration have remained key political issues, with an emphasis on restricting entry. In the Netherlands this reached a crisis after the 2004 murder of Dutch film-maker Theo van Gogh, whose film with Ayaan Hirsi Ali, a Muslim woman, criticised Islam as an oppressive religion for women. Since then there has been a resurgent debate over the protection of 'Dutch culture' against multiculturalism. By the 1980s the AFDC programme in the United States was focussed on low-income single women and their dependent children. This category was quickly added to the category 'Black'; the programme became racialised, and being on AFDC was likened to being lazy, irresponsible and unemployable.

It is thus an ironic social context for children's rights to have been placed on the table of governments at a local, national and European level. The issue of children's rights will be discussed more fully in the next chapter, but for now it is necessary to return to Marshall and social citizenship.

Conclusion

In terms of Marshall's ideas on social citizenship, we can see that, even in the 'golden age' of consensus and social citizenship in which Marshall wrote, there were ambiguities around the extent and partiality of 'social rights'. Furthermore, the other side of Marshall's (indeed most commentators') argument for social rights involves duties. Marshall's commentary on duties is fairly brief, consisting of duties to pay taxes and perform military service, both of which are unavailable to children under 16 years of age. The problem with Marshall's work is that the overall focus on the duty to work is inappropriate at first glance to children, who are 'protected' from work, although it needs to be noted, as Jens Qvortrup has observed, that children do, nevertheless, work; in terms of school work and the work involved in their own upbringing and reproduction (Qvortrup, 1994). The focus on paid employment and citizenship, of course, excludes others from citizenship, such as retired or disabled people and carers.

There are further limitations to Marshall's theory. First, as Oliver and Heater (1994) have argued, seeing social rights as part of, or equivalent to, civil and political rights is not correct. Civil and political rights are part of what Oliver and Heater call 'first generation' rights; that is, they are enshrined within the legal system and underpinned by (often international) law. This is not necessarily true with social rights, which are entitlements to services or income brought about by positive legislation, taxation and resources. Thus, this is mostly a matter of political will to undertake positive welfare policies. These are often, as Barbalet (1988) has shown, dependent upon professional bureaucratic infrastructures rather than intrinsic rights. The will of governments to welfare has been seriously challenged and reversed by monetarist governments that are more fearful of upsetting businesses and taxpayers than interested in selling the collective benefits of a welfare society. As Dwyer (2004) has observed:

> Marshall apparently believed that the public and politicians alike had come to some sort of consensus view that it was right and proper for the state to finance and provide extensive social provisions for its citizens and that this situation would always prevail. (p. 46)

Delanty (2000) has observed that Marshall's theory of universal equality of rights and responsibilities is too cumbersome to deal effectively with difference. Furthermore, his emphasis on the nation state and the specific social rights he discussed are both Anglocentric, in that they have limited use when viewing other welfare states (Mann, 1987) and democracies, and they do not give a handle to the increasing processes of globalisation.

However, it is not necessary to dispense with the idea of social rights. Although there are significant obstacles and shortcomings, as noted by Marshall's critics above, the contrast between social rights on one side, and civil and political rights on the other, is not necessarily so great. Indeed, all these forms of rights rely upon each other to some extent. Furthermore, some social rights do have legal force (such as education), and some civil rights can be reversed (such as age of consent and *doli incapax*). As Twine (1994) has emphasised, social, civil and political rights are necessarily interdependent, as individuals are through their lives. The welfare state is under pressure and subject to withering cuts across Europe. However, Lister and Pia's (2008) work questions the extent of this and advances the theory that, certainly in Western Europe, there is evidence of retrenchment and cutbacks, rather than a radical displacement of welfare ideals, even in the UK. They state: "many European countries have experienced some retrenchment of the welfare state, for most countries, *at the moment*, this is not of a significant scale" (Lister and Pia, 2008, p. 134). Whether this will survive the current cuts in public expenditure across the European and North American societies considered in this book, however, is yet to be seen.

Part II

5
Children's Rights and Their Limitations

In her seminal paper Onora O'Neill (1988) examined the legal and moral principles behind children's rights. She argued that children should be protected and nurtured because of their special vulnerabilities and thus should not and could not have full rights of citizenship. Huntington (2006) continues this view, arguing that children's welfare, or their protection, is not best achieved through the promotion of their rights, as children are not able to understand them, lacking the cognitive capacity or emotional maturity to make decisions. For Huntington, issues of poverty are more pertinent than rights in understanding an issue such as child abuse, and thus attention to poverty should receive greater priority. The argument offered here is a familiar one: children do not have full autonomy, and therefore rights as a mechanism for promotion of their welfare or access to citizenship are ineffective and inappropriate. However, as this chapter will argue, this is based on a misunderstanding of the nature and form of rights today. While the recognition of poverty and the vulnerability of many children is welcome, this is not the condition of all children, and fails to recognise children's own agency and the complex and interdependent manner in which human rights, including children's rights, have developed. This chapter explores the development of human rights and some of the ways in which children's rights fit, or jar against, general human rights. It explores the tensions in the relationships between children, parents and families, and the state in the operationalising of human rights. It also discusses the limitations and constraints of human rights for children's citizenship and identifies broader issues of power, rather than the technical identification, deployment and enforcement of rights, as defining children's citizenship.

Human rights

On the face of it, there is no arguing against human rights being inherently a good thing; however, human rights do have their critics, and this leaves room for the ambiguity of human rights applied to children to be explored. For instance, Marxists reject human rights as a false bourgeois view of human beings as selfish, self-sufficient, independent individuals separate from the social structures of communities. They also create the illusion of equality by diverting attention away from social and economic inequalities. However, under international law children are now rights-bearing individuals (Fortin, 2008), and it is worth reflection to ascertain what exactly rights are, and how they may correlate with ideas of citizenship for children. Some countries, such as the United States, have been established according to rights that people will have as a source of national identity. The case of the United States shows how progressive expansion of the term 'citizen' has been applied, with the result that, after the 1960s civil rights movements, black Americans were included on a more equitable basis. However, whether this was due to the effective use of civil rights is debatable; other forms of social change may have been more effective. Overall, children do not have the means to create national laws, as few countries allow children voting rights. However, there are some conceptual inconsistencies in practice. Some children, as we have seen, are responsible in the criminal law for the violence they commit, although the age of this responsibility varies enormously across space and time. Children do get prosecuted for murder; however, they have usually been taken as 'special cases' and have had sentences reduced, or even overturned. These are considered 'exceptional' cases, and the burden of proof for premeditation is higher than with adults. Furthermore, if an illegal taking of life by a child is committed as a 'war crime', this is seldom prosecuted, as, arguably, the state did not step in and protect them from becoming child soldiers in the first place (Grover, 2008).

The idea of a 'natural right' originates in Greek and Roman thought, but it was with Renaissance writers that the concept received the purchase it has today. Here people looked to claim their entitlements and enjoy the overall gains of natural law. Hobbes outlined the fundamental right of nature as being the right to self-preservation; following on from this was a theory of natural rights for individuals to pursue their own self-interests unimpeded. Locke, too, outlined a theory of natural law in which individuals were considered rational beings, and, as rational beings, had ownership of their lives and property and sovereignty over their own actions. The right to sovereignty was 'natural', as God had ordained, and it was necessary for men to be free to undertake their own business, although with some agreements for limited state interference. Thomas Paine later used natural rights to argue that, in addition to the freedom for men to undertake business unimpeded, men also had the divine right to resist forms of political oppression. Contemporary writers continue to find value in natural rights; for instance, Dworkin (1977) identifies rights as a natural *moral* category, in that people are born with rights and these rights are pre-social, absolute and universal. However, it is the very pre-social universality and absoluteness that require us to look beyond natural rights.

First, as Edmund Burke famously outlined, rights entail the inheritance and building up of a basket of freedoms that are organic and contextually sensitive, in marked contrast to the abstract, metaphysical and simplistic rights of declarations, such as the "armed doctrine" of the French Revolution (Burke, 1790/1969, p. 90). Similarly, T.H. Green found natural rights to be unacceptable because the diet of rights may not have been derived from that society; these 'alien' rights can be used against individuals, and rights become detached from the duties individuals owe (Green, 1895, p. 114). The claim, by natural rights theorists, of the self-evidence of rationality has been called into question by sociological evidence of the diversity of rationality (MacIntyre, 1988). Many rights are also being discovered. The rights of women, both as human beings and specifically as women, are still being spelled out in the rights compendia. The same could be said about other groups, such as disabled and mentally ill adults, homosexuals and, in our case, children.

Seventeenth-century rights theorists thus employed static notions of human nature, but in the nineteenth century evolutionary perspectives were grafted onto rights and an individual rights-bearer became developmental. Since the Ancient Greeks, the notion of *teleos* and the belief that cultural tastes, social theories and the unfolding range of attributes are central to the natural processes of growth informed rights theorists into the 'stages' discussed in previous chapters. Writers such as Mill argued that stifling such processes of development or artificially re-channelling these could inflict considerable harm on individuals and societies. The concept of liberty was conceived of as a freedom from impediment to our continual ability to express and exercise our development, whether deliberately or by accident; thus liberty became a well-established right of non-intervention. The sorts of civil liberties which we still normally think of when discussing rights tend towards the claims we make against the state to uphold our 'rights'. That is, a 'right' is something that we are able to do and which the state cannot take away. This 'universalling' of rights has clear shortcomings. For instance, the 'right' of children to carry a knife or offensive weapon to protect themselves has been curtailed in the UK by legislation, from 1953 up to the Violent Crime Reduction Act 2006, so that it is now virtually impossible for anyone under 18 to legally carry, buy or use any offensive weapon. In the UK this illustrates the 'unwritten constitution' by which citizens have the 'right' or 'freedom' to do anything which the state has not defined as illegal; this is very different from citizens having 'universal rights'.

However, towards the end of the nineteenth century this non-intervention was questioned. The right to the development of one's nature can be open to more than one interpretation: our human natures may well be a function of our own individual free will, or we may not be aware of our own needs for development. If development is more than our individual self-will, then intervention may not necessarily restrict development, but may assist or be essential to growth. What it means to flourish, of course, changes over time – we develop new capacities and shed old ones. Indeed, the concept of human flourishing has developed over the last 200 years, and Friedrich Froebel deployed the simile of our growth as a flower, emphasising the importance of the role of the gardener as an intervener guiding the maturation of individuals. This well-tended garden is in marked contrast to the widespread disorder of unregulated wilderness that characterises the negative libertarians. The limitations of our self-will have stimulated the growth of education as a way of enforcing the development of capacities in individuals.

Societies thus intrude on the rights debate in a number of ways, as they question the ubiquity of universalism and are the medium through which individuals associate and apply their rights. People have mutual sympathy and interdependence, wherein cooperation and expression of ourselves are impossible without the sustenance, support and moulding of others. Some go further and hold that humans are entities whose *essence* lies in group membership (Sandel, 1982). Such communitarian approaches place more emphasis on welfare rights than on choice rights, and welfare can only be catered for through intervention. Interventions today enter people's spaces in profound ways, from compulsory vaccinations to education provision to removal of children from their families.

The fact that human beings are social in nature, continue to develop and have specific needs has resulted in an ever-changing expression of human rights. All statements of rights change. The Universal

Declaration of Human Rights (1948) is perhaps the most influential and is very different from other declarations, such as those of the American and French Revolutions. The Declaration of Human Rights contains eighteenth-century notions of life, liberty and security of person, combined with twentieth-century sensibilities against the right to protection against torture or degrading treatment. It also includes psychological, social and mental rights, issues of housing, education, employment, trade union membership, and so on. All of these were underdeveloped in the eighteenth century. What is interesting is the absence of property rights from twentieth-century declarations. Furthermore, as experience of the declarations of human rights over philosophical diversity shows, human rights do not exist in nature but are human inventions; thus, they are not 'natural' or 'self-evident'; there are different conceptions of the good society, so there are no universal ideas of rights; and international human rights law is a product of political power, pragmatic agreement and a limited moral consensus. Thus, theories of human rights must *follow from*, not *precede*, a theory of a good society (Freeman, 2002).

It must also be noted that human rights are not the 'trumps' to other interests (Ronald Dworkin, 1977). As Freeden (1991) has argued: "In the final analysis it is not rights that have special protection but the attributes that they are designed to protect" (p. 10). This is reflected in Article 29 of the Universal Declaration, which outlines a limitation to rights to meet "the just requirements of morality, public order and the general welfare in a democratic society" (quoted in p. 61 of Freeman, 2002). Notions of 'morality', 'public order' and 'general welfare' are suitably vague to cover all sorts of embarrassments by states. Indeed, although democracy and human rights are sometimes connected, they are not necessarily symbiotic, as a benign authoritarianism can still support human rights. However, the limitations to rights are conceptual, as well as limited to the will of governments and the fact that rights might not be enforceable. Mostly it is far easier for people within communities to apply local laws than to appeal to higher international law or universal expressions of rights.

Jack Donnelly (1985), for instance, outlines a number of moralities that are higher than rights. First, the love that parents feel for children and *vice versa* is stronger than rights. Again, it is not helpful to think of love as a trump of rights; instead, rights are invoked for children when the values of love have failed. The need for placing rights within the context of other moralities is illustrated when we look at the example of freedom of speech; if this were applied dogmatically, there would be little to protect people's privacy or use a check to press intrusion. Rights, in their expression, need to be balanced with other values. The example of the press and freedom of speech also illustrates that it is not just states that need to be held in check through rights but also multinational companies, media corporations and 'nosy neighbours' that may intrude on our 'private sphere'.

Donnelly also cites the clash between rights and those moralities based around religion. Donnelly supports the 'modernisation' argument (cautiously): rights are more important than religion because they have an international consensus and can demonstrate a plausible theory about 'autonomous' human nature. However, Freeman (2002), among others, rejects the autonomy principles, as not all cultures value autonomy and even liberals disagree about the nature and importance of 'autonomy'. As Michael Goodhart (2008) argues, the universal principle of autonomy is questionable, since this principle will not apply to *all* human beings, as not all members of the human species have this capacity. These debates are far more extensively written about elsewhere and elaboration is not relevant in this context, other than to note the diverse and interconnected contexts in which rights are interpreted. Goodhart (2008) succinctly ends the dilemma by concluding: "instead of conceptual universality we should discuss the *inclusiveness* of an account of human rights and the *uniformity* of the rights it prescribes" (p. 189).

For children, we can acknowledge that they are humans and therefore have human rights, as do other, adult, human beings; yet children have specific needs and capabilities of their own, as children. This will be returned to in a discussion of recognition in Chapter 8. However, adult women have demonstrated that they are human beings and also have specific needs and capabilities. Like women, children, too, have the right to repair the social deficit of years of discrimination. Thus, children's rights are a special case. There are special categories of people recognised by the Vienna declaration, where the Universal Declaration on Human Rights was reaffirmed in 1993 – with categories women, children, minorities, indigenous people, disabled people, refugees, migrant workers, the extremely poor and the socially excluded.

Freeman (2002) has argued that rights declarations do refer to some universalised application to all humans: however, this also "entails some diversity of human-rights practice, since the concept of human rights presupposes the value of autonomy, which would lead to some variation in human-rights practice in different cultural and socio-economic conditions" (pp. 105–106); although, as Donnelly (2003) points out, the Universal Declaration model presents human rights as holistic and indivisible, yet each right is augmented by the presence of others. As article 5 of the 1993 Vienna Declarations puts it: "All human rights are universal, indivisible and interdependent and interrelated."[1] Expressions of rights are rarely declared without caveats, and it is in these caveats that contexts and interrelations come into effect. Take Article 8 of the European Convention on Human Rights, which declares: "everyone has the right to respect for his private and family life, his home and his correspondence." The article continues: "there shall be no interference by a public authority with the exercise of this right." However, the caveat allows a whole gamut of possibilities for public institutions to intervene in children's and adults' private lives by continuing:

> except such as is in accordance with the law and is necessary in a democratic society in the interests of national security, public safety or the economic well-being of the country, for the prevention of disorder or crime, for the protection of health and morals, or for the protection of the rights and freedoms of others.

The caveats lead to the almost perennial debate in the media over the right to privacy for the famous, rich and powerful from press intrusion against arguments of public rights to information. Children's rights to privacy from the press tend to be ensured through 'agreements' with the media or court guarantees of child anonymity, rather than specific rights. It is thus commonly accepted that children are a 'special case' when compared with adults.

Moving to the context of children's rights in general, part of the 'special case' includes different 'needs'. Writers such as Hartley Dean (2008) argue that a social rights perspective is "more effective than conventional human rights" (p. 3) as prescribed by the United Nations Development Programme and the Office of the High Commissioner on Human Rights to reduce poverty overall. This calls for a "welfare rights approach based upon a politics of need" (Dean, 2008, p. 1). There are problems here, as agreed 'needs' are not clearly measured, or agreed. There are further problems with implementing approaches to children's needs. In his work on the implementation of 'outcomes-led' approaches to children's needs in the UK, Bob Hudson (2005) notes the differential power that children have in relation to bureaucracies. Government agencies seek to engage children and young people into a 'partnership approach' to improve children's well-being. However, in reality this can only be achieved through inter-agency and inter-professional working. Hudson shows how professionals reinterpret the well-being needs and demands expressed by young people into their own institutional agendas. In a similar vein, Newman et al. (2008) argue that even the current modernisation of adult services around 'user-led' inputs has reduced the emphasis on structural and institutional changes and emphasises changes in the behaviours and roles of social care users. They argue:

> The current emphasis on personalisation, independence and choice in adult social care is now firmly embedded across government discourse, organisational missions and professional norms of good practice.
>
> (2008, p. 546)

Yet independence, choice and control shift power to 'self-governance'. Self-governance requires a long-term capacity-building process supported by user-led, peer and other community organisations. This involves effective mechanisms for information sharing, developing skills for decision-making and cooperative processes with a range of broader civil society actors. Such things are not cheap and do not complement professional pressures for short-term, measurable targets, not to mention high levels of demand in a climate of shrinking resources. In short: "aspirations for self-governance are also not easily reconciled with hierarchical governance regimes that emphasise consistency, standards, accountability and protection" (Newman et al., 2008, p. 548).

The policy literature produced today desires an 'adult', rather than dependent, conception of citizenship to work. This movement to self-governance is a trend towards governmentality that creates citizens and communities of 'governable subjects', critiqued by writers such as Nicholas Rose (1999). Welfare becomes individualised, rather than collectively managed, with service users managing their own risks as responsible citizens. Thus, the model of citizenship underpinning these reforms is one that emphasises responsibilities. These self-governing citizens operating through 'independence, control and choice' are more vulnerable to neoliberal reforms, fluctuations in the overall economy and personal crises. This is a problematic model, therefore, when applied to children, as some writers have argued (Middleton, 2006).

The sticky nature of human rights discourse, especially as it is applied to those in most need, has led Amartya Sen (1992) to progress a notion of 'capabilities', which are determined not by a measure of the resources someone has or the welfare they are able to derive, but are best determined according to their 'capability to function'. Or, as he puts it, welfare and justice should be concerned with a person's "actual ability to achieve various valuable functionings as a part of living" (1992, p. 30). A functioning is what a person can do or be according to their health, nourishment, self-respect, recognition and so on. Sen's view of welfare, as being based not upon an accumulation of needs but rather as 'lack of basic functioning', has been useful and influential in international aid programmes. There is also some talk of dignity. Martha Nussbaum (2000) has progressed Sen's theory of capabilities to include dignity, and presents a list of capabilities that are interculturally flexible and open-ended. They comprise the capabilities of hearing and seeing, as well as 'internal capabilities' that result from external conditions, such as social-isation and education. Nussbaum describes a theory of human nature that includes limits and needs; that is, all human beings are both capable and needy.

While the capabilities theory is still relatively new, there are two problems with this approach thus far. First, capabilities, although con-sisting of natural facts (such as the need for food, clothing and shelter), can nevertheless be morally bad; for instance, one can over-feed chil-dren (although one can identify minimal conditions of flourishing that can sort the good from the bad). Second, there is no guidance when one need conflicts with another, as is sometimes the case with finite resources. Finally, and perhaps most importantly, Sen and Nussbaum make it very hard to measure inequality or equality (Wolff, 2008); for this, more universalised measures are necessary.

Limitation to children's rights

David Archard (2003) characterises 'child liberationists' as a group of thinkers who claim that children should have all the rights adults have and should be entitled to the right to vote, the right to determine their own education, where to live or to take paid employment. In short, they argue against laws and activities that prevent children from having complete autonomy. The contrary view believes that children, because of their particular moral status, ought to be protected from all decisions and thus should be denied some or all of their rights. The standard view is that children have rights to welfare but there are curtailments of their liberty rights; by way of contrast, adults have rights to both welfare and liberty. Following Feinberg (1980), there is an argument for child-specific rights to, first, receive those goods that they are incapable of securing for themselves. Second, children need to be protected from harms that they may come to because of their vulnerability. Finally, children should receive those rights just because they are children, and this should cease once majority is gained.

However, as has been discussed, human rights are not a single entity but can be a whole amalgam of ideas – protections, entitlements or precepts that are usually closely interrelated and integrated into a number of different expressions of rights, locally, nationally or internationally. They can be rights that are recognised in law, or can be 'moral' rights, or those recognised by moral theory. Whether 'positive' or 'moral', children, in comparison to other groups such as women and ethnic minorities, are characterised by theorists and commentators who argue that they do not "have the capacity to exercise choice" (Archard, 2003, p. 5), along with the mentally ill or comatose. Thus, for many theorists, children do not have the *capacity* for rights. Archard characterises this view of children as follows:

> Children lack certain cognitive abilities – for example to acquire and to process information in an ordered fashion, to form consistent and stable beliefs, and to appreciate the significance of options and their consequences. They also lack certain volitional abilities – for example, to form, retain and act in the light of consistent desires, and to make independent choices.
>
> (Archard, 2003, p. 11)

However, this assumption does not include all children, and is premised on a universal process of development, whereby one grows into a series of competencies in a linear and chronological way. Instead, most societies have an almost arbitrary barrier between ages at which people are able to become holders of different rights at different times in life. For instance, there is no international consensus on the age of criminal responsibility, age of sexual consent, or age of employment, among others. Furthermore, as Archard (2003) has argued, even within one culture, "this is a point about liminal differences – about the extent to which real differences between classes are displayed by the members situated at the edge of each class" (p. 23). Thus, are there such profound differences between a 15-year-old and a 16-year-old in Britain in the ability to exercise independent choices around sexual consent? It is not too likely to be considered a chasm by the 15-year-old.

Another problem to be addressed with the graduated approach is the question when we can be sure that children have attained the capacity for rights. Testing for capacity and competence is extremely difficult, if not impossible, to achieve. It will be hard to agree upon the form or content of a test, and it will be difficult to administer. Furthermore, will all adults be able to pass these tests, and should they have to demonstrate that they are able to pass the tests in order to claim what they are entitled to?

The final difficulty in the graduated approach to rights can be stated as follows: if a child is considered not to have the capacity for making choices and expressing rights, who should do this for them? In the past this was considered the remit of fathers (or husbands), so, within a feminist-influenced world, does this transfer now go to both parents? In some instances, is it not better to entrust these rights to the state? Whom does the state appoint to act in the child's interest? Does the child have to agree with the decisions made by the entrusted person? These are a few questions among many testifying to the difficulty of entrusting a child's rights to others.

Thus, there is a differential line in which the graduated possession of rights appears arbitrary and unfair. However, this may be for legitimate reasons. Brennan and Noggle (1997), for instance, talk of 'role dependent rights', whereby different rights are given to those with a specific role or skills: for instance, doctors are given certain rights, such as the ability to prescribe drugs, which others are not. Similarly, those with car driving licences have rights to drive that others do not have. Thus, a graduated collecting of rights *per se* is not detrimental to rights as a group. However, as we have seen, there is a strong ideological construct of children as being incompetent, with exceptions, whereas adults are constructed as competent overall, with exceptions.

In terms of representing children in civil rights, Archard (2003) looks at the Best Interest Principle (BIP) branch of legal theory in the UK. The BIP looks to make judgements on what is in the child's best interest. The process of BIP is used in conjunction with the 1989 Children Act, which allows children's specific interest to be at the heart of legal judgements. However, there are a massive number of options, which can expand, like lining up a column of Russian dolls with no criteria for choosing which one. Furthermore, as Archard (2003) makes clear, the BIP does not take into account the interests of others; in short, "there is no determinate fact of the matter as to what is in a child's best interests" (p. 53).

Instead, Archard holds to the importance of the Right to be Heard, or for children to have a voice on matters affecting them; thus, the practice of children's meaningful participation. This right to a voice has the distinct advantage of considerable international agreement and forms an important part of the UNCRC, in Article 12 of which a child is to be given "due weight in accordance with the age and maturity of the child". In the UK the principle of children having a voice formed an important component of the Gillick case in 1986. The ruling in England is used to decide whether a child (under 16) is able to consent to her medical treatment, without the need for parental knowledge or permission. The ruling declared:

> The principle is that parental right or power of control of the person and property of his child exists primarily to enable the parent to discharge his duty of maintenance, protection and education until [the child] reaches such an age as to be able to look after himself and make his own decisions.... I would hold that as a matter of law the parental right to determine whether or not their minor child below the age of 16 will have medical treatment terminates if and when the child achieves a sufficient understanding and intelligence to enable him or her to understand fully what is proposed.

Thus, in Britain, the child does not acquire the right to decide on all matters affecting her interests, only those of which she displays sufficient understanding.

By way of contrast, adults, when consenting to medical treatment, just need to be informed and give consent, not a full appreciation of the decision being made for the future. Indeed, the requirement to display 'Gillick competence' is very high, and many adults would fail to display the maturity and 'understanding what is involved'. As Jeremy Roche argues:

> the law continues to sanction a situation in which children are not treated as fully human subjects entitled to the formal protections that adults take for granted and often when they find themselves in professional and legal arenas their voices and standpoints are systematically excluded.
>
> (2005, p. 47)

Rights talk for children, then, while very helpful in measuring children's citizenship and as a campaigning tool, is but a partial solution. Discussion of rights can also throw light on the roles and responsibilities of families and the state. Beginning with families, what are the relationships between children, families and the state? How have these relationships changed in the contemporary world?

The family

John Locke, as we saw in Chapter 2, looked at children's relationships with parents and likened them to "a sort of rule or jurisdiction over them". Thus:

> Paternal or parental power is nothing but that which parents have over their children to govern them, for the children's good, till they come to the use of reason, or a state of knowledge, wherein they may be supposed capable to understand that rule, whether it be the law of nature or the municipal law of their country, they are to govern themselves by.
>
> (1690/1986, p. 204)

During the time of 'nonage', parents, under natural law, have the right of "paternal power to parents for the benefit of their children during their minority, to supply their want or ability to manage their property" (Locke, 1690/1986, p. 206). Thus, parents, then as now, have the right to make contracts on behalf of their children. Contemporary writers, such as Robert Nozick (1974), build upon Locke's distinction to advocate a strong familial structure as a check to the state. This 'proprietarian' argument holds that parents produce children through their labour and are thus the 'owners' of the child. Thus, for writers such as Nozick, parents have clear ownership of and responsibility for their children. This notion of parental ownership is a powerful one in society and is assumed to be the case in many circles. There is a long ingrained attitude that parents should own, or have natural sovereignty over, their children. As Hugh Lafolette has argued, parents:

> exercise extensive and virtually unlimited control over their children. Others can properly interfere with or criticize parental decisions only in unusual and tightly prescribed circumstances – in all other cases, the parents reign supreme.
>
> (1980, p. 196)

In some degree of support for the proprietarian viewpoint, liberal democratic democracies, for instance, officially intervene in family life only when there is a clear failure to provide a minimum level of care. Thus, what we consider good treatment or parenting is not a right that children have, but is due to parents' agreement that they should have what is good for them.

Most political theorists, on the other hand, have tended to have a more nuanced understanding of parental responsibilities. Kant, for instance, in *The Metaphysics of Morals*, saw parents who bring a child into the world as having the obligation to make the child content with their condition. Parents can decide how to instruct the child, what books they read and what education they receive. Parents must, then, win the right to 'manage' and develop the child, but not a 'right' to ownership. The modern variant of this is that parents have a choice in deciding what a child should eat, read, watch on TV, what religion they should practice, and so on, but parents have no rights other than those necessary to discharge their duty. But duties are not rights: parents can't choose not to have the duty. As Archard says, "parents have, rather than parental rights, duties to care for their children and discretion in their discharge" (2003, p. 65). In today's liberal democracies the care of children offered by parents must reach a certain threshold, and after that it is up to the parents to provide for their child.

Nevertheless, parents are not just a passive agent in delivering a child's welfare; no moral theory must make parents just instruments of their children's good. As Archard says:

> Children need to be brought up. That is, they are essentially vulnerable, dependent beings who, at the early stage of human development, need dedicated care and nurture. Children do not simply grow up of their own accord and they cannot be left to their own devices.
>
> (2003, p. 73)

Murray (1996) offers the theory of 'mutualism', which argues that the good of the parent and child are intertwined; parents benefit from their child's flourishing and *vice versa*. It is thus a *relationship* where the well-being and happiness of both parent and child are mutual (Murray, 1996). There is little evidence to counter this view, but how would this be institutionally delivered? What form should 'the family' take? These answers are less easy to find.

Liberal theorists, such as William Galston (1991), privilege the nuclear family as the best way of "developing the capacities of children to ... the disposition to care for, and take responsibility for, oneself and avoid becoming needlessly dependent upon others" (p. 222). There have, nevertheless, been some profound criticisms of the family. Anthropologist Edmund Leach (1968), for instance, said of the private family: "Far from being the basis of the good society, the family, with its narrow privacy and tawdry secrets, is the source of all our discontents." Radical psychiatrists in the 1960s, such as Ronald Laing, noted the unbearable pressures from the nuclear family. Feminists and socialists both have condemned the private family as serving to perpetuate gender roles and transmit private property (Barratt and MacIntosh, 1991). We also know that those children born into different families with unequal prospects are likely to grow up and reproduce that inequality; thus, families reproduce inequality. Chris Paterson (2011), in a recent UK Government Report on tackling social mobility, has advocated a five-a-day strategy for parents, presumably mothers, to "tackle the opportunity deficit – creating an open, socially mobile society" (p. 4). He suggests:

read to your child for 15 minutes each day;

play with your child on the floor for 10 minutes each day;

talk with your child for 20 minutes each day with the television off;

adopt a positive attitude to your child and praise them frequently;

give your child a nutritious diet to aid development.

Whether these activities compensate for the passing down of gifts, elitist schooling, access to well-connected social networks, parenting styles, transmission of ambitious values and payment for higher education remains doubtful. In a similar vein, Okin (1980), drawing on Mill and others, shows that families are not necessarily the best place to train future citizens, as they are separated from the public world of politics and social engagement. Furthermore, recent changes in the past 50 years have questioned the normality of a private nuclear family, as new reproductive technologies have challenged the compulsory heterosexuality of the family. With increasing numbers of same-sex parents, the increasing numbers of women entering the workforce and the overall decline in marriage, there are strains on the institution of the family. Yet the ideology of the family remains powerful, and the adoption of human rights legislation in courts of law continues to sanction "ideas and practices concerned with family privacy and parental authority" (Roche, 2005, p. 46).

On the other hand, in today's society there are few institutions comparable to the family, whatever modern form this takes, as a moral educator and a place to bring up children. Families are the places where our identities are formed and equipped, and references made to wider kin. The alternative could be the Platonic 'state managed nursery', which is destructive to individual freedom and autonomy. Today, publicly looked after children's institutions, although striving to create a family atmosphere, largely fail to provide a similar continuity of care and stability to private families. From children's viewpoint the family remains an important forum for support, advice and help. When children need help their main point of reference continues to be their mother, or other family members, such as the non-judgemental listening of grandparents (Kufeldt and McKenzie, 2003). Research shows that children confide little to professionals such as social workers or teachers (Hallett et al., 2003). Brighouse and Swift (2006) argue that families, whatever form they may take, provide the best institutional way of delivering the social goods of physical, intellectual, moral or emotional well-being. The only problem is that 'family friendly' policies have tended to be rather family unfriendly, have served to place additional burdens on women and have not attempted to advance social justice. However, alternative policies that are better explained elsewhere can be adopted (see, for instance, Brighouse and Swift, 2008).

Protecting children 'at risk' pre-dates the emergence of modern welfare states. The responsibility for orphans, children in 'moral danger', homeless children and so on has, as we have seen, been a matter for public intervention. Children have become more of an economic burden on parents, as the demands for a child's education have expanded from preschool to extended education. Child-rearing also becomes more demanding and the emotional ties between parents and children grow more intense (Lasch, 1977). However, since the 1960s the experience of preschool children in public care has been increasing as both parents move into the workforce. Responsibility for the day-to-day tending, nurturing and care of children remains clearly that of the parents. However, the expansion of welfare state policy to supporting parents (and specifically mothers) into employment has meant that the state has an earlier involvement in the lives of children. Most mothers of children under three years of age are now in employment; over three-quarters in some countries, such as the Netherlands and Norway (Lister et al., 2007, p. 126). The addition of policies such as state-subsidised care, cash transfers, leave entitlements and others means that the state is a large stakeholder in the families of even preschool children. Transferring this into the language of social rights, we can say that a young child has a right to receive care and the parents have a legal responsibility to give that care, but this caring process requires support from the state. Fiona Williams (2004) has referred to this as parenting as a partnership between parents and the state.

Taking the example of preschool childcare, we note that in Finland a child has an individual right to be cared for, either by a parent or in state-subsidised day care. In the UK, the New Labour government and, so far, the Coalition government seem committed to make childcare a universal issue and a social right in the fight against poverty. Across Europe there is the assumption that a child over three has a 'right' to early education in a preschool setting, although practices vary, with Germany and the Netherlands lagging behind the UK and Nordic examples. There are still debates about whether children are best looked after by mothers or in public day care; however, very few ask the children for their preferences. Yet the experience of good quality and affordable childcare, and the possible advantages to a child of an educational start, improvement of language skills and opportunities for participation in wider society are something that can be placed as a social right. Preschool children have been, and continue to be, cared for not only by parents, other kin and the state but also by childminders, au pairs, domestic workers and nannies. Thus, there are more partners involved in care, and perhaps debates around care, rather than rights, should dominate discussion of children, their families, and the state's relationship to citizenship. This theme is picked up in Chapter 7.

European children, through the provision of preschool day care, are entering direct relations with the state, or those acting *in loco parentis*, at an early stage of their socialisation. Day care puts children in the hands of staff who are trained according to societal views on socialisation and children's competence. Those Nordic countries with a relatively long history of day care recognise the 'dual socialisation' of children at home, where long-term commitments to the child as special and unique can be contrasted with the institution, where staff may come and go, which inhibits deep involvement with the children (Dencik, 1995). What is clear, however, is the crucial role of the state as a player in children's citizenship.

The state

As the narrative of the book has shown, the nature and extent of children's citizenship rely on the interrelationships between the child, the child's family and the state. The term *parens patriae* refers to the parent of a country and is thus a definer of citizenship, although it must be acknowledged that this is mediated by other agencies in civil society, such as childcare professions, medical practitioners, civil society organisations or other local cultural practices. States today work within an increasingly interdependent world, bound together economically, politically and culturally with other institutions, such as private companies. The image of the state as an institution that could take children away as a Hobbesian form of retribution is not reflected in the reality of the actions of today's state.

Many citizens today, as in the past, treat state interventions in families with suspicion and resistance. Durkheim declared that that it was "the state that has rescued the child from patriarchal domination and from family tyranny" (1957, p. 189). The state interventions in the family, beginning in the nineteenth century, must not be mistakenly seen as the state replacing or subverting the role of the private family in society; indeed, in the USA, as Linda Gordon (2002) has made clear, American 'child rescue' interventions were "aimed as much to reinforce failing parental, paternal authority as to limit it" (p. 50). In Britain, Behlmer (1982) notes how nineteenth-century evangelists patrolled and interfered with industry, but the evangelical assumption was that interfering in a family was sacrilege. Even contemporary critical commentary sees family privacy as crucial, with titles such as Christopher Lasch's 'Haven in a Heartless World' testifying to the continued power and importance of familial privacy. Practices in liberal democracies assume that society will work better if individuals are left to just get on with it in families; it is certainly cheaper. Interventions as drastic as the removal of children from parental homes, occurring with a whole range of agencies (police, social work, medical, NGOs), are best simplified as 'official interventions', rather than state interventions. On the other hand, it is worth noting that legal notions of *parens patriae* are used in liberal democracies as parents 'in the last instance', but, once gained, the state's powers are greater than those of private adult citizens as parents.

The state's main role in children's lives is concerned with the reproduction of society: for good, such as tackling illiteracy, poor health and unacceptable housing; or for bad, such as the reproduction of inequalities. The most profound state, or official, intervention into a child's life continues to be around the role of children as future citizens. As Archard argues:

> the state has a role as *parens patriae* to protect the interests of children and a further distinct interest in ensuring that any current generation of children become society's future functioning adults. The state must thus ensure that children are educated to a certain minimum extent so that they can act as citizens. It must also, in its child protection

practices, show concern for the child's best interests but equally give weight to the child's own views.

(2003, p. 117)

The family is often presented as a benign institution, necessary for providing a communication system that stressed the moral principles that were necessary to encourage the infant into a civilised multicultural society. John Dewey (1938/1963) argued that in order to create an American democracy, with a diverse and increasing immigrant population, it was necessary to enable face-to-face interactions in communities where a 'civilising process' that enabled the valuing of each other in terms of their diversity would occur. Dewey did not want "to submerge individuality in mass ideas and creeds to produce a reverence for mediocrity"; rather, progressive schools could produce classes that were to value diversity over uniformity (Popkewitz, 2003). Respect for immigrant cultures would produce a healthy American culture, diverse and plural.

Recent liberal theorists argue that what is necessary for children is the provision of knowledge and capacities for critical reflection (Barry, 2001). Children must have enough autonomy to be able to make reasonable choices; they should be brought up with their parents' values and beliefs, but only if this exposes them to the range of alternative lifestyles and behaviours that could be open to them. However, this has led to some tensions with multiculturalism. The US Supreme Court, for instance, recognises the importance of the child as future citizen over and above the immediate interests of the parent. The state has a duty for "preparing citizens to participate effectively and intelligently in our open political system, to be 'self-reliant and self-sufficient participants in society'" (*Wisconsin v Yoder* 1972 quoted in Archard, 2003, p. 134). If parents wish, like Amish parents, to bring their children up as separate and protected from wider society, the state has a concomitant duty to overrule parents, bring children into state schools and "expose their children to a greater range of choice than they now do" (Gutman, 1980, p. 343).

In the UK, the need to prepare the child for a plurality of citizenship is also recognised. The Citizenship Advisory Group (1998) noted that the state needed to imbue children with concepts such as democracy, law, and so on, together with values of tolerance, equality and liberty; skills to understand and evaluate political arguments; and knowledge of how elections are undertaken and how the democratic political constitution and structures work. Advocates of civic education, such as liberals like

Gutman and Rawls, envisage that the preparation taught by liberal education, like political virtues and the capacity to reason, would 'spill-over' (Gutman, 1987, p. 571) into an education of personal autonomy. Amy Gutman draws on the work of John Rawls to outline a primary good of civic education. She argues that as children we would want "adequate nutrition, health care, housing, familial affection, and an education adequate to choosing among available economic and social opportunities and to become informed, democratic citizens" (Gutman, 1980, p. 340). It is Gutman 1980 not Rawls. However, this liberal approach illustrates how children are not to be considered as players in citizenship. She argues that we:

> do not consider children – or at least young children – to be rational beings; that is, people whose present values and preferences demand respect or whose value can provide discernable, independent standard for justifying our present actions towards them. In fact, since we believe that many young children are generally not in a position to give consent, many things we do to them are perfectly acceptable even when they explicitly refuse consent.
>
> (Gutman, 1980, p. 339)

This forms a problem for legitimacy, as the notion of consent, according to classical liberal social contract theorists, justifies authority that children are not in a position to give.

An alternative analysis, and one in contrast to the 'partnership' of the state and family, sees the state as a way of 'governing' by 'policing' their well-being, where policing is "not understood in the limiting, repressive sense we give the term today, but according to a much broader meaning that encompassed all methods for developing the quality of the population and the strength of the nation" (Donzelot, 1980, p. 7). Policies towards families were not necessarily benign gifts of the state for the welfare of children, but a series of policies through which the state could legitimately intervene in families in order to control them. Philippe Meyer declared that

> through the development of a code of children's rights. The child had become the essential part of the family, its most precious burden. The proliferation of control procedures for indigents, and for the regulation of parental authority, defined the child's rights as the index of family duties. In the war waged by the State against irregular families ... the child is no more than a pretext and a hostage.
>
> (1977, p. 11)

The policing of families gives rise to the 'naturalness' of childcare by families/mothers and the genealogy of 'need' identified by Fraser and Gordon (1997). The task was to "govern the autonomous, flexible, and self-managing child" (Dahlberg, 2003, p. 265). Most liberal theorists, following Mill's arguments on the education of women, look at how education would lead children to be autonomous or, as Archard puts it, "to have an open future" (Archard, 2003, p. 135). Schooling came to be an important form of modernisation, but also colonisation, as the 'modern' child was to be spread across the world. First through English and European languages, followed by a menu of rights, children could become the vehicle that forms 'world development'. The neoliberal image of a 'child citizen' is reinforced through the World Bank or the International Monetary Fund, which insist on decentralised, privatised and community-based family policies. The neoliberal policies of the US, the UK, Australia and Canada were targeted at post-Soviet, Asian, African and Latin American countries, as if they were the same. This included discourses of responsibilisation and autonomy that would enable citizens to take care of themselves and their families in communities.

By way of contrast, communist welfare policies were focussed on building a collective nation and ideology that would produce good models of citizenship and family. Thus, schools, childcare centres and families were encouraged to produce a unitary model of education and belonging. The 'cradle to grave' policies were similar to those developed by social democracies, but were explicit in the way they wished to educate children, control conduct and ensure adherence to a rigid hierarchical and centralised system.

Nicolas Rose (1996, 1999) has argued that the national social state had legislated and transferred the care of children and others to the state through knowledge and new cultural ways of thinking about citizenship and belonging. While the social state was developed to take care of citizens, the new 'knowledge based' or 'networked' societies required communities and individuals to take care of themselves. The new discourses of state policy and the economic, political and technical changes mushrooming in recent years are part of international change. The adaptability of a centripetal social state providing a robust public care system is called into question. The result has been the dispersal of decentralisation of government, the valuing of private, individual autonomy and responsibility, and the focus on uncertainty, flexibility and choice in times of instability. For Rose, the late twentieth-century focus of governmentalities continues to centre on the natural good of the private over the public, localised knowledge and community-based decision-making over central government. Thus, there is an urge to bring in marginalised 'voices' and highlight civil society or community. For instance, the norms expressed in the Third Way (Giddens, 1994) argue for a policy that can produce autonomous, responsible, self-sufficient children and families. On the other hand, those who are attached to welfare, perhaps inevitably given the inequities of modern societies, are considered failures in this social order and are viewed as personally responsible for their poverty.

Conclusion

It is effective for rights to evolve out of specific activity by citizens debating and arriving at agreements. The influence of women entering the world of paid employment and politics in the twentieth century has applied the notion of rights to new arenas, most notably the 'private' sphere of the family and social goods, such as welfare and education. This change is partly due to the political processes that women have entered, rather than merely a series of externally imposed judgements. Thus, the diversity and complexity of modern life are best expressed through the act of democratic politics and have altered what it is to be a citizen, who can be a citizen, and the type and nature of influence over political decision-making.

However, popular democratic political participation is not necessarily one of progressive inclusion. The conservative elements of majority decision-making have arguably inhibited progressive labour legislation and health in the United States when compared with Western Europe. The requirement for a change in the minds of the majority of citizens remains imperative. The US Supreme Court ruled against segregated schools in 1954, yet ten years later only 12 per cent of Black children attended desegregated schools in the southern states. It was only after the majority black and white populations agreed to pay for progressive elements that tackling racial poverty was realistically challenged. The lesson of this is that it is only through the influence of being a citizen in the fuller, political and economic sense that genuine rights can be generated. This is not to reject the importance of cosmopolitan or international rights, but emphasises the obligations on states and citizens to ensure the possibility of the exercise of citizenship and political community for all.

Human rights have global appeal and are available to everyone. "It is an aspiration, not a moral truth" (Goodhart, 2008, p. 191), especially for those who have no other recourse. Thus, the global appeal of human rights is aspirational: "human rights are neither relative nor universal. They are legitimate because of their global appeal. That is enough" (Goodhart, 2008, p. 193). Or is that enough? The exclusiveness of the concept of rights does not rely on what it protects (whether choice capacities or welfare) but rather in its being simultaneously prioritising, protective and demanding action. It distinguishes through a combination of these properties rather than the specific content. As Freeden (1991) explains:

> a human right is a conceptual device, expressed in linguistic form, that assigns priority to certain human or social attributes regarded as essential to the adequate functioning of a human being; that is intended to serve as a protective capsule for those attributes; and that appeals for deliberate action to ensure such protection. (p. 7)

Threats to human rights, capacities, choices and welfare come from bureaucracies and markets, as well as states. But also threats come from parents, officials, landowners, and religious and social authorities; in other words, from those with *power*. Rights have become an important tool in identifying where power lies and have had some impact, especially when viewed on an international level. It is this internationalising of rights that has led some to argue that national citizenship has been superseded by international citizenship and a new cosmopolitanism. This will be explored in the next chapter.

6
International Citizenship

The nineteenth century, as far as the development of children's rights and citizenship is concerned, can be seen as what Milne (2008) refers to as the 'prehistory' to the present. As we have seen, there were sweeping changes to child protection and controls on the age of sexual consent, amongst other aspects of children's status. However, it was during the twentieth century that these developments really accelerated. Drawing on the social context of religious zeal, philanthropy, paternalism, feminism, socialism and the developing sciences of psychology, psychiatry and paediatrics, the 'children's rights movement' became internationalised. It is with this, and an internationalising context of human rights, that children's citizenship is intertwined. We have moved from a nineteenth-century world of nation states setting the agendas to one in which states are enmeshed with each other. With such issues as climate change and the series of financial crashes, among others, the nation states' citizenship systems are no longer able to cope with global issues (Held, 2010). The following discussion takes a very European-focussed viewpoint, and, while one must be suspicious of European colonialism, the discussion of rights in this chapter only traces their origins in the West, not necessarily a final endpoint of dominion. It must also be acknowledged that the history of concern with individuals and individual rights, while present in a tradition of European thought, is rooted equally in other discursive cultures. For instance, India is the largest democracy precisely because democratic ideas were already embedded in its culture preceding the British Empire; democracy and rights were not necessarily imposed upon India by a hegemonic West (Held, 2010).

One can scarcely find a sociology or political science textbook today that does not feature the concept of globalisation. With the recent dynamic changes in information and communication technologies, jet travel, trading blocks and multinational corporations, there are significant limits to the nation state, although, as Hirst and Thompson (1996) quite rightly alert us, we need to be sceptical of the death of the nation state; trade and investment patterns are still based around core economic concentrations in Europe and North America, with the Pacific rim and the economic growth of Brazil, Russia, India and China to be shortly added to these lists. The G20 is nevertheless an exclusive and powerful club of nation states. However, in the twentieth century there were some profound challenges to nation states and patterns of globalisation that affect us all.

First, the gaps in wealth between the rich and poor nations are still stark, and possibly accelerating. In this sense we can discuss polarisations between economies. This is crucial, as the effects of these inequalities in basic subsistence, and access to rights and liberties offend a global sense of social justice. The global inequalities impact upon rich as well as poor countries, with migration and crime closely associated with these inequalities. Second, international patent rights have meant that genetic materials, including seeds, medicines and species, are obtained within a context of monopoly property rights. The laws of contract extend beyond nation state boundaries and become enforceable across the globe. Third, while writers have talked of the triumph of liberal democracy and the principles of the 'free market' since the fall of the Eastern Bloc (Fukuyama, 1992), processes of liberalism are still challenged by a variety of forms, notably religious fundamentalisms. Fourth, Faulks (2000) talks of the internationalisation of 'global risks'. Unlike the global market and values of liberal individualism, there are planetary risks, including infectious diseases, international crime, nuclear power and ecological damage.

A response to this has been the return to ideas of 'cosmopolitanism', a doctrine going back to the Ancient Greeks and Romans. The Greek derivation of the term originates from a *kosmos* (world) *polis* and gives rise to a political form of world citizenship that has few adherents today, as the size and almost infinite diversity of forms would make this impracticable. Rarely do national governments use 'direct' forms of democracy; Switzerland is perhaps the closest in Europe to 'direct' forms of participation. At a global level it is quite likely that citizens would feel distant from decision-making and would feel disempowered. Citizens' sense of being outside forms of governance and citizenship has led to growing problems in existing nation states, with minorities, such as those in Belgium or Canada, seeking to form states outside (or within) existing national boundaries. The trend in this sense is perhaps more local than global.

Immanuel Kant feared that global governance would lead to a 'universal despotism'; such fears explain, perhaps, why contemporary cosmopolitanism tends to adhere to a series of international agreements between existing nation states held together by universal principles of justice and international law, rather than striving for a global Leviathan. Thus, the United Nations Declaration on Human Rights in 1948 and the European Convention on Human Rights declared in 1950, discussed in this chapter, have a Kantian make-up of individual states, being the primary unit of political authority, held together by a series of international moral obligations under human rights.

It is perhaps for this reason that most adherents to cosmopolitanism tend to be associated with the Roman form of 'legal citizenship', in which a contemporary group of 'patricians' will maintain stability and social justice on a global scale, bonded together by the legal glue of treaties, alliances and agreements. There remains the problem of enforcing rights and treaties through an international legal authority when government responsibilities fall short of international law. These legal prescriptions tend to be understood through the prism of specific and different cultural and ideological beliefs. Supranational courts handling cosmopolitan disagreements will tend to make highly controversial and normative judgements over whether or not individual rights have been infringed. It is true that national governments are in a similar predicament; however, national governments tend to have a large body of case law that has been evolved and shaped through the national political culture of politicians, media and the general public. The imposition of rights in internationally legally protected constitutions that are separate from political influence can end up undermining the actual exercise of democratic citizenship.

The concept of 'cosmopolitanism' has become an important term in theories and politics of sustainable development. Beck (2006), for instance, argued that individuals are able to raise their aspirations from their localities and develop a broader, hence cosmopolitan, outlook. For theorists working on international development, globalisation does not just refer to the impersonal development of capitalism but has emotional and ethical consequences too. The intensity and drastic nature of global concerns urge people to act together and to recognise a shared sense of dangers to future generations. Schools and the media are significant for the development of such a perspective, because both have the capacity to increase awareness of the relationship between the local and the global. Such global issues also seem to touch a nerve with children across the globe, with children seeming to have a particular readiness to accept universal forms of social justice. Within international children's organisations, at present, a global concern and international movement seems to be restricted to a limited set of wealthy children but has the potential to develop, especially under the guidance of supranational organisations (Larsson et al., 2010). Supranational organisations have also developed with the project of intervening in the lives of children. Just like the nineteenth-century reformers encouraging the nation state to adopt a more direct interventionist approach towards children, international organisations have identified children as being a cause that gives them competencies to intercede in countries and contexts previously considered independent or beyond their influence.

International citizenship

Writing on the tenth anniversary of the League of Nations in 1929, the biographer of the organisation, John Eppstein (1929), declared that the 1924 *Declaration of the Rights of the Child* was pushed through by the Director of the Social Question Section, Dame Rachel Crowdy. Milne (2008) emphasises the role of sisters Eglantyne Jebb and Dorothy Buxton, who formed the Save the Children Fund, as being fundamental to the drawing up of the 1924 *Declaration*. Both perspectives are probably correct; the work of campaigning men, and especially women, was key to the development of international practice. Both writers, however, fail to refer to the pioneering work of the 'social purity' movement in England in the 1870s and 1880s, in particular the work of Josephine Butler and the 'London Committee for the Suppression of the Traffic of British Girls for the Purposes of Continental Prostitution'. Indeed, the League of Nations continued to use the title 'International Conference of White Slave Traffic' up until 1921, when it was changed to 'International Conference of Traffic in Women and Children': "in order that women and girls of colonial races might be protected" (Eppstein, 1929, p. 167). What the conference achieved from the beginning was a number of 'guiding principles', including the setting of an age of consent to be 'trafficked' at 21.

By 1929 the League's Child Welfare Committee, under the chair of Rachel Crowdy, established the twin aims of "returning to their homes of minors who had escaped the control of their parents or guardians, and the other with the public assistance of children, stranded for any reason in a foreign country and in need of relief from public funds"

(Eppstein, 1929, p. 169). Thus, the Child Welfare Committee campaigned around child protection but also child welfare, reflecting in some sense the concerns of late Victorian campaigners around children's sexuality and control of children's labour. The issue of social welfare, as we saw in Chapter 4, also developed amid concerns about maternal welfare. Save the Children was established with the motivation of ameliorating the suffering of Austrian and German children after World War I. Another important development was the establishment of the International Labour Organization (ILO). Thus, there were the twin achievements of guidance that "raised the age of consent in many countries and the age of marriage in some" (Walters, 1952, p. 187) together with the "endeavour to secure and maintain fair and humane conditions of labour for men, women and children, both in their own countries and in all countries to which their commercial and industrial relations extend" (Article 23, League of Nations). The Child Welfare Committee undertook three major international enquiries between 1928 and 1932 into juvenile courts, national legislations on the legal age of marriage, and the welfare and training of blind children (van Ginniken, 2006).

If we take a snapshot of the 1932 Child Welfare Committee, there were 12 government representatives, all of whom were men. Of the 13 'assessors', on the other hand (who were representatives from NGOs, the ILO and the League's Health Organisation), ten were women. A note on those women's backgrounds is telling.

First, Estrid Hein, who was Danish, had been a doctor since 1906 and was recognised as an eye specialist in 1918. She was an active feminist, a member of the Danish Women's Society and the Scandinavian Family Law Commission, and the first female member of the Danish Institute for the Blind.

Gertrud Bäumer was a German politician who actively participated in the feminist movement. She was also a writer, contributing to the newspaper *Die Hilfe*. She was head of the Federation of German Women during World War I, and after the war she joined the German Democratic Party, for which she was a Reichstag member between 1919 and 1932. She was later appointed counsellor for education and youth in the Weimar government's ministry of the interior (Bell and Offen, 1983).

Grace Abbott was a sociologist interested in collecting data relating to child labour and juvenile delinquency. She obtained funding for over 100 social research investigations. In 1929, in response to the Depression, she advocated for federal aid for relief, and collected relief reports from 203 cities and distributed them to national agencies. She worked for the Children's Bureau in the United States and served as President of the National Conference of Social Work and on the committee organising the first Conference on Social Work, held in Paris in 1928.

The Uruguayan Paulina Luisi, a socialist and feminist, was honorary vice-president of the Pan American Conference of Women. She was the first Latin American woman to participate in the League of Nations as a government representative. She acted as delegate of the Uruguayan Government to the Commission for the Protection of Children and Youth and in the fight against the trade in women and children. An interesting aspect of Luisi's moral reform platform was a campaign for obligatory sex and health education programs in the public school system. She suggested having these programs first introduced in primary schools and then continuing on to the secondary level. She defined sex education as the pedagogic tool to teach the individual to subject sexual drives to the will of an instructed, conscientious and responsible intellect. As opposed to sex education, health education classes would focus more on the scientific aspects of reproduction of the species, natural history, anatomy, personal hygiene and the prevention of venereal diseases.

Helen Burniaux was a Belgian trade unionist. She combined her trade union work with a full-time occupation as a school inspector. She was a member of the Belgian *Comité National d'Action Féminine*, and president of the International Federation of Working Women for the year 1923–1924.

Another medical doctor was Italian Fanny Dalmazzo of the *Union internationale des ligues feminines catholiques*, which was a youth group charged with carrying out its apostolic mission among young girls from the working class. In 1919 the French branch advocated for women's suffrage and for a women's trade union. However, according to de Grazia (1991), the group as a whole was considered quite reactionary; Fanny Dalmazzo, for instance, did not think women should have the vote, although the organisation she belonged to certainly did have radical ideas, albeit shaped within a religious framework.

Emilie Gourd, who represented Women's International Organisations, was a Swiss women's rights activist, and from 1912 to 1928 she was President of the Swiss Federation of Women's Suffrage (*Schweizerischen Verbandes für Frauenstimmrecht*).

Charlotte Elizabeth Whitton, representing the Social Service Council of Canada and Canadian Council of Child Welfare, was a Canadian feminist and the first female mayor of a major city in Canada, serving Ottawa from 1951 to 1956 and again from 1960 to 1964.

The British Dame Katherine Furse represented the International Scouts and Guides, and Dame Rachel Crowdy herself was the only high-ranking woman in the secretariat of the League of Nations (van Ginneken, 2006).

It is difficult to say whether there was any influence of women on the League, but, as Geert Van Goethem (2006) notes, the resolutions of the International Congress of Working Women (ICWW) had a determining influence on the results of the International Labour Conference and on the working of the first conventions. Van Goethem maintains: "It was mainly in their committee work that these women exercised their influence, and it was precisely there that the recommendations of the ICWW proved useful. It should come as no surprise then that the final conventions on the eight-hour working day and the protection of female and child labour differed only slightly from the resolution adopted by the ICWW, although this in itself cannot be taken as a measure of the authority of women workers" (2006, p. 1040).

United Nations Convention on the Rights of the Child

The fate of the 'Geneva Declaration' of 1924 went the way of the rest of the social and other missions of the League of Nations; there were a good deal of friendly favours from the members, but it got lost amid the issues of the Great Depression and starting of World War II. Little, really, was achieved for children in practical terms by the League. The League was eventually succeeded by the United Nations (UN), the kernel of which developed from the 26 allied states signed up to the Washington Pact in 1941. By 1948 the United Nations had drafted, published and declared the United Nations Declaration of Human Rights. This was a considerable achievement, as there were enormously contrasting philosophical positions, ranging from Gandhi's emphasis on duties leading to earned rights, to positivistic views of rights as universal categories, to the social rights discussed in Chapter 4. Thus, the UN introduced a declaration of human rights just at the time when there was no philosophical agreement about the idea of human rights, their nature or how much they should encompass. The declaration was passed by individuals within the UN, who were able to bypass the theoretical divergences across the globe by working towards practical agreements. Although the context of the Cold War discouraged states from directly interfering in sovereign territories, other pressures, notably from decolonisation and the civil rights movement, introduced new principles of rights, concerned with racism, asylum-seeking rights and other social rights.

The United Nations in 1946 created the International Children's Emergency Fund, later to be named the UN Children's Fund (UNICEF). UNICEF was the first intergovernmental agency exclusively concerned with the interests of children. That is, a specific agency was set up by a number of states to carry out projects and plans specifically around children. Within the 1948 Universal Declaration of Human Rights it was accepted that children must be recognised as a subject of special care and attention. The special needs of children were also built into the Conventions relating to the status of refugees in 1951 and the elimination of all forms of discrimination against women. All of this led to the United Nations Convention on the Rights of the Child, among other international legal frameworks protecting children. We will return to these soon.

In the 1960s the General Assembly approved the notion that 1979 was to be the International Year of the Child. In the run-up to this in 1978 the Polish delegation, led by Adam Lopakita, tabled the motion that the UN should formally adopt a convention on the rights of the child. Lopakita was firmly influenced by the ideas of Polish paediatrician and pedagogue Janusz Korczak. In 1911 Korczak had been director of a Jewish orphanage in Warsaw, where: "he formed a simple children's republic with a small parliament, court and newspaper within the orphanage" (Milne, 2008, p. 48). In 1926 he helped children establish a newspaper that formed a supplement to the main national Jewish newspaper. The newspaper survived into World War II.

The ratification of the UNCRC in 1989 by all bar two member states established a clear diet of rights for children. It is made up of 54 legally binding articles, covering many aspects of children's lives, such as their families, their health, education and also their right to a nationality. A thorough review of each of the articles is beyond the task of this book and has been handled very well elsewhere (see Alen et al., 2006; Freeman, 2007; Reynaert et al., 2009). What is clear is that the "UNCRC is an important set of international standards which is comprehensive and detailed but not without flaw" (Kilkelly and Lundy, 2006, p. 12). One of the rights (article 3) identifies that the child must be a primary consideration and "all actions concerning the child shall take account of his or her best interests". For commentators such as Lansdown (2001), this goes beyond the child as passive recipient of welfare at the behest of parents and professionals. The Convention makes it clear, Lansdown argues, that all decisions concerning children must take the whole gamut of the UNCRC as a package of rights. She argues that the child's best interests must be assessed to the:

> extent to which all their human rights are respected in any particular policy, action or legislation. In other words the rights embodied in the Convention must provide a framework with which to analyse the extent to which proposals promote the best interests of children.
>
> (Lansdown, 2001, p. 94)

Lansdown gives the example that a child protection team's attempts to protect a child from abuse must respect the child's right to privacy (article 16). Lansdown, interestingly, points to the right to education (article 28) and how this must be placed within the context of children's right to express their views on matters that concern them (article 12). Similarly, Verheyde (2006) explores the ways in which the UNCRC encourages questions of who pays for education and how equality can be promoted through education. The education system in the UK does not give children these full rights and denies children the right to shape the curriculum or to participate in school councils and teaching methods, among other things. These concern important questions of not only children's rights *to* education but also children's rights *in* education. Howe and Covell (2005), in the Canadian context with wider, global implications, discuss not just children's rights to education but the sort of curricula they should follow if they are to be fully empowered and engaged in citizenship, not as now, when children have a fairly minimal understanding of their rights during childhood and are ill-equipped to understand them when they reach adulthood. Since its adoption in 1989 there have been a number of supplementary protocols adopted onto the UNCRC, in particular for vulnerable children. These include The Optional Protocol to the Convention on the Rights of Child on the Sale of Children, Child Prostitution and Child Pornography, and The Optional Protocol to the Convention on the Rights of Child on the Involvement of Children in Armed Conflict, both protocols adopted in 2002.

Milne (2008) has argued that the UNCRC centres around the 'Three Ps': protection, provision and participation. Protection of children from harms of violence and sexual abuse, together with provision of the minimum requirements, is relatively uncontroversial. However, the provision of rights to participation, under article 12, where 'due weight' should be given to children's views, is not. Article 12 of the Convention is interesting and pertinent, as it includes a right to participation, so important in terms of citizenship. Or, in Lansdown's words, participation and the right to be heard are necessary if children "are to move beyond their traditional status as recipients of adult care and protection and become social actors entitled to influence decisions that affect their lives" (Lansdown, 2001, p. 95). The issue of participation will be discussed in more depth in Chapter 8 of this book. For now it is worth noting that participation has different meanings and the various theories of participation can lead to children's views being 'manipulated' or being directly linked with broader theories of citizenship, democracy and representation (Thomas, 2007). This, realistically, has amounted to a number of clashes between adults and children over children's right to decision-making.

Thus, children have had to draw upon the support of sympathetic adults to improve and realise their specific rights and link to broader claims to citizenship. Within the context of the United Nations, "NGOs have been essential partners from the beginning" (Beigbeder, 2007, p. 521); included in this are organisations such as the ILO and intergovernmental organisations, such as the United Nations Educational, Scientific and Cultural Organisation (UNESCO), the World Health Organisation (WHO) and UNICEF. NGOs have found human rights rhetoric to be a crucial way of discussing ethical issues in the overall dominance of *laissez-faire* capitalism among the nation states that form the membership of important international organisations, such as the UN and the EU. As Conor Gearty (2010) has argued, human rights are used: "as a rallying cry for ethical action, not a term of legal art to be interpreted in court" (p. 28).

Most of the academic literature has focussed on the gap between the rhetoric and ideals of the UNCRC, and the reality on the ground. Ennew (2008) has argued that the UN has recognised the rights of children as in need of protection, "but has been slower to consider them as citizens, only recently paying partial attention to their political actions and potential as a global force" (p. 67). Indeed, some writers, such as Yasemin Soysal (1994), have argued that in the post-war era the unfolding of universal rights has replaced the notion of a national political subject with "universal personhood rather than national belonging" (Soysal, 1994, p. 1). The language of human rights becomes central to the world of government and citizen affairs, and social membership is increasingly based upon the properties of a person rather as a citizen of a country. Thus, migrants to countries become party to some social rights within the receiving political community; for instance, they have an international civil right of representation in courts. Furthermore, international bodies, such as the European Court of Human Rights in Strasbourg, produce rulings, such as in the case of the child murderers of James Bulger in England, Robert Thompson and Jon Venables. It was judged that the nature and extent of their custody should be depoliticised by transferring these decisions from the political Home Secretary to the more impartial judiciary.

In this sense, does children's universal status as recipients of international rights make discussions of citizenship superfluous? While children do have some social and civil rights, they still do not have political rights. The inadequacies of political participation even in international contexts make children the objects of policies rather than the active participants. As Kilkelly and Lundy (2006) argue, "the need for and benefits of consulting children and young people about their experience of their rights" (p. 13) remains a limitation of the UNCRC. Human rights, even article 16 of the UNCRC, do not by themselves ensure the development of participatory frameworks necessary to create common institutions of governance. The institutions will therefore be and appear alien to them.

A great problem of human rights and their declaration through international agencies is that children's 'rights' to shelter, water, respect and health care can be overturned by national courts under the guise of 'national interests', 'fiscal responsibility in difficult times' or the clash with the economic rights of others (i.e. the rich). The UN's talk of rights is nearly always couched in terms of 'available resources' or 'cultural limits'. Furthermore, appointments of those having the statutory obligations for inspections are political appointments, often agreed with the nation state's approval. Thus, the enforcement of rights remains within the national legal framework.

Citizenship based around national identity retains its importance in that, as Habermas (1994) has argued, the national state remains the institution most able to concentrate economic, military and communicative power. National citizenship holds on to its importance because it is also the expression of the relationship between rights, responsibilities and participation, so crucial to governance. Rights, responsibilities, participation and belonging are expressed largely within the local context; while recognising processes of globalisation, the operationalisation of governance remains with national governments. The international paradox is that elements of our economies and laws are supranational, while identity and representation remain local and tied to national identities. The changes and nature of international problems make people wish to retain local control and local representation.

Although nation states working within the liberal market remain the key controllers of power and citizenship, the need to move away from this is becoming striking. The awareness of the organic processes of birth, growth and finite resources gives rise to 'ecological' perspectives on citizenship (van Steenbergen, 1994). The usual liberal concern with welfare, rights, property, liberty and the market is countered when the destructive elements of the market are recognised on a global scale. It is not just the poor and disadvantaged who are harmed in this. Ecological approaches also, like feminism, make links from the intimate to the global; the ethical decisions we make as consumers, or whether or not we use birth control, make it apparent that issues around embodiment have global ramifications. Thus, the private and public divide so important to classical liberalism is challenged. Ecological citizenship, as opposed to classical liberalism, changes the form of responsibilities that we undertake. The choices we make over recycling, consumption patterns, Internet use and our connections to those overseas make duties non-enforceable, and thus the nature of responsibilities cannot be delivered by the conventional framework of educational and political institutions. New forms of government and education are necessary. The nation state has been changed to the extent that writers such as Lister (1997) have looked to understand citizenship in a more complex way, in which all persons must be international and 'multilayered'. Citizenship, then, for Lister, must be able to be located on a spectrum that can move from the local to global via the regional, national and supranational.

European citizens

Europe, once one of the most belligerent parts of the globe, suffering two major world wars between European nation states, has through the European Union (EU) been able to put aside its differences, and now the thought of two major European countries being at war with each other is highly unlikely. The EU, unlike the North American Free Trade Agreement or Association of Southeast Asian Nations, has looked to create political and not just economic institutions. The European Parliament, for instance, is trying to create new networks of participation by encouraging closer cooperation between political parties, a system of pressure groups, social movements, NGOs and 'steering' policies across national boundaries. While the UNCRC is an important symbolic banner for children in European countries, the European Union and the treaties between nation states have real legal ramifications for children in Europe. Indeed, there has been an accumulation of legislation, legal acts and court decisions which constitute the body of European Union law, known as the *Acquis Communautaire*, although, to begin with, these were largely confined to relatively modest legal and judicial measures. For instance, in February 1982 the European Commission and the Court of Human Rights found the UK government in breach of the Human Rights Convention by "not respecting parents' objections to corporal punishment" (Newell, 1989, p. 14). Note that this was in response to *parents'* objections, not those of their children. This had implications for the UK, which followed by abolishing corporal punishment in 1987.

The EU's attention to its 97 million children is increasing, especially since the publication of the 2006 communication 'Towards an EU Strategy on the Rights of the Child' and the inclusion of children's rights in the Treaty of Lisbon, which will promote "solidarity between generations and protection of the rights of the child". It has established a series of social rights, including those around the protection of children and competence around the trafficking of children. The EU has developed a whole range of policies that affect children both directly and indirectly, and almost every aspect of EU law has an impact, either directly or indirectly, on children (Ruxton, 2005). Children's rights lobbyists have been instrumental in raising the profile of children's issues across Europe (see Lansdown, 2002).

EU law has specifically focussed on child protection, but not on those aspects that are deemed to fall within the competence of national governments, such as generic child protection; the issues the EU focuses on are those such as campaigning against child labour and sexual exploitation, with a view of coordinating police and judicial efforts across nations, rather than guiding those within nation states. The EU has also introduced a number of 'soft laws' aimed at combating child pornography on the Internet and a singe six-digit hotline (116000) across the EU for reporting missing children. Since 2000, and the introduction of the Lisbon treaty, the EU has paid attention to the causes and consequences of child poverty, setting up a series of action plans and processes throughout the 2000s. For instance, the 'EU Task-Force on Child Poverty and Well-Being' was established in 2006 and a number of detailed comparative research reports on child poverty were commissioned (see Directorate-General for Employment, Social Affairs and Equal Opportunities, 2008). These policies were not so much top-down requirements, but more to do with the new governance strategies of cross-national cooperation, knowledge and skills transfers across states, and encouraging a more proactive response from Member States.

The 'Lisbon Agenda' has served to link some young people across the EU in friendship and to formulate cultural links, but has done so in the guise of 'improving economic efficiency', thereby retaining the liberal conception of citizenship. The new thinking of the European Union also distinguishes between 'children' and 'youth'; for the latter, in the words of the European Youth Pact of 2005, member states would have a commitment "on promoting young people's full participation in education, employment and society". This was followed up in May 2007 with a 'Memorandum of Understanding' between the Council of Europe and the European Union whereby the two institutions will "campaign to empower young people to participate actively in the democratic process". In this sense there is an attempt to link young people into a form of solidarity and participation. This is demonstrated by initiatives such as the 'Youth in Action Programme', set to run between 2007 and 2013, which aims to encourage civic participation of all young people but specifically targets disadvantaged young people, including those with physical or mental disabilities.

The forward march of European integration, if there was such a thing, has been checked by the 'No' votes in 2005 in France and the Netherlands, and by the recent fallout of the economic tensions of sovereign debt within the Euro. Yet even by the mid-1990s the progress of social policy across the EU had begun to slow down, as noted above, with 'hard' European laws being replaced with 'soft' laws of guidelines and common goals, leaving implementation to individual Member States. Nevertheless, in addition to the soft laws on child protection and poverty, there are some key European measures on childcare (1992), parental leave and part-time work (1997) that have somewhat compensated for the perceived reluctance of some national governments to reform. The influence of the EU on children in Western Europe since the 1990s has still been profound, albeit low-key. Indeed, Lister et al. have suggested that, under the influence of the EU, "legislation and policy recommendations have redefined the young child's need for care as a responsibility of both the state *and* parents" (2007, p. 109). The massive investment in preschool care for children in the West is in marked contrast to the relative decline of those services in Eastern Europe, previously known for its investment in preschool provision. From the perspective of the EU, childcare policies are key to further social integration, participation and belonging, especially for those from migrant or ethnic minority backgrounds. The concept of gender equality is on the European agenda as a result of the actions of the feminist movement and female officials, referred to by Lister et al. (2007) as 'femocrats', thus reflecting the actions of the League of Nations and the United Nations; the increasing influence of woman in organisations tends to lead to a greater focus on children's lives and welfare.

There are also attempts at symbolic aspects of shared belonging, such as the burgundy-coloured passport of the EU, the driving licence and number plates, as well as a European anthem and postage stamps. The Copenhagen *Declaration on European Identity* of 1973 strongly emphasised the 'common European Civilisation', the 'common heritage' and 'converging approaches to life' across Europe. Lister and Pia (2008, p. 181) also note the new European emblem and flag in 1986, with the 12 gold stars forming a circle that has a striking similarity to a Christian halo. Other efforts to provide aspects of a common European identity include the European Weeks and European Years associated with various EU-chosen themes and programmes, such as the Capital of Culture awards.

Others include the fostering of civic partnerships of young people through the Youth in Action Programme and the external policies of the EU through the use of human rights as a lever in foreign policy (see Delanty, 2008). With the export of European-style human rights, some commentators see this as a way of uniformly universalising identities that sweeps over local cultural identities. However, the new adoption of a European identity, Sassatelli (2002) notes, has a discourse of 'unity in diversity' as a motto of the EU, in an attempt to grapple with aspects of globalisation and the growing migration across and into the EU. A Council of Europe statement, quoted in Sassatelli, declares: "diversity lies at the heart of Europe's cultural richness, which is our common heritage and the basis of our unity" (2002, p. 29).

It must also be kept in mind that the language of rights in the EU context has been grounded in a conception of good that is based around economic integration. As Stalford (2003) notes, children "have always been regarded as merely incidental and, indeed, instrumental to the mobility of economically active adult migrants" (p. 1). The citizenship that the EU is associated with is the liberal citizenship of rational, self-interested economic actors able to move themselves and the factors of production across national boundaries. Thus, the type of citizenship encouraged is 'active' in that it relies on the working and taxpaying citizen model; while there is an improvement in that it is not defined in terms of military service, it is tied down to economic efficiency. For children, this has implications in terms of how much choice they have in moving across borders, reflected in the European Union's legislation, which locates accompanying family members across borders as dependent. While this does entitle the 'dependent' member to social, welfare and educational rights, they remain dependent upon the migrant worker (see Stalford, 2008). Despite the concern for competence in child trafficking and the resources spent on this, very little is spent on children's views of parents moving across boundaries.

Children's lack of choice in crossing boundaries leads to the way in which the rights around citizenship are deployed. Rights may attempt to provide the glue of citizenship belonging, but active citizenship is something beyond the claiming of rights, and involves participation. Thus, the enjoyment of rights that adults and children have is private and passive and removed from the participatory element. Indeed, the failure of the EU to embed its laws on children within the UNCRC, and specifically Article 12 on participation, results in:

> little prominence attached to younger children's interests and needs, and to the value of their contribution to the day-to-day life of the EU. The focus, instead, is on a relatively narrow set of themes centred around employment, education and political activism.
>
> (Stalford and Drywood, 2009, p. 169)

The citizenship encouraged by the EU looks to steer nation state policy and to encourage the movement and geographical connection between groups of older children, under the youth programmes. Thus, the free movement principle may, for some, encourage a development of support and friendship networks. A problem arises in consistency across Europe, as the standard mechanisms for monitoring the rights of children remain weak and piecemeal. The Europeanisation of professional practices may further the normalisation processes of children and young people, as national standards become integrated into 'European' standards of practice.

The way in which the EU establishes a rights-based European policy has implications for the nation state. There is a decided shift towards universalist rights and treating people as people in an abstract manner, rather than as persons within national contexts. However, despite the attempts, such as the Maastricht Treaty 1992, to sever the link between nationality and citizenship, the EU remains at heart statist and exclusive in character. As O'Leary (1998) has pointed out, the EU has limited the expansion of the EU and has attempted to encourage a mythical European identity. The economic protectionism characterised by the Common Agricultural Policy produces environmental harm and disadvantages poorer regions of the world. The Amsterdam Treaty of 1997 firmed up border controls and restricted both economic migrants and asylum seekers. Furthermore, the Amsterdam Treaty limited the

European Court of Justice to interest in law and order and 'national security'. As Gerard Delanty (2008) has argued, "rather than a shift from nationality to a postnational kind of citizenship, what is occurring is a transformation of nationality as a result of Europeanization" (p. 61). The EU, by formulating a rights-based package of citizenship, needs to encourage a more participative and inclusive public sphere in a world where blame for non-participation is placed upon children and young people in terms of the 'democratic deficit' and 'apathy'. As Bellamy and Warleigh (2001) have argued, the public sphere needs to "be reinvented as an instrument of political engagement: a tool for the expression of opinions and the resolution of problems rather than simply a batch of entitlements" (p. 13). The public sphere of the European project must reform itself to effectively ensure children's rights and encourage a real form of children's citizenship engagement. There must be:

> more inclusive and meaningful interaction with children on a broader range of issues. This demands enhanced structural and financial investment in a more far-reaching communication strategy, more...widespread engagement with civil society. Additional consideration should also be given to how such processes can genuinely inform decision-making and to how the impact of any ensuing measures on children might be monitored in the long-term.
>
> (Stalford and Drywood, 2009, p. 170)

The citizenship employed by the EU must be more than and *beyond* the claiming of rights as citizenship. The enjoyment of rights is a specifically private or passive activity and EU citizenship must, as Jo Shaw (2007) argues, emerge from the conjunction of rights and membership. The process of belonging is the active or public aspect of citizenship that the EU needs to address, for children as well as adults. The EU can be an important tool for children in Member States, as well as those in families, in particular through the actions of the European Court of Justice. The processes at a European level must challenge: "deeply embedded cultural attitudes towards children and childhood and...children's citizenship status in a manner that extends far beyond nation-based and EU formulations of citizenship" (Stalford, 2008, p. 169).

Conclusion

Citizenship over the past half-century or so has eased, allowing a larger number of groups into citizenship who have traditionally been excluded due to sexual and racial barriers that have been largely, although not completely, removed in Western societies. Thus, territory has been raised as a more significant criterion than descent and place of birth as the signifier of citizenship. This has resulted in a more diversified society, and the traditional notions of social rights to citizenship have been replaced by different forms of rights, such as the right against discrimination and the right to multicultural recognition (Kimlicka, 1995). This, in turn, has had a significant effect on citizenship identity and the degree to which citizenship becomes separated from ethnic, racial or cultural affiliations. This has certainly given rise to concerns over unity and integration of ethnically diverse societies, and has resulted in attempts at re-tightening of access to citizenship (Joppke, 2008), although these have been curtailed by the limitations on the nation state.

The issue of cosmopolitanism and citizenship claims is affecting all debates around human rights and international citizenship. Clearly the nature of the nation state has changed significantly. Just as ideas of citizenship changed when applied to those beyond the city walls, citizenship is being modified now as decisions, collective or otherwise, move beyond the power of nation states. In some respects this is a good thing, as national governments are held to account for their actions amid the wider, global political community. However, there are still significant obstacles and difficulties. Johan Galtung (1977) argues that individual responsibility for human rights violations, as expressed in international law, do not hold structures and practices of globalisation to account, as structures cannot be arrested. Cornides (2008) also cautions that NGOs and international bureaucracies pretend to have the authority to make and monitor human rights; however, this only serves to shift the power of monitoring and enforcement to unelected bureaucracies. Tara Collins (2008) looks at the current monitoring of human rights and finds broad problems with recent approaches. She argues that monitoring tends to be 'linear' in that a rights issue is chosen, data is collected, the data is analysed and a final report is produced. Such an approach has many potential faults. First, governments can influence the approach and keep the focus away from human rights by deflecting issues, such as the imprisonment of children, away from the rights of those children arrested to the experiences of victims of crime. Second, data collection tends to rely on official statistics, anecdotal or press reporting, so that the voices of children are marginalised from the production of reports. Third, the approach to monitoring tends to be reactive, rather than proactive, and the agenda tends to be set by the powerful. Collins argues that such a form of monitoring tends to elide the focus on human rights, whereas rights should be at the root of monitoring, reinforced by robust and reflective tools. A tighter emphasis on the violation of rights and the experiences of those whose rights are violated becomes the primary concern, rather than the perspective of external rapporteurs coming in cold to the subject. In a recent analysis of the academic literature on the UNCRC, Reynaert et al. (2009) caution that issues reflect the concerns that look good in the global children's rights industry, rather than what necessarily is the prime concern for most children. The increasing focus by NGOs on children as victims of violence and abuse, while not denying the importance of the issue, does not necessarily reflect the concerns of children across the globe. Children are worried about their rights while in employment, education, the need for transport, access to health and so on. The right to protection is not necessarily the most important issue for all children.

Part III

7
Inclusive and Differentiated Citizenship

Karl Mannheim in the 1920s argued that generations are formed when members of a particular age cohort go through the same historical events and experiences that are significant and shared among the group. Through having the same or similar shared experience, generations develop a world view or consciousness. Mannheim believed that young people develop a 'fresh contact' onto the world, which develops over time into something that is recognisable and identifiable to themselves and to outsiders as a generational world view. Each generation will share a historically positioned outlook, a similar socialisation and a comparable identity formation. In ways similar to Marx's analysis on the development of social class identity, generations share life-chances and also positional interests. As Mannheim puts it:

> The fact of belonging to the same class, and that of belonging to the same generation or age group, have this in common, that both endow the individuals sharing in them with a common location in the social and historical process, and thereby limit them to a specific range of potential experience.
>
> (Mannheim, 1952, p. 291)

Mannheim here looks at generation as a specific social group. In everyday life and in social sciences we talk of childhood and adulthood as two categories, or 'stages'. Jens Qvortrup (1987) went further and argued that 'children' and 'adults' were not some descriptive shorthand but structural elements attached to a particular social status. The different categories had shared interests within themselves and between other groups, notably adults.

Developing Mannheim's analysis of generations, Thomas Olk (2009) identifies four different ways in which generations are structured. First, there are generations that exist at a 'snapshot' of the here and now: that is, generations of children, adults and 'elderly' people are generations at specific historical points. In this sense, age groups can be classified as 'classes' or categories. Olk's second concept refers to the succession of different generations over time. These are often associated with specific historical events, such as the 'children of the great depression' or 'baby boomers'; such factors shape the generation as something distinct, recognisable and different from previous and succeeding generations. A third concept compares the balance sheets of specific age cohorts and contrasts the surpluses and deficits between them. Thus, the balance of the elderly generation today can be compared with those who lived in the past or are to receive the benefits of the future. The final forms of generation that Olk identifies are the generations living in the future and the burdens each generation produces to limit the chances of future generations.

What Olk does by reflecting on the way generations are defined and understood has implications for issues of social justice. For instance, a focus on generational matters can identify current welfare regimes that seem to skew resources to elderly people, such as the United States and Japan, and those that are relatively 'youth oriented', such as Denmark, Sweden and Ireland (Lynch, 2006). Other countries hold positions in between. However, in all modern societies the elderly are the main recipients of *public* income transfer programs, while children, even taking benefits of child allowances and the costs of education into account, are mostly financed privately by their parents (Kohli, 2006). What is intriguing is that this is not done in a deliberate manner, by one generation being consciously aware of their clash of interests. There is, to date, scant evidence for this. Rather, it is a consequence of policies. Olk suggests that those welfare regimes with universal citizenship-based systems tend to be youth biased, and those with occupation and insurance-based welfare systems tend to be developed in the interests of the elderly (Olk, 2009, p. 196), but these systems are not developed intentionally to reward one generation over the next.

Olk (2009) argues that empirical indicators suggest that the incomes of children in the West between 1985 and 1995 have declined in comparison with other age groups. In terms of per capita income, children as a group have lower incomes relative to the economically active population, at a time when the retired population's comparative income has improved. Furthermore, in most advanced countries, the poverty rate of the under 18s is higher than that of the elderly.

However, investment in children and a good childhood is not part of a zero sum calculation whereby a good childhood will mean a poorer active or elderly population. Indeed, as Esping-Anderson (2002) has shown, the welfare of the elderly primarily depends upon the welfare and well-being of current children, as they are tomorrow's workers. The productivity of future generations of workers will shape the welfare of future generations of old people. Thus, there is a close interrelationship between investments in children and the well-being of future generations of elderly people.

It is important to note that families and societies create continuity and change. Where children, parents and possibly grandparents live together and care for each other, this militates against any feeling of generic generational conflict. Generations thus become the site of social reproduction and social change, offering the possibilities of both stability and renewal. Leena Alanen (1994, 2001, 2009) has developed the concept of generation into a framework for sociologically understanding the situation of children. Generations, for Alanen, are produced and reproduced in interactions between adults and children, whereby adults and children produce the social structures of generations, thereby give children active agency in the constructing process, in marked contrast to the constructions of passive children by other commentators. Alanen outlines a 'generational order' that is:

> a system of social ordering that specifically pertains to children as a social category, and circumscribes for them particular social locations from which they act and thereby participate in ongoing social life. Children are thus involved in the daily 'construction' of their own and other people's everyday relationships and life trajectories.
>
> (Alanen, 2009, p. 161)

While children are active in constructing the generational order, adulthood is the standard against which children are always measured (Alanen, 2001). Power is differentially distributed, and Alanen explores how adults develop 'standard expectations' of how children behave and it can be charted and compared. Similarly, Jenks (1996) notes adult responses to children who represent a challenge to conventional adult definitions; they are demarcated as something else and labelled as something 'other'. For instance, in crime and disorder the usual marker of childhood 'innocence' is removed from these children and greater severity of sentencing is deployed.

Importantly, Alanen develops her analysis of generation from a feminist perspective (Alanen, 1994) and builds upon feminist uses of the term 'intersectionality', where generations are simultaneously gendered, classed, raced and so on. Importantly, being 'generationed' forms an important element of understanding intersectionality, and generation can be a legitimate 'lens' through which girls and boys share positioning in terms of age but 'gendering' the lens can show different forms of ordering. Similarly, the lens of class or race can develop a fuller conceptual framework.

While the analyses of generation by Qvortrup and Olk demonstrate how categories of generation are related according to macroeconomic structures, these miss important elements of structure that are more cultural and interpersonal. Alanen draws on the work of Rob Connell (1987), whose analysis of gender does not begin and end with the categories of gender; rather, it is only the starting point of interest, where the constructing, reproduction, maintenance and sustaining of the categories are made in the relationships between groups. If the categories are left as they are, there is a danger that analysts can slip into false universalisms or biological constructions. Instead, age, like gender, is 'practice based' in the interactions, relations and interdependencies of generations. The interdependency and maintenance of generations occur within structured interactions of parents and children, or between teachers and children, mostly around principles of care. The role of parent or teacher can only exist if there are children to parent or teach; thus their statuses are symbiotic, although the relationship is not symmetrical but based on asymmetrical structural power.

Thus, it is necessary to develop an analysis that, first, looks at how structures of childhood or adulthood are produced. Blatterer (2007) takes a similar approach to unpack the category of 'adulthood' and how the terms and status of this generation are asymmetrically interdependent upon children and the category of childhood. Second, attention needs to be paid to the *everyday* practices of generational (re)structuring. Finally, consideration needs to be paid to the meanings "through which existing generational categories and their interrelationships are produced and rendered culturally meaningful" (Alanen, 2009, p. 169). Mayall (2009) adopts a similar approach to generation, one informed by feminism, to understand the structuring and restructuring of modern families. Mayall notes that in contrast to the 'old days' when children passively obeyed their parents, there is an expectation that children can discuss a variety of issues with their parents; they are better informed and, although having less physical autonomy, have more intellectual freedom. Mayall notes the important contributions from children to housework and caring for family members, thereby keeping the family a relatively healthy organism.

With people living longer and in welfare states, children, parents and grandparents have to live within kinship spaces far longer than before. Yet the family retains generational relations, although these have markedly changed. While women have entered the world of paid work in ever increasing numbers, Mayall notes the continuing role that mothers still perform in the unpaid work performed across the generations. Thus, patriarchy retains a powerful hold over women and children as "aspects of child–parent relations remain constant: the pivotal role of women in caring work; the authority and responsibility of parents; the parental teaching role; children's dependency; continuity of care and concern over time" (Mayall, 2009, p. 181).

Thus, a focus on generations demonstrates the ways in which taking a narrow economic focus, while highlighting structural tendencies, can only be explained in the light of interconnections, interdependencies and principles of caring. By looking at how generations and their intersections with other structures such as gender operate, broader processes of inclusion and exclusion can be discerned. By utilising analytic tools used by feminists, more nuanced and sophisticated analyses of children's citizenship can be brought into play.

Arguments for group rights: Children's differences

One series of debates, begun by feminists, centres on whether there should be specific 'group rights' associated with belonging to a specific social category. Roger Smith (2010) identifies a group of commentators, notably traditional developmental psychologists, who suggest that "childhood is a distinct phenomenon, recognizable aspects of which are shared exclusively by all those to whom the term applies" (Smith, 2010, p. 2). Indeed, a good many within the 'children's rights' movement were moved towards including all children within an over-arching and protective umbrella term to incorporate all children and avoid excluding some of the most vulnerable. The UNCRC, for instance, has an all-inclusive category of all those under 18 years of age. This serves to focus attention on some of the more vulnerable aspects of children aged up to and including 17 years. It also solidifies calls for 'group rights' for all children, irrespective of their age, class, gender, ethnicity and so on.

Iris Marion Young (1990) criticises liberal conceptions of citizenship in terms of their claims to universality. While it is a desirable end for democrats to aim for the equality of all to participate in shaping their own lives, this will be easier for some than for others. However, due to the inequality of resources, some groups of people will be able to better shape their lives, sometimes at the expense of others. Relatedly, the structures in decision-making, if they do not set out to actively seek the views of the marginalised, will listen to the voices of the powerful more than those marginalised. Despite the claims to universality, the structures of inequality in societies mean that 'universalism' works in favour of a group of people with a particular identity: that of middle-class, white men. There is thus, Young argues, a bias supporting a deep-rooted imperialism and patriarchy "because its rational and universal status derives from its opposition to affectivity, particularity, and the body" (Young, 1990, p. 117). The latter aspects are associated with those falling short of the ideal; the focus of Young's argument centres on women, but can include others. Indeed, some theories of multiculturalism perceive the lack of recognition of difference as being one of the major forms of oppression (Taylor, 1992).

In order to combat the excluding discourse of 'universality' and 'rationality', it is necessary for groups to form together and be taken as a group in itself. This is similar to arguments put forward by Will Kymlicka (1995) for group rights based around culture and ethnicity. However, Young's view differs from liberal pluralist commentators, such as Kymlicka, in that only marginalised and excluded groups take the form of a specific group of people with *positional* difference, whereas Kymlicka's *cultural* differences see groups more or less as a set of differences among equals. Young's later work (2000, 2008) expands on this to show that, through structures, the division of labour, hierarchical decision-making and, one can add, processes of representation and recognition, there is an inhibition of "the abilities of some people to develop and exercise their capacities while offering a wide opportunity to others" (2008, p. 78). Traditional liberal pluralism based on cultural differences alone does not make structural inequalities, such as gender, class or generation, visible and open. Policy structures can be put in place to accommodate improvements to structural inequalities. By way of contrast, Young does not see the centre of domination of groups according to the distribution of resources; for her, the starting point begins with institutional constraints on 'self-determination' or 'self-development'. This is helpful in understanding the domination of generations, as rich children are also dominated institutionally, due to their social position *vis-à-vis* 'universality' and 'rationality'; this they have in common with poorer children.

Ideas of group differences can also allow positive levels of identification in addition to those characteristics supposedly lacking. Jean Bethke Elshtain (1998), developing Young's argument, lauds the distinctive qualities that women possess *as women* and contends that these should not be quickly sacrificed in the race for liberal equality. First, liberalism and active engagement in the public sphere lead to bureaucracy and rationalisation into all spheres of life, including those of the private world of women. The public sphere is concerned with the monopolisation of power, hierarchies, and the overriding of civil liberties and traditional local identities. The public world is marked by "impersonal, rational and abstract standards" (Elshtain, 1998, p. 367) and the suppression of alternative identities. This would, according to Elshtain, be detrimental to the lives of women.

The argument put forward here builds upon earlier feminist work in the 1980s with the publication of Carol Gilligan's (1982) *In a Different Voice*. Gilligan offered a critique of the previous conventional moral theory associated with the developmental psychology of Lawrence Kohlberg that offered a reductive series of characteristics associated with gender. In contrast to Kohlberg, and the then common assumptions of child development in which reasoning 'develops' at specific 'stages', Gilligan drew on Nancy Chodorow's (1978) gendered 'object relations theory' to arrive at the sense where girls adopted a different set of moral reasoning from boys. For Chodorow, newly born babies develop their ego in reaction to the dominating figure of the mother. Boys push away from their mothers and repress their sense of intimacy and tenderness and formulate their sense of independence easily by relating to the freedom of their father. The girls identify themselves with their mothers more strongly and less separate from themselves. The girl's ego formation is restricted with the intense bond with their mother and thereby more fully develops a capacity for care than boys. Translating this to moral theory, Gilligan argued that girls develop a different capacity for empathy and sensitivity, whereas boys define themselves more or less entirely in terms of independence and autonomy. According to Gilligan, " 'masculine' moral reasoning utilises mathematical calculations and the adoption of hierarchical rules, by way of contrast girls look to more concrete, relational issues to adjudicate moral dilemmas" (quoted in Cockburn, 2010, p. 30).

Pushing this view even further, Virginia Held (1995) argued that the highest model of moral human association is typified in the mother–child relationship. Held noted that the mother–child relationship has six fundamentally superior elements to 'contractual' theorists: first, the relationships are not voluntary – both mothers and children readily accept the obligatory strings attached to the relationship; second, these relationships are typically permanent and non-replicable, so they cannot be 'exchanged' like the morality of the market place; third, the relationship is based between unequals and, rather than individuals measuring each other's 'rights', the relationship is above this and is based on cooperation, solidarity and love; fourth, the relationship is not based on the 'rights' of non-interference but on a conception of positive rights of what is good and to the benefit of all; fifth, the relationship is not built upon the atomistic ethic of individual gain but is based upon creating a symbiotic community; finally, in contrast to the relationship of economic men seeking to 'equalise' their relationship so that they will not lose out, the caring/relying upon relationship is something that is accepted and cherished.

Held's privileging of the mother and child relationship is, quite rightly, not without its critics; Tong (1997), for instance, argues that this can be essentialistic and further limits women's choices and their ability to resist and change patriarchal structures. Baier (1994) highlights the dangers of valorising the mother–child bond and applying it to other contexts, especially in the public sphere, which would lead women to rely on trusting too much; in a highly competitive, patriarchal society, this could leave people open to betrayal. Carol Gilligan noted that differences between the sexes and women's subordination were centred on the different moral 'strengths' of men and women. However, dominant notions of science have also stressed the differences of groups from the adult, white male norm, such as representations of women and children, and also of 'non-white' races, different religions, abilities and so on. As Nancy Leys Stepan has argued, "it is no accident that 'race' and 'sex', in their modern, primarily naturalised or biological meaning emerged in the eighteenth century, when the new political concept of the individual self and the individual bearer of rights was being articulated" (1998, p. 30). The ontologising via embodiment of sex and racial differences renders groups as distinct and differentiated from the white, male norm. Thus, communities and individuals will continue to be placed outside the liberal universe of freedom, equality and rights. Not everybody, including and perhaps *especially* children, could position themselves as an abstract individual. Feminists such as Leys Stepan have convincingly argued that the science of human difference is not something that belongs to the past but is re-created in the scientific practice of today. Such scientific traditions in early forms of developmental psychology have placed children as ontologically and irreducibly different from adults. This focus on embodiment, history and science is reflected in recent reappraisals of the ways biological and psychological science have represented children (Hendrick, 1997). Children's bodies are represented as becoming, with the introduction of terms such as 'development', 'schooling', 'paediatrics' and so on that place an emphasis on the differences between the bodies of adults and children. It needs to be noted here that it is not just feminists who have been concerned with this denigration of difference.

While it is instructive to place the category 'children' under similar scrutiny and to deconstruct the category, there are, nevertheless, a number of problems with group rights. First, it is necessary not to replace a static, essentialist and universalistic definition of one social group, white middle-class men, with another, such as women or children. All social identities are dynamic and unstable, and categories shift according to place and time, as we have seen with the category 'child' in the above chapters. Second, intersectionality, when aspects of an individual's identity may cross over each other or be in tension, makes it hard to deploy a monolithic system of group rights of children; for instance, how would we assign group rights to a black girl living in contemporary Europe or North America? Third, might group rights around childhood actually reinforce dominant constructions of children as 'victims' or as vulnerable? Fourth, Young (1990) argues that women, as a subordinated group, have a superior form of knowledge compared to dominant groups. But is it helpful to argue that children's 'standpoint' is superior to an adult's, or is it just different? Can't children's and adult's 'standpoint' be the same on some occasions? Finally, individual children are, by their social situation, members of their social group, and can suffer from what Martha Minnow (1990) has called "the burdens of group membership" (p. 49). This involves the negative labelling of themselves as members of a socially subordinated group. This usually victimises children's and young people's viewpoints by dismissing their views because they differ from those of the wider group. Minnow (1990) has argued that the dilemma of difference is deep-rooted, and membership of a negatively labelled group is often unavoidably going to be characterised in disapproving terms. Thus, differences are often defined as deviant rather than just 'different'. It has been clearly demonstrated by Thorne (1987) that children are defined by characteristics exactly opposite to those that dominant groups value in themselves. It is those values that need challenging and changing directly, rather than retreating into ideals of group differences. Even the youngest children are capable of rationality and autonomy, as adults, on the other hand, are susceptible to vulnerability, emotion and irrationality.

Arguments of group rights, therefore, avoid an important lesson on the development of a more nuanced, inclusive and progressive form of citizenship. Take Hegel's classic discussion of the master–slave relationship. Hegel argued that the oppressor is also enchained by his or her oppression. Marx took this up with his discussion of the alienating aspects of capitalism for the capitalist, as well as the worker. Thus, it is necessary to develop forms of relationships that can overcome forms of oppression by fostering trust between groups, as well as within groups. With the development of rights, obligations and dialogue, empathy is built up between individuals who may well share many common experiences and formulate mutual interests in building a communal life. Maintaining differences and valorising one group's statements and negating another's, even if it is to compensate for years of oppression, interrupt communication, dialogue and trust. It is an unlikely strategy for children to break free of the social silos in which they are placed, separated from the 'important' spaces and conversations they should be engaging with. How else are powerful adults going to learn that you need to speak differently with children? Carole Pateman (1992) correctly noted that feminist campaigners for women's citizenship, such as Mary Wollstonecraft, argued for equal rights plus their differences from men to be acknowledged. Instead of groups speaking to each other from separate communities, it is better to be *relational* and acknowledge excluded groups.

Richard Bellamy has argued (in his case these are ethnic minorities but the principle is equally applicable to children) that equal treatment can only come from within political communities. He argues:

> Excluded groups tend to look within existing political culture for reasons justifying how they might be treated the same or differently to others in order to achieve equality of concern and respect with them.
>
> (Bellamy, 2006, p. 246)

There are clearly advantages in working as a group. Yardley (2009), for instance, discusses the support required for teenage mothers, who possess a diverse range of support needs. However, the needs are best expressed through a group than on an individual one-to-one basis. Group support allows more of a social mix and a sharing of experiences and helps to integrate young mothers into an area. With the mixture of the group, individuals are able to share advice, bolster their confidence and manage the possible stigma attached to young motherhood. However, this does not necessarily mean that there should be separation and separateness; quite the contrary, acting as a group allows the individuals as a collective to speak and have dialogue with others more effectively.

While essentialist notions of 'group rights' have their limitations, the deconstruction of categories is a necessary and important stage. Chantal Mouffe (1992) argued that a deconstruction of the essential identities is a "necessary condition... in order to theorize the multiplicity of relations of subordination" (p. 77). Thus, for Mouffe, there is a requirement for a radical rethinking of citizenship to include the consideration of the equality and liberty of different groups, not just women. It is necessary, before this is done, to explore the ways in which categories are constructed as subordinate, and Mouffe concludes, *contra* those who retain the simplicities of the equality/difference debates, that a category that "permits us to understand how the subject is constructed through different discourses and subject positions, is certainly more adequate than the one that reduces our identity to one single position – be it class, race or gender" (Mouffe, 1992, p. 88).

Feminist ideas of citizenship and the concomitant recognition of difference have been applied to understanding children's citizenship by Mehmoona Moosa-Mitha in her adoption of "a difference-centred theory of children's citizenship rights" (2005, p. 369). This assumes difference across the board according to age, and also transgender, anti-racist and non-classist differences that need to be recognised and incorporated into the spheres of children's lives. For Moosa-Mitha, the 'adultist' construction of power needs to accommodate children in a form described by Nigel Thomas as a way that "encourages marginalized groups to express their perspectives" (Thomas, 2007, p. 210). The form that this should take is explored further in the next chapter on participation, but for now the shortcomings of existing democratic spaces (in the physical, social and psychological senses) for children need to be acknowledged. A more genuinely inclusive sharing of power that requires more than just tinkering with procedures and a request for more rationalism is needed. Instead, an inclusive sharing of power needs spaces for proper deconstructive struggles among a plurality of interests where children's voices are both protected and listened to.

This feminist critique fits in with what Habermas (1987) says about the modern neoliberal 'System' of commerce, government, law and clientelism which colonises and absorbs the personal and civic life of the 'Lifeworld'. Alderson (2008) shows how this happens through the British 'Children's Agenda' in the 2000s, whereby active and agentic citizens became passive clients of state services, consumers and recipients of pervasive mass media. Habermas believes that this encroachment of the 'System' into our Lifeworlds results in a fragmentation of shared meanings, loosens social bonds and leads to anomic feelings of helplessness, disempowerment and alienation. The encroachment of the system into children's spaces makes charities; children's centres and schools act and behave more like tightly regulated businesses than social movements which are there to engender flourishing communities (see also Fielding, 2008).

Care and intimacies

So, if the liberal, autonomous, adult, worker model of citizenship is unfair and disadvantageous to children, what other models are out there? Again, children's political movements can learn from the experiences of other groups, with which feminism has direct and pertinent parallels. I have written elsewhere about the possibilities of the 'feminist ethic of care' and the usefulness of the concept in promoting the interest of children (Cockburn, 2005, 2010), and here I discuss how it forms an important conceptual tool in rethinking children's citizenship. The framework moves beyond an individualist 'balance' between rights and responsibilities that places an over-reliance on a rationalistic moral framework. Carol Gilligan's work on difference was hugely influential in this framework and was built upon by other moral theorists, such as Joan Tronto in *Moral Boundaries*, who developed a feminist ethic of care (FEC) to include a total world view which covers:

> everything we do to maintain, continue and repair our 'world' so that we can live in it as well as possible. That world includes our bodies, our selves and our environment, all of which we seek to interweave in a complex, life-sustaining web.
>
> (Tronto, 1993, p. 103)

This is a very contrasting model of human nature to the narratives of the state of nature produced by early liberal thinkers, such as Hobbes, Locke and Rousseau. It is one that is social, interconnected and in tune with our current concerns with the fragility of our planet. For Tronto, definitions of care are placed within broader social and political concerns rather than essentialised into an individual gendered psychology, like Gilligan's. The process of caring is a complicated phenomenon that must include the position of others' needs within its frame of reference. Tronto develops four ethical elements of care: *attentiveness* to the process of caring about someone; levels of *competence* involved in giving care; *responsiveness* of those receiving care; and *responsibility* to those that we take care of.

First, Tronto (1993) identifies the importance of 'attentiveness', by which she means an ethic of thoughtfulness and comprehending the needs of the self and others. The attentiveness people bestow usually occurs in the private sphere, beyond the sight of others, and is rarely seen as an element of citizenship practice. It has traditionally been associated with the role of women. Rousseau, for instance, perhaps had attentiveness in mind when he declared that the task of Sophie's education must prepare her:

> To be pleasing in his sight, to win his respect and love, to train him in childhood, to tend him in manhood, to counsel and console, to make his life pleasant and happy, these are the duties of woman for all time, and this is what she should be taught while she is young. (p. 328)

Thus, Sophie's education consists of 'attentiveness' to the care of a husband, and later writers assume that this attentiveness will be bestowed upon children. By way of contrast, Emile's education is about curbing his passions and equipping him with knowledge of a range of subjects that enables him to be a deep-thinking, humane and autonomous citizen in the public world. Fortunately, few in advanced societies today would restrict girls' education to this, but it does draw attention to the privacy of attentiveness. However, it is worth noting that in the 'free' market attentiveness to children and adults is characterised by low status and poor pay (for further discussion see Low Pay Commission, 2011). The ethic of attentiveness is crucial to the sustenance of societies and gets little direct attention. A reappraisal of the term is necessary for a better sense of social justice.

Tronto also draws our attention to the levels of competence involved in giving care. Tronto's discussion focusses on the invisibility and devaluing of the competence of some carers by virtue of the fact that the bulk of caring is performed by women in the private sphere. However, children are represented and perceived as 'incompetent' in most mainstream discussions. Indeed, the political structures today *assume* children's incompetence, and this is presented as a major reason for their exclusion from full citizenship. However, sociological studies of child-hood have challenged this assumption of incompetence (see Hutchby and Moran-Ellis, 1998). Furthermore, sociologists have shown that children are not passive recipients of care but, on the contrary, are often active *givers* of care (Evans and Becker, 2009). This ability of even the youngest children to give care demonstrates that children and young people's competence can only be determined within the social context of their own meanings; and that children are active contributors to society in terms of their own work in reproducing themselves. Tronto's feminist ethic of care can then be deployed to re-evaluate children's own active involvement in the process of care and to other issues.

Tronto then explores the concept of responsiveness to and from those receiving care. She notes that true responsiveness is highly skilled and greatly devalued. Responsiveness is a skill carried out not just in families but also by members of communities and by practitioners. The most responsive ethics are those that are informal and immediate and can be contrasted with the more bureaucratic 'professionalised' responsiveness that is closer to bureaucracy and clientelism, rather than to love, care and attentiveness. Following on from this, feminists have argued for spaces where there is less attention to rationalistic 'choices', but, rather, to reformulate public forums to allow more expressive and responsive communication to occur (Pajnik, 2006).

Finally, Tronto draws our attention to the responsibility we have to those we care for. Here, Tronto's ideas are in contrast to the traditional notions of duties in discussions of citizenship, where they are presented as a 'balance' to rights. However, these debates become tautological and prevent a focus on the immediate processes of engagement, as they are premised upon individuals formulating some form of 'equation', weighing up giving responsibilities and taking rights. Instead, constructive participation does not involve the bare expressions of rights. Although human rights and responsibilities are important for children and young people to place on the agenda, effective responsibilities always involve considerations of others. As Sevenhuijsen (2004) argues:

> this approach usually offers little space for reflection about how people actually experience or 'do' responsibilities, or for the moral considerations they employ in this respect. The discourse on responsibility in fact becomes a strategy of 'responsibilization' ... in which 'responsibility' is in fact equated with 'obligation'. (p. 26)

For children, and indeed for many adults, this move to responsibilisation has significant drawbacks. In the criminal justice field the move to responsibilise and punish, or, in Barry Goldson's word, "adultize" (Goldson, 2002a, p. 690), child offenders in the UK, there is a skew towards the responsibilities of children by minimising the overwhelming evidence that young offenders are drawn from underprivileged backgrounds and damaged communities.

Tronto's work shows that at all times a carer must take on board the perspective and interests of another person; there is not just an isolated, autonomous, self-interested, taxpaying voter here. Instead, Tronto acknowledges the power differentials involved in caring, where tending and taking care of people are often the duties of the powerful. By way of contrast, Tronto notes, the concrete giving and receiving of care are left to the least powerful in society. Furthermore, the process of caring about others is not a fixed state, but fluctuates. People may have strong feelings of caring about others because of particular experiences and events during the course of their lives. Caring may be shaped in the formative period of the life course: it could flourish or be compromised as a result of early primary relationships and, as Hollway (2006) has argued, extend across the life course and pervade most institutions and relationships.

Tronto's contribution to citizenship theory is an important one, as she identifies three 'moral boundaries'. First, traditional moral theory separates public and private life. Children are cared for in 'private' spaces and they are absent, excluded or 'protected' from public life. While issues of privacy are, of course, fundamental to women's and children's lives, feminists, as we have seen in Chapter 3, have shown that private spaces are often sites of loneliness, violence and abuse, experienced by both women and children. The challenge to the public/private distinction leads to the second 'moral boundary', which challenges the separation of morality from politics. Politicians have long been prone to scandals and have thus been subjected to moral constraints. However, deeper moral questions such as the nature of education, the feelings of the sick, the experiences of children in day care and social questions beyond economic and political efficiency are essentially moral questions. Due to feminist and other challenges to political life, moral issues, such as the sexual abuse of children and the exploitation of children's work, have entered the political realm, even at an international level, and led to important reforms. The final 'moral boundary' concerns challenges to abstract accounts of morality and builds upon Gilligan's critique of technical and expert-led solutions to social policy and constructions of citizenship. Instead of top-down, technocratic, 'expert'-led definitions of children's best interests, often defined within quantitative frameworks, that are separated from the lifeworlds of children, a fuller understanding of giving and receiving care is informal, intuitive and context-specific.

The feminist ethic of care, therefore, in addition to being theoretically effective, is not as unworkable or utopianistic as it appears at first viewing. Today political and legal institutions accept that there is no strict separation of the public and private, and that the state and law can and do intervene in accordance with the child's best interests. The Gillick decision, discussed in Chapter 5, does allow a child, if 'competent', to take part in decisions, including contraception and residency with parents. Thus, the feminist ethic of care should not be used uncritically; indeed, recent developments of the approach have argued that it is not *the only* approach to developing citizenship. Principles according to justice, economics, materialism and 'science' also have important contributions to make in furthering children's well-being (Sevenhuijsen, 1998). Access to adequate care should be perceived as a human right, even with the dangers of its technocratic manifestations. In their analysis of babies in neonatal units, Alderson et al. (2005) show us just how embodied and closely connected to physical desires human rights are. They are interactive in that they take "meaning from relationships between two or more people, or between individuals and systems" (p. 79). In this sense, 'rights' are shown to be emotional and to occur within personal and relational contexts of care. The authors argue:

> Adults described babies' preference for care by their parents or by sensitive nurses that the baby knew well; it was not only techniques of care that necessarily mattered to the babies, as much as who gave that care and the quality of the relationship between that person and the baby.
>
> (Alderson et al., 2005, p. 79)

What is of overwhelming importance is to place all moral theories into some sense of dialogue. Sevenhuijsen (2004) correctly advocates placing ethical and moral debates within the context of pluralism and democratic citizenship, where technical, 'expert-led' forms of knowledge are questioned, challenged and debated rather than merely accepted. Similarly, Porter (1999) describes the example where:

> if you are surrounded by the demands of small children, the confusion of teenagers or the needs of ageing relatives, then the

considerations needed to make moral choices differ from those who only need to consider themselves. (p. 5)

The feminist ethic of care is an important element in analysing children's citizenship today, as it demands that policy dilemmas cannot be divorced from the immediate realities and emotional complexities of people's lives. Thus, it is central to understand the processes of caring by focussing on actual, concrete and connected settings. Instead of care being a distinct policy, separated artificially from education, health and criminal justice, it should, as Brannen and Moss argue, "become a way of acting and a habit of mind informing education, health and other domains – a manifestation of a 'caring' society applied across all public services and other human service agencies" (2003, p. 199). The connected nature of caring must be aware of the 'moral deliberation' associated with care (Sevenhuijsen, 1998, p. 128). Caring involves differential elements of responsibilities and need which often include conflicting agendas. Thus, a caring ethical framework must be deliberative and involve situated social practices that are "open-textured, dialogic, open to criticism, self-criticism and debate" (Sevenhuijsen, 1998, p. 128). Here not only top-down knowledges require watching, but also those within the concrete contexts of caring for and being cared for.

Feminists are not alone, although they were the first, in focussing on issues of care and 'primary relationships' as an important platform for understanding 'higher' relationships, such as those based around rights and citizenship. Axel Honneth (1995) utilises the concept of 'love', which refers to relationships including sexual, parent–child and friendships, mostly within affective and private contexts where "human beings are recognized as concrete creatures of need" (1995, p. 25). For Honneth, these relationships are the site of intense and complex emotional interactions that involve trust, attachment and affection, but are also balanced out with the more individualistic 'self-assertion'. Ideally, these interactions are affective and intuitive, forming relationships that encourage the self-confidence that enables the perception of 'autonomy' necessary for public life. It is worth noting that for Honneth, as for feminist ethicists, it is the processes of love and care that lead to the mutually desired demarcation of individuality that is necessary for the "cognitive-formal relationship of recognition found in law, they are recognized as abstract legal persons" (1995, p. 25). Honneth here accepts Marshall's notion of civil rights and the modern legal term of moral rights and individuality, along with Kant's notion of rational autonomy.

While the reciprocal nature of recognition extends the status of legal personhood and allows a degree of flexibility, as seen during the nineteenth and twentieth centuries, it also illustrates the under-privileging and shame associated with those who were denied subject status, such as those excluded up to the civil rights movement, and those who continue to feel a sense of shame and inadequacy, such as children.

Again, similar to Marshall's shift from civil to political citizenship, Honneth theorises the State or solidarity of the system above the legal civil society or the love manifest in the family. However, unlike the singular compromise between capitalist and working classes characterised in the post-war Marshallian state, Honneth's state should respect subjects because of their individual particularity "that they do not share in an undifferentiated manner with others" (Honneth, 1995, p. 125). Honneth's sense of social relations is highly complex and involves an unpacking of ideas of 'dignity' and 'integrity', and, one can suggest, ideas of the good citizen, from a legally defined person to one based upon the degree of social recognition. Modern social systems are open to cultural conflicts over what the abstract ideas of modern society are and the interpretive practice involved in operating them. Dominant interpretations of societal goals depend upon the success of groups in publicly interpreting their own accomplishments. He argues:

> abstract guiding ideas of modern societies provide so little in the way of a universally valid system of reference with which to measure the social worth of particular traits and abilities that they must always be made concrete through supplemental cultural interpretations before they can be applied in the sphere of recognition.
>
> (Honneth, 1995, p. 126)

Honneth suggests that this may lead to social tensions as these cultural ideas are contested and new ones compete with them.

Other theorists have also noted the inadequacy of the notion of liberal citizenship and personhood as it is applied to more intimate spheres. Writers such as Jeffrey Weeks (1998) have focussed on the private sphere to raise issues around 'sexual citizenship' for homosexual people struggling, first, to have their sexuality decriminalised and then to seek equality with heterosexuals. This has traditionally been seen as something in the private domain, but has public implications. Ken Plummer's (2003) phrase 'intimate citizenship' opens the doors in another way to debates around citizenship, this time from the perspective of intimate relationships. The feminist challenge to the depoliticisation of the private sphere, captured in the phrase 'the personal is political', thus shines a light on the power relationships within the private sphere and how this has public ramifications, not just around gender and childhood. Other social theorists, following feminists, have also looked into the private sphere and suggested a 'democratisation' of private lives. Giddens (1992), for instance, notes that families have become 'democratised', particularly with the evening out of power differentials between men and women and the renegotiation of personal relationships. This process of enquiry must continue.

Manfred Liebel (2012) in his characterisation of 'citizenship from below' focusses on the importance of children who suffer from social structures and power relations coming together to push for common social action. It is through these actions that social transformations can take place. Here children in the rich world can follow the successful lead of those children in the developing or majority world who have established organisations and social movements. Children in the majority world, like children in 'the West', suffer from status deficiencies and are not taken seriously. In the majority world few children have the educational privileges or the welfare of children in Europe and North America, and, with the combination of racism and status discrimination, they have few opportunities for those positive experiences that are so important in establishing positive social recognition. It is often under circumstances of crisis or when backed into a corner that children combine together and challenge the existing social order. As Liebel argues, the "necessity to do something in order to survive leads many children to take part in spontaneous formation of groups whose self-help is frequently denigrated…in the more organized forms of children's movements a marked sense of justice arises. Children act intrepidly, expressly demanding the realization of rights" (2012, p. 188).

By drawing parallels to African children accused under colonial laws against 'hawking' or 'loitering' (which was discussed in Chapter 3 in the context of nineteenth-century Manchester), Liebel (2012) argues that contemporary African children combining into a social movement create a daily practice of citizenship where they experience a sense of mutual respect and a formulation of their own rules, demands and rights. These demands for rights are not expressed on their behalf by NGOs according to abstract rights of the UNCRC but are "primarily founded on their own experience, and are immediately related to the reality of their lives. They are not formulae of compromise or general principles that leave broad, almost unlimited scope for interpretation, but concrete programmes of action in experienced or conceivable situations in life" (Liebel, 2012, p. 188). Moosa-Mitha (2005) makes a similar point in her discussion of the everyday social spaces children live in, where all children "respond, mitigate, resist, have views about and interact with the social conditions in which they find themselves" (p. 380); thus, all children practise citizenship.

It is, however, important to recognize that children, as well as being disadvantaged as children, may also suffer additional social disadvantages. Again drawing on positive examples in the majority world, Liebel (2012) identifies ways in which children, through self-help, establish different ways of working and rewards that look more to solidarity or a 'social economy' rather than a competitive market.

Conclusion

In this chapter we have seen that new perspectives of citizenship have moved the discussion from classical citizenship theorists, and the earlier theorising of moral and political rights. A more complete analysis of children's citizenship must move away from individualism towards new forms of citizenship that will accommodate group identities and intersectionalities between groups. We have seen how a look at generation and recognition of positional difference allows us a more nuanced understanding of children's citizenship. Indeed, the care perspective of feminism has provided a richer conception of citizenship relations that is extended both into the private sphere and beyond superficial 'contractual' relations theorised within liberalism. The role of adults as advocates is, of course, crucial as they can act as a pull on issues. Success by advocates can be linked together to form a sort of 'movement' of voices coming together. This can form a sort of coalition of specific advocates around a particular issue. As Sarri and Shook (2005) have observed, a narrow issue can be easily solved and has more chance of success. A single issue that is easily solved can encourage children and young people to get involved with raising a politics of childhood. Seyla Benhabib, in referring to the exclusion of children, suggested that the interests of those "who are not full participants in moral discourses ought to be and can be effectively represented in discursive contexts through systems of moral advocacy" (2004, p. 14). Better understanding between groups is the vital component, and good advocacy is a means rather than an end in itself. However, this must be a second preference to the self-advocacy and mutual support in the political participation within 'children's social movements' described by Manfred Liebel.

A broader understanding of how groups are represented supplements, rather than replaces, the distributive paradigm outlined in Marshall's idea of 'social citizenship' (Lister, 2008). As Fraser and Honneth (2003) has suggested, the institutional context of social structures first determines how resources are distributed in the first place; second, analytical attention needs to be applied to non-material social goods, such as respect and recognition; finally, looking at broader systems of representation emphasises the processed, dynamic and historical nature of social and power relations. It is the experience of disrespect, rather than the distribution of resources, that "comprises a central principle of social justice" (2003, p. 352).

Could children be capable of such recognition and push their voices into the public sphere? As the literature around the sociology of childhood has shown, children are able to demonstrate that they are not only able to receive care, affection and love but are also able to give it; they are also bearers of rights and are able to recognise and respect the rights of others. Looking to where children can become full members of a society based on shared values and recognised with sufficient esteem to provide their own accomplishments, there seems to be a long way to go. Children's contributions to society continue to be belittled and devalued, and not accorded the respect and recognition of being involved in mutual esteem and solidarity. However, there are ways, I would argue, in which this may be reversed. Through a reinvigoration of participatory forms of democracy, such as those striven for by children in the majority world, there may be a format in which children's voices can be more clearly heard and recognised. Hannah Arendt (1973), in *On Revolution*, muses on the ideal public spaces offered in New England town meetings, and describes the dangers associated when people participating do not come together as equals to discuss matters of common interest. Real interactions based on commonly recognised individuals, she argues, are the way to negate the negative effects of the mass media and the ideologies that appeal to our anxieties and antipathies. A strong and healthy public life requires individuals to constantly weigh up and consider the viewpoints of all members. How this can happen when the recognition of children is so maligned is taken up in the next chapter.

8
Participatory Citizenship of Children

Participation and democracy

Debates around citizenship in the early twentieth century were not so much concerned with who should or should not be a citizen; rather, commentators were more interested in the attributes of a 'good' citizen (Harris, 2004). The virtues of citizenship shaped the work of T.H. Green, and his writing reflected the view that involvement in politics and public life was more of a privilege than a public right. Participation, as such, was an elitist activity, at first restricted to a handful of aristocrats and later, reluctantly, extended to a bourgeois few. It was believed that participation should be restricted to those who were deemed to possess virtue and a demonstrable capacity to participate. Education and property were the original qualifications of the franchise in the nineteenth century, and excluded were those who were believed to place private interests over the public good. Others were excluded for the standard reason that they were 'irrational', frail and dependent upon others, thus capturing most women and all children. Extending participation has a long history of resistance. The idea of the social contract or natural rights is just too static (Faulks, 2000). The inclusion of people into citizenship has been a result of active campaigns against injustice and extending citizenship to previously excluded groups. Thus, social change and social justice arise from the combination of the exercise of rights and responsibilities among the citizenry. The requirements of the community and nation are aspirational and liable to changes over time. They are also constrained by the power of the 'free market'.

It was J.K. Galbraith who commented that responding to the views of the 'contented majority' would reflect the downward spiral of engagement with society (1929/1973). This is because people see their needs and desires satisfied through the market in a short-term way, rather than broader and more reciprocal ways in which they receive the benefits of social goods. Thus, better-off people are inclined to wish for a privatisation of previously public goods, such as health, education and transport, where utility is satisfied through the private contract of the consumer. This privatisation has resulted in an undermining of civic attitudes whereby such goods become matters of private consumption rather than collective responsibility. The 'new' consumer attaches their interest to narrower campaigns and the private support of pressure groups and single-issue campaigns. This has been compounded by the growing gap between the rich and the poor, so that the former are tempted to see the latter as an expensive problem, not as fellow citizens within a shared system based around cooperation and civil equality. As Jacobs et al. (2004) say, talking of the USA, but applicable elsewhere:

> The privileged participate more than others and are increasingly well organised to press their demands on government. Public officials, in turn, are much more responsive to the privileged than to average citizens and the least affluent. (p. 1)

Furthermore, this has an impact on associating and formal participation, with those from families earning more than £75,000 per year being twice as likely to volunteer as those from families earning less than £10,000 (Office for National Statistics, 2004). The important point being raised here is that poverty and other forms of social exclusion have been associated with lower levels of trust, feelings that citizens can't influence decisions and a weaker sense of 'collective efficacy' (Kitchen et al., 2006). Poorer people spend more time and energy simply trying to secure adequate services and striving for a comfortable standard of living. While recognising that children may need help through participatory practice in developing their social and cultural capital (Pinkney, 2006), research raises significant questions about the extent to which participation promotes inclusion. Indeed, the Victorian legacy in Britain around 'visiting' and 'improving' shows that active citizenship can have a detrimental effect on those receiving charity.

Commentators on citizenship tend to focus on the exclusions: women, workers, and so on. But, equally, citizenship can bind people together, as Bellamy (2006) argues, "through the inclusive logic of the practice of citizenship" (p. 245). The process of democracy redefines the similarity and dissimilarity between people, but mechanisms must exist so that each is given equal concern and respect. Children are not given the same levels of concern and respect, and are not included in the process of democracy. However, children and young people display some political attitudes; as Hayward (2012) points out, environmental issues and peace initiatives attract over 70% approval ratings by young people. A recent analysis of the 2010 General Election by Whiteley et al. (2010) found that approximately 49% of young people aged 18–25 voted, up from 37% in 2005.

Children have also participated in politics, such as the 2003 anti-war demonstrations in the UK and in other parts of the world where children grow up within a "politically charged environment, where protests, marches, and sit-ins, press photo calls, and hunger strikes are all part of their childhoods" (Smith, 2007, p. 50). Ann-Marie Smith's research among indigenous children in Loxicha, Mexico, looks at the widespread political participation of children and the distortions of children's political participation by the media and NGOs. The media presented children as victims of the circumstances but did not present them as contributing family members, often looking after younger siblings, let alone participating in political marches. Instead, children's political participation gets shoe-horned into 'approved' and 'safe' forms of participation that are often provided by governments or other adult agencies.

Participatory forms of citizenship, sometimes referred to as republican forms (Lister and Pia, 2008), emphasise the importance of participation in government as the foundation of citizenship and the promotion of the social good. Those who favour a participatory approach argue that attention to participation makes liberal ideas of citizenship seem too fragmentary and short-focussed, and the communitarian level seems too absorbed in the individual community, or local identities, rather than wider civic goals. The issue of participation recurs in theories of social capital, such as those of Robert Putnam (1993), who offers a Rousseauian ideal of participation through clubs and civil society that leads to greater participation and healthy government institutions.

In Chapter 1 we saw how the ancient Greeks viewed political participation as an intrinsic part of citizenship. In order to have a sense of civic equality, it was essential for all citizens to play their part in political processes. This was the underlying principle that Aristotle maintained in his political theories. However, if we view much of the commentary in Western Europe there is a widespread dissatisfaction with democratic politics, as exemplified by low voter turnout at elections and declining trust in politicians (Norris, 2011). For young people this is particularly apparent, with a seeming unwillingness to engage in direct deliberative

politics, exemplified in a decline of young people's membership of political parties and other civil society associations. Thus, there is a decline
in the 'ideal' or 'thick' forms of direct democracy, where all become
involved in making and administering the law, plus a lack of trust in
the narrower account of citizenship in which we are reliant on a class
of benevolent rulers who administer the state in a way free from private
interest and prejudice, akin to the Platonic 'Guardians'.

For younger children, there is a *de facto* handing over of decision-
making capacity to those whom one hopes would be benevolent
guardians, be they parents, carers, institutions or the state. However,
there is no way in which all decisions will be made in an objective way
to ensure that children's viewpoints and interests are taken into account.
It is unreasonable for us to assume that this will happen in all, some
or even most cases. This is not because of any inherent perniciousness
of those in power over children – most people in positions of responsibility arguably do make decisions that they think are in the child's
interest – but because on most moral issues even experts disagree with
each other. Second, there is no guarantee that those acting on behalf of
children will make decisions for others over and above their own, possibly conflicting, interests. For adults in democracies, the best guide to
social and political decisions is those decisions made by representatives
reflecting the expressed and evolving choices of citizens made under
conditions of political equality. Even in the 'thin' level of democracy
in England, where Rousseau observed that the people were only free
once their votes were being cast, representatives are still to some degree
held to account. Thus, some form of recognition for children as equal
partners, albeit (like adults) with evolving levels of expression, must be
developed. It is no surprise that so much of the children's rights movement based around the UNCRC focusses on article 12, on the right to
participate on decisions that affect them.

Civil society

Participation needs to occur in as many spaces as possible. In a recent
report Frances Cleaver and I emphasised that there is a spectrum of civil
society associations for children and young people, ranging through private to public life (Cockburn and Cleaver, 2009). Young (2008), in her
politics of positional difference, notes that traditional theories of cultural difference have tended to focus narrowly on state policy and what
the state allows, forbids or remains silent on; thus tending to ignore
civil society as a crucial site for the working of injustice. Young notes

that civil society is an important arena where non-governmental institutions exercise exploitation, domination and exclusion. Similarly, Seyla Benhabib has noted how a focus on "social movements.... Civil, cultural, religious, artistic, and political associations of the *unofficial* public sphere" (2002, p. 21) should form a 'dual track' approach to critical politics.

A focus on civil society in the 'advanced capitalist' societies has been stimulated in recent debates by Michael Walzer (1998), among others. For instance, the European Commission since 2001 has been concerned with including civil society into its own structures. The dominance of recent debates, mostly by American scholars, is centred on waning social capital, increasing social mistrust and the turning away from political authority. However, this thesis has been critiqued for failing to account for current forms of solidarity, connectedness and political engagement, for instance, around the Internet (Ester and Vinken, 2003), and, in the context of this discussion, those of children and young people. Rhys Farthing (2010), in his helpful analysis of youth politics, characterises the ambiguity of young people's participation as being "simultaneous engagement and disengagement" (p. 182).

There is a requirement to update older theories of civil society and association to properly understand and make sense of children and young people's contributions (Morrow, 2004). Studies of civil society from conflict zones or the developing world show that focussing on the knitting together of society remains vital (Kabalo, 2006). Bruegel, in her research on improving children's friendships across ethnic and faith divides, concluded: "that day-to-day contact between children has far more chance of breaking down barriers between communities, than school twinning and sporting encounters" (2006, p. 8). In a similar vein, research by McGrellis (2005) in Northern Ireland also saw the importance of cultural divides being bridged by children and young people and that investment is better placed in young people's leisure and nightlife industries rather than formal projects.

Michael Edwards argued that in order to facilitate a healthy civil society it is necessary to generate: "an inclusive associational ecosystem matched by a strong and democratic state, in which a multiplicity of independent public spheres enable equal participation in setting the rules of the game" (Edwards, 2004, p. 94). For this to happen, two things are necessary: the first is to strengthen the preconditions in which interactions can take place and the second is to support innovations in the public sphere. One can, perhaps, go further and search for dialogues occurring in the 'free-spaces' of civil society networks and see how they can be supported, listened to and heard in a context that is "fragile and difficult to maintain" (Baiocchi, 2003, p. 55).

When exploring issues around 'civil society', it is worth keeping in mind the caution that Morrow (1999) encourages us to have, and to reinterpret and retrieve the way social capital is applied to children. She argues: "in much existing work on social capital, children and young people are constructed as the passive recipients of culture, their agency is denied and there is no acknowledgement of how children actively generate, draw upon, or negotiate their own 'social capital' or even provide active support for parents" (p. 74).

This is useful in balancing the excessive focus on formal mechanisms for association in civil society and in recognising the possibility of children's active agency exercised also through other channels. One study found over a thousand youth groups dedicated to some form of 'social action', including youth wings of larger organisations, youth councils, campaigning, community-based and support groups (Roker, 2002). These did not include children's groups, and the researchers found it impossible to clarify 'youth-led', 'youth managed' or 'youth involved' projects. It is important also to note that many projects are short-term, are close to collapse or have been superseded by other projects. The broader volunteering literature reflects the interests of formal charities and voluntary associations, and figures are highly eclectic and inconsistently defined. Furthermore, any statistics collected are more likely to be skewed towards white, higher social-class groups. Indeed, a paper by the European Volunteer Centre notes: "the lack of quality evidence on volunteering, the failure to adopt consistent definitions" (2004, p. 16).

In both the UK and the Republic of Ireland, there was concern in the 1990s about the relatively low level of volunteering by younger people compared with middle-aged groups. However, this assumption has been challenged as underestimating the contribution of children. At a European level, Gaiser et al.'s (2010) review found that amid the:

> concern that younger generations are increasingly disinterested, uninformed, skeptical and even alienated from the political class, structures and processes. Against the generally pessimistic evaluations and predictions of the public, the relatively simple assumption of a linear decline of youth participation does not hold true in the face of European survey data, which rather show complex patterns of relationships and change. (p. 443)

In the UK the Home Office Citizenship Survey (Home Office, 2003) found that the rate of young people's community participation, including formal and informal volunteering, rose from 18.8 million in the UK in 2001 to 20.3 million two years later. There have been similar trends across Western Europe, where "membership in all types of civic organizations (spanning welfare, religious, cultural, youth and sports organizations) has increased with the exception of youth organizations" (Gaiser et al., 2010, p. 443). Furthermore, young people aged between 16 and 24 in the UK were more likely to be engaged in informal volunteering than any other age group. This might suggest that it is the 'hidden' aspect of young people's involvement that is important to recognise. The hidden nature of volunteering, where more *informal* action occurs, may also explain the overemphasis on white, middle-class participation in formal organisations, whereas poorer people and those from ethnic minorities, in addition to children and young people, are more likely to be involved in 'informal' activities with families, friends and networks than formal charities. There is a requirement to redress the excessive focus on formal institutional mechanisms for participation and on procedures, policies, processes, practices and techniques. Researchers and practitioners are beginning to realise the importance of 'the informal sector', of peers, parents, friends and less formal networks. For instance, Yuen et al. (2005) note the importance of leisure activities in providing a foundation for the development of shared meanings through the familiarisation of participants into social learning that leads to the emergence of social capital. Haste and Hogan (2006) have helpfully extended the analytic focus of 'civic engagement' from the narrow confines of voting, and, one can add, formal volunteering; to include helping (in a broad sense) and struggling to make one's voice heard.

Young people are spending an increasing amount of time with peers (Dixon, 2006) and it is therefore important to focus on this aspect of their lives. All the research shows that friendships are important and crucial to children's well-being (Layard and Dunn, 2009) and that rejection by other children can lead to depression, aggression and antisocial behaviour (The Children's Society, 2007). Young people themselves cite relationships with their peers as one of the most important aspects of their lives, especially when they go wrong. Policy needs to focus on supporting children's and young people's peer networks.

Currently the media have a preoccupation with children and young people in groups, or 'gangs'. Most groups of young people or 'gangs' are not involved in criminal activity and, furthermore, can form an important part of children's and young people's association. Nancy

Rosenblum (1988), for instance, in her discussion of civil society, argued that it is necessary to include a wider group of structures into discussion, structures not included by other commentators on civil society. She includes not only identity-based groups but also street gangs, and points out that within these groups young people learn other associational skills, such as taking turns in talking, and reciprocity. The connection of gangs with identities is reinforced through other research; for instance, Les Back (2005) showed the connections between social identities and local spaces. For young people, the spaces gangs would identify with were those where participants in gangs felt safe. The young people in Back's study operated a sophisticated local knowledge. He notes:

> The maps that are produced to document the contours of safety and danger cannot be reduced to typologies or clunking correlations between ethnic categories or gendered identities and the social inequalities of a given place.
>
> (Back, 2005, p. 40)

Back notes the fluidity in gang membership, in that 'Black gangs' also comprised a few women and white men.

The role of families in children's civil society associations is often forgotten. Lopes et al. (2009) point out that only a handful of studies have looked at parental influences on shaping citizens, and the role of families in young people's attitudes to political participation is often neglected. However, it is vital to recognise that children have dual lives, in public and private. It is important to note the crucial role of the family in terms of a) whether or not children and young people receive family support; b) whether the family members serve as role models for young people, in terms of getting them active and involved; and c) whether families form such a vital role in children's identity. Youth projects have noted the importance of building upon family connections to bolster young people's involvement in wider structures; however, caution must be applied so that this is not done in a way that reinforces the status quo (Bailey and Jones, 2006). Family circumstances also affect young carers, who find the opportunities to participate in wider citizenship structures very limited, given the enormous pressure of time and energy from their caring roles. Often these caring duties remain unnoticed by teachers, practitioners, policymakers and political commentators (Barnardos, 2006). However, with young carers we see a direct and important contribution of duties that we can re-evaluate as providing an important social function.

Sports clubs are also a site of social capital. Putnam and Coleman, in their classic accounts, refer to the importance of adult sports clubs, but children's sports are rarely given an equivalent level of attention. The group of young people up to the age of 19 is most likely to engage in some sport (National Statistics Office, 2004). This enables young people to gain experience of associations, place and cooperation. Sport also relies heavily on volunteers and is an important element in sustaining social capital. A cautionary note needs to be made that engagement with sport often does not provide space for dialogue about wider matters. Access to sporting facilities is also shaped by wider social inequalities. For instance, and in contrast to expectations, Pakistani/Bangladeshi, Indian, Black Caribbean and Black African people were less likely to have engaged in at least one sporting activity in comparison with white people; this was particularly striking for Pakistani/Bangladeshi young people (Sport England, 2004). In addition to this, participation in sport was less likely for women, disabled people and those from low-income families.

Citizenship education

As we have seen in Chapter 1, 'citizenship education' has existed for literally thousands of years. In the subsequent chapters the nature and type of education have shifted according to the ideas and demands of citizenship. There has been recently interest in citizenship education in the UK and elsewhere in Europe, with particular emphasis on the nature of citizenship education in British schools (Citizenship Advisory Group, 1998). Schools have the potential to provide a ground-breaking forum for furthering children's participation in society. They have the attention of all children aged between 5 and 16. They can offer mechanisms such as school councils, and citizenship education on the national curriculum, that can provide children with the skills to influence things around them. Davies et al. (2007) note that participating in decision-making in schools can: boost academic achievement; make children feel better; give feedback to teachers, thereby boost their professionalism; enhance pupils' communication skills; facilitate better relations with the school and community; improve behaviour; encourage parental participation; and enhance children's interpersonal and political skills.

However, citizenship education as currently practised has been criticised by some writers for being ambiguous about children's rights, and the good feelings of participation are undermined by the undemocratic nature of schools (Lockyer, 2003). Attitudes to school are remarkably different according to social class. Sutton (2007), for instance, noted that for 'estate children'[1] "[a]ttitudes towards school were generally negative: school was controlling and boring; somewhere they tried to spend as little time as possible" (p. *viii*). This has implications for citizenship education in schools, where practising social responsibility will probably be seen as an extension of 'more of the same' by those from less well-off backgrounds. Wyness (2000) notes that it is within the school that 'generational conflict' (Alanen, 2001) arises. Wyness argues: "the timetable and the curriculum are overlaid with codes of conduct and modes of self-display, with rules and regulations" (2000, p. 90) which separate children from the decision-making in schools. This excludes children from active participation in decisions, and any notions of dissent are immediately defined as 'deviance'. While some adults have attempted to democratise schools, on the whole pupils have found them disappointing amid a rule-bound culture that is "profoundly undemocratic" (Mayall, 2002, p. 101). Schools, therefore, remain a place dominated by adult concerns, with little opportunity for children to express themselves freely.

In terms of encouraging active citizenship, Holford and van der Veen (2003) have identified only minor effects of school-based citizenship education programmes on the extent of active citizenship of young people. Yet they have also pointed out the benefits of extra-curricular activities for processes of informal learning in civil society and the process of active citizenship by these groups.

Citizenship education in school is not the only option for improving children's participation in their wider communities and decision-making (Lopes et al., 2009). First, work needs to happen before children get to school. It is necessary to provide a framework for children under five, as well as those who are older, to explore and communicate their perspective (Clark and Percy-Smith, 2006). The previous section raised the importance of family encouragement for engaging with civil society. The practice of citizenship needs to be developed at as early an age as possible. Second, it is necessary to make use of support from the voluntary sector and the youth service, as they have a better record at offsetting the effects of citizenship education in schools, in order to ensure that as many young people as possible are included. The Office of Standards of Education (OFSTED) in England points to the important educational contribution from youth work (OFSTED, 2007), especially in the field of 'making a positive contribution'. Other longitudinal work also points to the importance of local youth services in inhibiting social exclusion and providing a positive influence (Feinstein et al., 2006).

This is very challenging at the current time of swingeing cuts to youth services and voluntary organisations. The education of young people into citizenship is also undertaken by voluntary organisations such as Children's Rights Alliance England, A National Voice and Funky Dragon, among many others. Youth workers in faith-based organisations – many of which have high levels of participation by young people from Black and minority ethnic communities – can assist in facilitating youth-led opportunities (National Youth Agency, 2005). Children also have a feeling of self-control of commercial spaces such as shopping centres, where children and young people feel that they have a sense of 'ownership'. Leonard (2007), however, shows how even spaces conventionally seen as innocent children's spaces, such as streets, parks and other public spaces, are imbued with relationships of power that often result in children feeling unsafe and challenged.

In short, citizenship education is an important opportunity to improve children's participation. However, this is not to take place only in schools, but must complement wider elements of participation in society. As the Irish Taskforce on Active Citizenship argues:

> Dialogue, participation and responsibility are formed at home, at school and in the wider community. Through participation in formal education young people need to feel part of a community working towards shared objectives and a common good and not just merely isolated individuals pursuing their own interests.
>
> (Taskforce on Active Citizenship, 2006, p. 41)

As Susie Weller (2009) has argued, "citizenship education is not only about creating future citizens but also about institutionalising, controlling and shaping the kind of participation in which teenagers may legitimately engage" (Weller, 2009, p. 20). By way of contrast to the environment of schools, which is based on hierarchies, testing, discipline and individualistic competition, it is perhaps better to pay closer research attention to processes of informal learning and the beneficial process of encouraging active citizenship by socially excluded groups.

Spaces for participation and democratic renewal

Recent political theorists have unpacked the operation of citizenship in society and have looked to see how people's views are best 'represented'. Virtually all commentators accept that how citizens communicate with each other and resolve issues is in a poor state of repair and imbued with selfish individualism and the one-way operation of power. Habermas

(1990), for instance, looks to how 'intersubjective' or 'communicative' representation becomes open, inclusive and shared, but this happens in contexts that are in marked contrast to a political life where individuals battle it out asserting their claims and interests. This only leaves a lifeworld colonised by the powerful, separated from citizens, where decisions are made. Benhabib (1998) also problematises representative procedures that are dominated by a few, and at times singular, voices. Instead, Benhabib wishes to look at spaces that are more like a conversation. Similarly, Wyness (2009) questions how children's representational structures can *represent* the interests of all diverse and unequal children within School and Youth Councils in the UK.

It must be remembered that the participation of children in democratic structures is not a recent 'sixties', 'postmodern' or 'trendy' idea generated in the last 40 years or so. The French statesman Turgot in the eighteenth century believed that those ten years of age could be fully equipped to be participative citizens. However, these voices have been drowned out by the cacophony of voices throughout the 'modern' period advocating that children should be 'shielded' from society and from the potential harms that may be inflicted upon them. However, shielding children presents its own dangers and is a form of abuse in itself. Children's initiation into democracy must not be ingrained through a narrow curriculum in schools, but must be practised. John Stuart Mill, who admittedly advocated the 'protectionist' approach towards children and democracy, believed that it was only by involving women and working men in politics that they could develop a self-generating and self-improving process of citizen education. Mill points out:

> We do not learn to read or write, to ride or swim, by being merely told how to do it, but by doing it, so it is only by practicing popular government on a limited scale, that the people learn how to exercise it on a larger scale.
>
> (quoted in Pateman, 1970, p. 216)

The exercise of citizenship is crucial for the development of a person's moral maturity, and a person grows as a social being, improves their judgement, and dispels inertia only through participation. In a similar vein, Tocqueville declared:

> far from thinking ... that men can be instantaneously made citizens by teaching them to read and write. True information is derived from experience, and if the Americans had not been gradually accustomed

to governing themselves, their book-learning would not assist them much at the present day.

(Tocqueville, 1994/1838, p. 120)

The heart of John Dewey's writing in the twentieth century was that authority and tradition were not the source of learning. Children learn by doing things themselves. It is this questioning mind that is needed by responsible and active citizens. Modern societies require a generous attitude of mind to change with the rapidly changing environment of modern life. For Dewey, the mode of learning was more important than the content. Civic efficiency and good citizenship are "neither more nor less than the capacity to share in a give or take experience" (1916/1961, p. 120).

There have been experiments in school democracy before. Homer Lane's school in an American slum for delinquent children tried to provide a 'little commonwealth'. A.S. Neill, reflecting on his experimental school in Summerhill in England, claimed: "self-government works. Each child has a vote and a voice, irrespective of age ... the children are learning to live with others by interacting with their peers, being judged by their equals, and not by fathers and mothers and teachers" (quoted in Adams, 1972, p. 137). More recently, Johan Galtung has argued: "one could not teach democracy forever in school without practising at least some of it ... Young people have heard many *words* ... and they may be more interested in the teachers *life-style* and how [democracy] is *practised* in everyday reality than in a million or two extra words" (1981, p. 187). The spirit of democracy, as Beck (1998) has declared, "is a spirit of society" (p. 71). A spirit is enacted through socialisation and a curriculum but also through the deeds of practising, rehearsing and exercising political freedoms. Such freedom "perhaps only microscopically, shifts the power relationships of a society gradually into democratic reality" (Beck, 1998, p. 72).

Children have been, and probably will continue to be, constrained in what they do. Indeed, all of us, whatever our age or social power, quite rightly have constraints. Hannah Arendt characterised the problem of freedom as "an essentially political phenomenon, that it is experienced primarily neither in volition or thought, but rather in activity and is thus dependent on a political space prepared for this activity ... and refers back to highly authentic experiences which people have had with politics" (1958, p. 14). The 'new modern' world, which Beck (1998) refers to, has shifted ideas of citizenship away from the nation state towards 'particularities' of gender, family, class, ethnic group and so on.

The other aspect of 'post-industrial' sociology, as already identified by feminist theorists discussed in the previous chapter, is the questioning of the 'naturalness' of categories based around gender, ethnicity and a 'reflexivity' towards traditional scientific epistemologies (Bourdieu, 1992).

Children are today granted the right to act on their own, in accordance with their age and developmental status, except in the sphere of politics. The goals of society, and each individual within it, are not to be drilled into young people, at least not in the narrow curriculum and pedagogic sense in which they currently are in schools. This is not applicable to the complexity of twenty-first-century society. There is no uniform rite of passage today, if there ever was one. Instead, children and young people are subject to processes of 'individualisation', whereby young people form a 'biographisation' of themselves in an active struggle of designing their own story or narrative. Young people, Beck (1998) suggests, are "avant-gardists of their own lives" (p. 78), conceiving of themselves and organising their personalities. It is in these spaces that generations perhaps interact and communicate with each other, thereby form part of a new 'generational order' (Alanen, 2009). The intersection of this generation is an important point. Fielding and Moss (2011) discuss the choices that children and young people have in terms of 'empowerment', which is today associated with the ways in which individuals as consumers are offered options. However, Fielding and Moss (2011) point out that consumerism is far more narrow, short-term and restricted than broader democratic ideas and emancipatory practices associated with the civil rights movements. However, as the above discussion notes, democratic practice, in terms of the technocratic formal procedures, is not something that excites children and young people; but practising it is.

What is it about these processes that seems to particularly disinterest children and young people? One such idea is that children are unsuited to these rationalistic and technocratic forms. Some anthropological evidence exists to support this. Anthropologists have long studied rites of passage across cultures. Victor Turner (1969) looked at puberty rites and the 'liminal' period of adolescents, where young people go through dialectical initiation processes that inscribe upon the child wisdom and knowledge of the group. Thereby, children reach adulthood by undergoing the initiation, often in ceremonial formats. Turner draws on the work of Mary Douglas to illustrate that the liminal period is often one that is fraught with communal ideas of 'pollution' and 'danger'; this perhaps provides an insight into the way girls' sexualities and 'yobbish behaviour' in boys have been understood in histories described in this book. Turner's conception of a rite of passage assumes the neophyte to be a *tabula rasa*, or a blank slate, on to which the adult knowledge is inscribed. However, developmental psychologists, such as Piaget and Vygotsky, have long questioned assumptions of a *tabula rasa*, and it is quite unlikely that the childhood/adulthood transition is ever so binary or abrupt. Adult feelings and competencies occur before any *rite-de-passage*.

Interestingly, anthropologists have also looked at how liminal occasions illustrate the order of society and often serve to disrupt and challenge. One example is the Boy Bishops of the Middle Ages. The custom of electing a Boy Bishop from the children of monastic schools prevailed in most Catholic countries, with the consent of civil and ecclesiastical authorities. He was elected on St Nicholas' Day (6 December), attired in full pontifical vestments and processed around the parish, blessing people. He presided over ceremonies. The custom was suppressed by the Council of Basle in 1431 but persisted until its eventual abolition in England under Elizabeth I in the sixteenth century. Huizinga (1949/1970) notes that this custom of electing a Boy Bishop was symptomatic of the medieval culture, which was brimful of play; it was with the nineteenth century and the birth of modernism that culture went sour. Nietzsche in *Birth and Tragedy* mourned the passing of a passionate and joyous era to one that was meaningless and one-dimensional. As Huizinga says:

> all Europe donned the boiler-suit. Henceforth the dominants of civilisation were to be social consciousness, educational aspirations, and scientific judgement... This grotesque over-estimation of the economic factor was conditioned by our worship of technological progress, which was itself the fruit of rationalism and utilitarianism after they killed the mysteries and acquitted man [sic] of guilt and sin.
> (1949/1970, p. 12)

Stripped of the playful and the sacred, human beings are left to a tawdry and banal industrial world. This is comparable to Max Weber's 'Iron Cage' of bureaucracy, where social life becomes routinised and mundane through the bureaucratic generation of taxonomies and systemic organisation. The social world becomes disenchanted as bureaucracies dominate both humans and nature; change is managed without the need for 'liminalities'; but change is an integral part of the scientific and technical arrangement of the world.

Play challenges disenchantment and subverts order and boundaries. Hegel likened play to the free descent of water in a waterfall. Huizinga declares: "child-life performances... are full of imagination. The child is *making an image* of something different, something more beautiful, or more sublime, or more dangerous than what it usually is" (1949/1970, p. 32). I am not wishing to place some essentialised notion of children as playful, as children are quite as capable of seriousness and procedures; adults also play, and adult play forms the vast majority of examples in Huizinga's book and those of other anthropologists of play, such as Handelman (1990) and Bateson (1972). What this does do is identify just how unappetising formal democracy is to anyone, child, youth or adult. Furthermore, play, and the subversion and remaking of politics from this, forms a healthy and important part of the operation of democracy and the initiation of children and young people into these processes.

Instead, there is an underlying assumption that young people will be willing and able to share their wishes, beliefs and views with bureaucrats if they are offered any structures and spaces in which to do this. Yet it is important to pay attention to the specific spaces into which children and young people are invited and to ask questions about whose terms are defining these spaces. This can be very time-consuming and requires enormous commitment by policymakers to getting it right. Investigations into what young people want to improve their lives emphasise the desire for more 'informal' space (Elseley, 2004), both safe and free of adult supervision.

Young people are less likely to express themselves in more formal contexts, and only a few feel that they could do this meaningfully (Mayo and Rooke, 2008). Indeed, even the most articulate and older young people require support by adults in expressing themselves. The more formal the space, perhaps within institutions with hierarchies and invested with power relations, the more young people were put off. As Weller (2009) has found with 'school councils'[2] in England, only a minority of young people feel comfortable in these surroundings, as they are still subject to existing staff–student power relations and staff listen more to the voices of particular (favoured) students. These spaces are in marked contrast to the informal spaces provided by the local youth service, voluntary sector and sports clubs that young people value most. It is thus important to focus analytic attention onto how participatory spaces are presented. For instance, 'provided' spaces, such as council meetings, are paradoxically disempowering to local people. Those subject to discrimination and exclusion entering these spaces can find them intimidating. How they talk, what they talk about, may be seen as incoherent, irrelevant or even disruptive by those adults offering these spaces. Here we can contrast these 'provided' spaces with 'claimed' spaces where associations occur in a more 'organic' process. For instance, in the developing world, street children, perceived as victims within the West (Panter-Brick, 2000), appreciate the notions of freedom that life on the streets offers them, often in marked contrast to the cloistered and at times abusive relations in the family home (Butler, 2008).

Social media are perhaps a site of radical change in young people's associations. A focus on social media is beyond the remit of this chapter, and, as Livingstone and Haddon (2009) demonstrate, there is a burgeoning literature elsewhere. However, the danger may be that in these new spaces children may also be just talking to people 'like them', rather than opening up dialogue with others. However, with the help of adults, children can use the new media to raise the visibility of an issue and can gain access to the wider mass media (Schechter and Bochenek, 2008). Sophia Rosenfeld (2011), reviewing the ideal forms of public life discussed by writers such as Arendt and Habermas, warns against the way in which the Internet does not serve as a medium where equal individuals enter together to arrive at common ground. Instead, the anonymity of the Internet encourages mud-slinging and maliciousness, and allows participants to dip in and out of discussion rather than arriving at some understanding.

The wider literature (Morrow, 2005; Harris, 2009; Weller, 2010) looks at the successes and failures of participatory spaces, focussing on whether those in power listen to or act upon young people's voices. *Listening and acting* on the voices of young people is of utmost importance. It is also important for those engaging with young people to accept that children's participation is constrained by adult providers, and to be careful not to overly criticise those young people engaging with these structures; they are not to be dismissed as being too cosy and uncritical of policymakers, but those young people are worth listening to (Faulkner, 2009, p. 103).

Education for democracy

It is now accepted within sociology that, if we wish to speak of the present or the future of the economy, it is necessary to talk of a 'knowledge-society' (Beck, 1992). Sociologists have noted the ways in which an increasingly technically oriented knowledge has enabled an unprecedented domination and mastery over nature. Manuel Castells, in his three-volume work charting the move towards a 'network society'

(Castells, 1996), shows how capitalist production methods have led to an attempt at coordinating global capital while work becomes increasingly atomised and individualised. The economic and social changes have transformed society and freed (some) individuals into more expressive forms of work. This has led to a dramatic change in the role of the worker, from one who is generic and passively receives skills to one who is "self-programmable" (Castells, 1998, p. 341). Thus, education is not a form of technical instruction, as technologies can quickly change, but a form of transmitting knowledge able to equip citizens with a completely different practical set of premises that require fundamental specialised retraining. What is required, instead, is a form of education that produces a person who is flexible and adaptable to this radically changing context. Thus, for Castells:

> Education, in distinction to looking after children and pupils, represents a process through which people...develop the ability to constantly redefine the necessary abilities for a given task; it also concerns abilities to provide oneself with access to the sources to learn these techniques. An educated person, at least in a corresponding organization environment, can reproduce themselves in regards to the endlessly changing tasks of the production process.
>
> (Castells, 1998, p. 341)

However, this has come at a cost to social relationships. While humans become politically emancipated, there is a concomitant individualisation process by which individuals become isolated from society. What is more, the development of knowledge-based capitalism, by emphasising technical knowledge and management skills, creates the context of some winners and also a considerable number of losers with unseen but increasing levels of poverty. Giddens (1990) also notes that the expansion of the social distribution of knowledge and the greater sophistication of that knowledge do not mean the average citizen feels as though their everyday lives are transparent, understandable or controllable; quite the opposite. What Castells is interested in is the gap between our technological overdevelopment and our social underdevelopment (Castells, 1998).

So where does social change come from and what can a 'radical' education look like? First, it cannot be according to the traditional Marxist approach that relies on a conscious revolutionary middle class willing and able to connect to the rising proletariat. As Marxist sociologists Bowles and Gintis (1987) have shown, even a modest 'reforming' or 'redistributionist' agenda will not cater for the changes in production, lead to greater democracy for all, and enable a mature and socially aware consciousness ready to compete with the domination of all areas of social life colonised by capitalist formation, individuation and marketisation.

One approach put forward by Paul Gagnon looks to replace the self-serving reflexive individual, ready to adapt to technological changes, with one who is socially aware and willing to turn themselves to public issues. He argues:

> Schooling for work is a 'conservative' function, demanding disciplined mastery of tasks from the world of work as it is, not as we wish it to be, and objective testing of student competence. Schooling for citizenship, in contrast, is a 'radical' activity, egalitarian and sceptical in style, mixing the hard study of history and ideas with free-swinging exchange on public issues. The school nurtures both teamwork and thorny individualism, at once the readiness to serve and the readiness to resist, for nobody knows ahead of time which the good citizen may have to do.
>
> (Gagnon, 1995, p. 74)

This will prove mightily difficult, as education in general, including schools, is still maintained by the prevailing interests of those who established it. As we saw in Chapter 3, it was established by a self-confident 'high culture' that wished to produce a workforce designed for economic reproduction and the maintenance of an elite. Although heroic and emancipatory ideas continued to be put forward (from Rousseau, Pestalozzi, Fichte and Dewey), an education that will provide all children with, as Carole Pateman describes, "the intellectual, emotional and moral capacities [to] have reached their full potential and they are joined, freely and actively in a genuine community" (1970, p. 40) seems a long way off for all children. As Heinz Sünker (1997) has shown, there is a difference between the '*Erziehung*' type of education, which stresses conformity, affirmation and conventionality, and the German ideas of '*Bildung*', an education that is reflexive, aesthetic and aims at maturity, responsibility and the development of society, or 'societalisation'. The current education, based on producing elites, develops few who have the skills of reflection and responsibility; as Benhabib has argued, today's citizenship education should not be one that overly encourages "reconciliation and harmony, but rather political agency and efficacy, namely the sense that we have a say in the economic, political and civic arrangements which define our lives together, and what one does makes a difference" (Benhabib, 1989, p. 389).

This is a task too difficult to deliver in schools; it must extend out to where children can experience democracy in their everyday lives, in institutions such as the family, community and school. As the sociological theories of Beck, Castells and Giddens have shown, it is not a decline in social groups as such – after all, social classes and inequalities remain as obdurate as ever; it is the increase in the gap between the social elites and the rest that has produced a crisis of political representation.

There is nothing necessarily wrong with encouraging autonomy, independence and individualistic thinking. After all, as Theodor Adorno noted, the "single genuine power standing against the principle of Auschwitz is autonomy...the power of reflection, self-determination, of not co-operating" (1998, p. 195). However, these principles must not be confined to an elite; autonomy must be placed within the web of interdependence and caring where we all live and, hopefully, thrive.

Recognition, expression and dialogue

It is necessary for all children's education, at whatever age, to recognise their voices, to support them in expressing themselves and to facilitate a meaningful dialogue with others, as far as the child's capability allows. Honneth's (1995) theory of recognition links identity formation to three intersubjective conditions: first, self-confidence, so that children are able to express their needs and desires in a way that is not threatening. The second intersubjective condition that Honneth argued was necessary for identity formation was self-respect; this is more than feeling in harmony with oneself, it also has a sense of universal dignity and self-reflexive agency of persons, that is, having a sense of oneself as a person. The third necessary intersubjective condition identified by Honneth (1995) is self-esteem, which is a sense of one's uniqueness and difference, that which makes a person feel valuable.

Honneth's three conditions for identity formation are not inconsistent with a large body of research that identifies key elements of children's resilience, including their need for security, self-esteem and self-efficacy (Graham and Fitzgerald, 2010), or with those of the women's and broader civil rights movement in the 1970s, which also emphasised security or safety, self-esteem and self-efficacy or consciousness. This was a certain success of the movement in the 1960s. For children, hearing their voices or accessing their views, experiences, dreams, fears, desires and uncertainties holds out the possibility for children to discover and negotiate the essences of who they are and their place in the world.

Baraldi (2008) has also noted 'self-expression' as a key concept for sociological studies on childhood, since it is the cue for children's self-socialisation, autonomous participation and agency. Children are thinking beings who create and give meanings to the world around them, such as in the family, in school and among peer groups. The construction or expression of these meanings interacts with those of others and becomes an important part of their positioning in society. For Baraldi, promoting children's agency and social participation requires their self-expression to be facilitated in their interaction with adults. However, these expressions of identity are often very difficult to achieve in the real world. Within broader society, children's expression tends to be a struggle around being listened to, misrepresented or plain ignored. The concept of struggle in sociology tends to be associated with the Marxist notion of class struggle. There have been only a few notable analyses of struggles between younger and older people, such as Mannheim, Qvortrup, Alanen and O'Neill. However, young people participating in public structures and citizenship retain a distinct feeling that their voices are being oppressed or marginalised in adult structures. It is small wonder that children and young people become associated with 'struggle' and have a preference for direct action and more confrontational politics. The inclusion of children's and young people's 'voice' is being initiated in a number of public contexts. However, the representation of those voices (if they are gathered) is a crucial part of the process, and this can be done in either tokenistic or empowering ways (Hart, 1997).

Children's participation in citizenship, in the broadest meaning of the term, consists of the importance of recognition and the concomitant struggles that children and young people have in the expression of their identities. However, despite the continuing negative portrayal of young people generally, there are possibly some improvements in attitude at both local and national levels. Where these advances have happened is within conditions where dialogue takes place. The importance of dialogue with children has long been recognised by practitioners and advocates for children (Kirby et al., 2003). However, the processes of dialogue with children and young people have only recently begun (Graham and Fitzgerald, 2010). The development and nurturing of dialogue is vital to a good civil society, and expression, together with dialogue, forms a fundamental part of the process of identity formation and social recognition. Meanings are constructed through dialogue, and, interestingly, cultural theorists have commented on the way authority is challenged and changed through irreverence (see Bakhtin, 1981). Such a challenge through irreverence perhaps explains some of the adult resistance to children's and young people's participation.

Two-way communication is essential to effective citizenship. There is a gap in the literature where little is known of the 'private' associative processes, such as children's and young people's dialogues within and between families, friends and associates. There are a few exceptions (see Holland and O'Neill, 2006) of studies of dialogues in families, and even less is known of the dialogues that occur with peers and within schools and neighbourhoods, even though family background and relationships with peers, schools and neighbourhood are so crucial to how an individual acts and reacts in communities and civil society. Such a theorisation acknowledges the power practices at work within and around participation and citizenship as a more complex endeavour which must identify and analyse *networks* of power. In other words, any analysis of children's participation must recognise power within a broad range of practices ranging from the home, to schools, to the street and to politics.

It is also important to focus on dialogues between groups of young people. Here there are obvious connections in dialogues between different groups of young people around ethnicity in terms of the social cohesion debates. Given the high profile of issues around 'social cohesion', one would expect more empirical findings in this regard. However, for a discussion around citizenship it is necessary to stress the importance of dialogue across all social categories, including those around different incomes, geographical spaces, gender, ethnicity and health. Thus, the importance of bridging social capital becomes acute, and this should be facilitated by policymakers. Whether interest is in children's and young people's participation in service delivery, in how local government decisions are made, or in how children and young people can shape advocacy groups, there is considerable literature looking at the successes and failures of these processes, some of these focus on the effectiveness (if it exists) of the dialogues that occur (Kirby et al., 2003). Basically, success or failure depends upon whether those in power actually listen to or act upon children's and young people's voices. Despite the plethora of interested parties seeking children and young people's 'voice', there are deep problems in the dialogues between adults and children. This is perhaps especially so in the formal forums of decision-making.

In short, the chance of a fulfilling dialogue occurring relies on children and young people feeling comfortable in being citizens. Successful citizenship depends largely upon a young person's educational background, a wide social network, the encouragement of parents, adequate support from professionals and positive experiences of previous associations throughout the processes of a young person's life and within and between the different associative circles (Cockburn and Cleaver, 2009).

Conclusion

This chapter has looked at the way citizenship today manifests itself for children and some of the factors inhibiting children from expressing themselves. The overall constraint for children continues to be the lack of social recognition; children's perceived passivity and the constant marginalisation and devaluation of their activities render them invisible to many. Indeed, commentators continue to be bothered about children's and young people's 'apathy'. This is largely apportioning blame to children; instead, the chapter discussed the flourishing contributions children make to their families and communities. It is just that these activities are not recognised. To take the example of child carers, some estimates number 175,000 young carers in the UK, including 13,000 who care for over 50 hours a week (Evans and Becker, 2009). This does not include the caring for younger siblings undertaken by older brothers and sisters. Yet there is barely a whisper of this in the mainstream media.

The spaces for participation are rarely 'child friendly', and usually consist of the formally structured and hierarchical forums that most adults shun. Instead, it is necessary to understand where children choose to participate; this is often in relaxed and private spaces or those 'liminal' spaces where children and young people have time that is free from adult supervision and control. A large body of research work on participation spaces is now being developed, and there is a need for policy-makers to engage with this literature that maps the complexity of children's participation practice (Percy-Smith and Thomas, 2010). This has a profound impact upon how we understand civil society for children; there is a fluidity of children's lives, as they move from familial spaces to places where they see their friends and then interact with formal structures.

The formal structures with which virtually all children interact are schools. Since Plato, the issue of citizenship education has been an important part of theorising citizenship, yet it is rarely asked what works for children, and the views of children have been, until recently, entirely absent from accounts. Recently, Block (2012) has shown how schools in the USA in the nineteenth century served to foster consensus and conformity. The argument put forward in this chapter is that currently schools are not best constituted to meet the demands of children in their preparation for democracy. The hierarchical nature of schools, and their tendency to view children's voices as unimportant, or even as a problem, do not best prepare children for deliberative aspects of citizenship. In the worst-case scenario, the perception of schools not listening to children can foster cynicism and disappointment with participative structures. The future tendency of educational policy is towards more narrowly defined goals of preparing children for paid employment, rather than as critical thinkers feeling comfortable with all communities and trusting in democratic structures.

Perhaps most importantly, it is necessary to focus more on policy-makers engaging in a dialogue with children. It is very difficult for policymakers to act on the voices of children, even if they are both-ered to listen to them. There are far too many more powerful voices and pressures on policymakers for children's views to count; this further reinforces children's and young people's cynicism over participating and deliberating with policymakers. Looking at the structures with which children interact, there is little chance of dialogue for children with pol-icymakers. School policies emphasise 'parental choice', whereby parents carry the risks of finding their children in schools not of their choice. Successful schools will continue to adhere to government-set agendas and qualification league tables; those schools perceived as 'failing' are for the losers of the system. In this context, the voice of individual children becomes marginalised. Although dialogues can and do hap-pen within schools, as Wyness (2006) has argued, children have limited degrees of autonomy in schools and are marginalised from the decision-making processes. This is not to say that children need or want to be treated as adults, or want to make final decisions about their future, but they do wish to make claims and have preferences that are listened to. Decisions on the future of schools and what they will be like to study in can, one can assume, only be improved if children's preferences are taken into account. Lawy and Biesta (2006) note that children's lives are shaped and firmly integrated into the social, political and cultural make-up of society, and their citizenship manifests itself in children's everyday practices. Citizenship is not something learned as such, but rather exists in the everyday; thus, 'citizenship education' cannot be a preparation for some magical *rite-de-passage* to be engineered and possessed but is a practice embedded in the everyday for all, including children.

Conclusion

The arguments advanced in this book have suggested a rethinking of children's citizenship. This reconsideration has been primarily stimulated by the recent developments in the sociology of childhood that have called for a re-evaluation of children's agency, competence and contributions to society (James and James, 2004). Sociological studies of childhood have challenged the trivialisation of children's actions that has served to render them invisible in academia. Until very recently children were considered 'non-citizens' and had not appeared in discussion about citizenship theory other than in the context of 'citizenship education'. Yet children do participate in some aspects of citizenship, and this increases according to their 'evolving capabilities'. Children have responsibilities to themselves, their friends and families, and it is only the way children are represented that depicts these responsibilities as invisible. The responsibilities of child citizens are graphically illustrated in the UK, as they are more and more drawn into having responsibility for crimes they have committed, and there is also reduction of welfare by punitive justice principles by the state (Goldson, 2002b).

Citizenship, from its very inception until today, is defined in terms of its exclusion of others. Commonly, this exclusion counts those outside a specific geographical boundary as 'other'; however, we have seen that this also includes an 'othering' of those *within* boundaries. In this final chapter, I will first review the arguments that have led to this rethinking of children's citizenship and discuss the formation of citizenship ideas that coincide with placing 'internal others' outside citizenship. I will then discuss how the 'dependency' that children have been constructed with is characteristic of all human beings in this complex, fragile and interdependent world. This interdependent human being, giving and receiving care, is a better and more realistic starting point for citizenship than ideals of the 'unencumbered self' that have been superseded by more recent theories of citizenship.

The development of children's citizenship

As we saw in Chapter 1, citizenship developed in two ways. In the Greek city state of Athens citizenship was *participative*, amid a network of civil society associations, culminating in *phrateres* arriving at important decision-making which determined the course of Athenian policy. Children, we can assume, participated in their own way as family members, and with their evolving capabilities became workers and, in the case of boys, entered *ephebes* to begin their military and formal citizen training. Thus, the Greek model of citizenship, especially that promoted by Aristotle, is reflected upon as being an important lesson in participative citizenship, in which society is bonded together by all citizens having responsibilities throughout civil society. In this sense all had a stake in society, and participative responsibility was a value pervading all decisions. With the advent of writing and philosophical discussion of citizenship it also became clear who was outside these considerations, and the main thinkers were at pains to declare who was incapable or undeserving of citizenship. Children, along with women and slaves, were represented as human beings carrying traits that excluded them from citizenship and were presented as incompetent, incomplete and even possessing 'dangerous' characteristics.

The second model of citizenship, and often presented by way of contrast to the Greek model, was the Roman idea of citizenship. This was far more passive, in that citizens rarely directly shaped policies. Instead, the Romans developed a system of laws that presented citizens as subjects who possessed a diet of rights. The nature of the Roman Empire, fostered by the development of Christianity, began a process of universalising citizenship and presenting a thinner but more inclusive model that understood citizens as having rights by virtue of being human. This is not to say that each had equal rights; children were still defined largely in terms of their 'incapacities' and their place under the jurisdiction of families, in particular fathers. However, even the humble slaves, as well as children, had some rudimentary rights to life and treatment as human beings under the sovereignty of Rome. Roman ideas formed the bedrock of what was later to be understood as natural rights.

Theories of citizenship developed alongside other intellectual movements. With the Renaissance and Enlightenment new and more sophisticated ideas of citizenship were established, giving rise to concomitant practices of exclusion. Chiefly, the social contract theories concentrated on the ways in which contracts are made and by whom. Pertinent to citizenship, Hobbes, Locke and Rousseau were interested in the contracts made between the people and the state, but this developed alongside legal changes. Citizenship was understood as being like a contractual bargain between the citizen and the sovereign, so that those who could and could not write political contracts with a sovereign coincided with those who could and could not write legal contracts. In somewhat of a contrast to civil and case law, in which there was some recognition of children's evolving capacities – children from a very young age could participate in the contract of consumer exchange and then labour exchange – theorists still represented all children as being in some form of incubation for citizenship. Thus, ideas of the *tabula rasa*, education and parental responsibilities put forward at the time were premised upon a model of children as *always* passive and dependent. There was no understanding of children as growing into citizenship, the best was through nothing other than rather arbitrary ages. However, social contract theorists, especially Locke and later Thomas Paine, established the principle of equality and the indivisible rights to life, liberty and property.

Children were included in some rights, albeit filtered through patriarchal structures of the family, specifically the right to life and protection, and liberty to a lesser extent. However, children were *de facto* excluded from holding property, except the right to their own labour. It is ironic that, just as children were being written out of and excluded from formal citizenship contracts by social contract theorists, the system of industrialisation came into being, built upon an ever-expanding body of workers that included children from a very young age working in trades, workshops and later factories. Thus, children did contribute as wage earners. However, as we saw in Chapter 3, children were, for highly honourable reasons, excluded from contracting their labour directly by a series of legislations and indirectly through the introduction of compulsory schooling.

Liberal conceptions of equality, then, clearly did not provide equality, security and justice for all on equal terms. During the nineteenth century liberal ideas of citizenship were challenged; it became apparent that liberal equality was largely abstract and did not offer these rights equally to children, women and working people. The radical movements of the nineteenth century recognised that structures like the family, economic production and decision-making institutions all played a significant part in determining the nature and extent of citizenship. In Chapter 3 I discussed the three important processes through which children were further removed from 'formal' liberal citizenship by having their labour power curtailed, and movements of protection, although challenging patriarchy and taking a social responsibility for *all* children, placed children in a linguistic space where specific children became defined by their innocence and vulnerability. This vulnerability was explicit in the child protection campaigns and implicit in the *tabula rasa* 'schooled child' (Hendrick, 1997).

Children in the twentieth century were the recipients of a number of significant 'social rights' to education and indirectly, through parents, to other welfare benefits. This certainly led to a better economic and material life but still relied on gendered, informal care in the family to support an unequal market economy. Those engaged with unpaid informal care remain unrecognised and undervalued in comparison with those in paid work (Lister, 1997). Symbiotically, those who are the targets of such informal care (young, disabled, sick and elderly people) remain defined simply in terms of their passivity, dependence, vulnerability and inability to 'contribute' to society. Furthermore, while children within families broadly have happy relationships with their kin and those in proximity to them, they are further defined and judged by a host of 'experts' and 'professionals'. These judgements mostly reinforce the passive, vulnerable and naïve image of children, and they downplay children's agency and competence.

I do not wish to present a vulgar and simplistic process of an ever-expanding development of children's dependence and exclusion from citizenship. This would be unfair to the real-life activities of parents, policymakers, professionals and other adult citizens who genuinely care enormously about children. Indeed, on a daily basis the agency that adults as well as children display in the real world often counters this process. Parents want to see the clever and competent activities of their children; professionals do work hard in forming equal relationships with children and giving them as much as they can in decisions; policymakers, too, are trying to listen to and even 'empower' children in as many ways as possible. However, these are largely gifts to children and run against the ideas of autonomous, rational, individualistic and competitive citizenship that lie beneath our societies today.

Dependency, interdependency and citizenship

So where does this leave children's citizenship today? How can children's citizenship be understood and how can we move forward? Some writers, such as Young (1990) and Kymlicka (1995), have argued for special 'group rights' for disadvantaged groups. Young, for instance, shows how we form our identities and capabilities from specific locations in communities and groups which may be oppressed. For children, their identities and capabilities are always curtailed, although occurring in a dynamic and incremental way. So Young argues that oppressed groups should have special rights of representation and veto in relation to policies that affect them. Thus, Young refers to a 'differentiated citizenship' that reflects and represents more equitably the real interests of a diverse society. Lister (1997) builds upon this in her formulation of 'differentiated universalism'. This is a way of building a view of citizenship founded on a politics of need based on agreed, overarching, universal principles premised on equality, and these needs require particular attention at specific times. Thus, a proactive form of social citizenship can hone welfare institutions to counter disadvantageous positions of certain individuals. Notions of group rights and differentiated citizenship are attractive to apply to children, as liberalism has hidden and denied children from political theory and decision-making. However, as we saw in Chapter 7, there is a greater danger that this can reinforce children's differences and leave them further from the forms of social and political recognition argued for in the previous chapters. As we saw in Chapter 5, children already have some 'group rights' in that there are legal rights for children's 'interests to be paramount'. The state is charged to intervene actively to prevent any risk of violence to children, and does so perhaps more quickly than when there are similar risks to adult women. Children also have rights to free education and welfare that are unavailable to adults. However, the continuance of these 'privileges' continues to define children passively and negatively. Thus, debates around needs, universal values and equality need to take place, and in these *every* single citizen is to be recognised as equal "citizen . . . institutionally entrenched and practiced" (Bauman, 2002, p. 326). Thus, the project of recognition moves to centre stage.

How might this social recognition be taken forward? One way is the internationalisation of citizenship and the movement of child rights issues to an international level. As we saw in Chapter 6, globalisation is certainly having an impact on the ways that people experience citizenship and think of rights. However, this is in the context of a continuation of the primacy of the nation state. The process of globalisation and global awareness has not necessarily led to an expanding level of human consciousness. Global institutions, Dwyer (2004) has noted, "may not automatically promote increased civic human consciousness and a concern for the welfare of all humanity. It may well enable a higher level of oppression and exploitation of the vulnerable" (p. 184). Within the UN powerful nations, such as those that are members of the Security Council, continue to override the needs of developing nations (Heater, 1990) and this may even lead to greater polarisations between the developed and developing world (Faulks, 2000). It is perhaps more realistic to view citizenship in a globalised world as containing multiple levels of citizenship, as citizens engage in a host of institutions at a range of levels: local, national and supranational (Faist, 2001).

In times of economic adversity and 'credit crunch', plus the prospect of a double-dip recession, children's rights and citizenship must not be placed in a side-room waiting for prosperity to return (Morrow, 2009). It must be recognised that children and young people are the major sufferers in these hard times; young people are the largest group experiencing unemployment and fiscal tightening. The recent 2011 street disturbances in the UK have seen children's rights being eroded in the spirit of reaction. The impression given in the UK press is that the rioters are children and youths, yet, according to the Children's Commissioner for England, 75 per cent of those charged are over 18 years of age. The nature and context of social rights are under severe attack for all, not just children. However, as Marshall (1950/1992) originally posited, the full enjoyment of civil and political rights is difficult without things such as an adequate benefits system, free and accessible health care and a challenging education system. The state still has an obligation to provide the necessary support for these rights, or citizenship is incomplete. However, fiscal demands clash with these social rights and are, contrary to Marshall's optimism, relatively insecure and subject to sweeping changes.

Following the September 11 attack on the United States, and the concomitant reaction to limit political freedoms and increase executive political power, the continued requirement of social rights is to maintain a firm argument for other rights to freedom and protection from the state. Thus, liberalism still has many redeeming characteristics; liberal thinkers' emphases on freedom, pluralism, tolerance and fairness are key issues that must not be dispensed with. However, children must be considered in these aspects as human beings in their own right and the myth of the 'unencumbered selves' must be challenged. We are all, as Fred Twine (1994) observed, firmly interdependent upon each other; particularly as we all, in the privileged parts of the world, are living longer and our children and young people are remaining dependent into their twenties. As Fiona Williams (1999) argued, we need to "recognise that we are all necessarily dependent on others, but at the same time challenge institutions, structures and social relations which render some groups unnecessarily dependent" (p. 667). Geraint Parry (1991) notes this sense of 'dependence' as a good thing, as it enables us to be aware that we are all part, or should be part, of a 'mutual society', living in environments where we rely on the contribution of others for the opportunities of a good life. This recognition of interdependence is a foundation stone of a civic society that is vibrant, tolerant and welcoming.

The argument in this book has been to shine a light on the negative aspects of liberalism, which, from its foundations, has been reliant on exclusions. This sometimes manifests itself in territorial divisions, and it is necessary to foreground the liberal, plural and 'postmodern' "flexibility of mind required to perform citizenship in a variety of contexts [which] underlines the dangers of associating citizenship with only one narrow aspect of identity" (Faulks, 2000, p. 167). The other negative aspect of liberal citizenship, which silenced women and continues to negate children's contributions, is the state and public–private divide. The consensual relationships in the public realm were reliant on force and coercion in the private sphere. It is necessary to maintain the values of rights and responsibilities in both private and public contexts. As was suggested in Chapter 7, a consideration of an ethic of care, or intimate citizenship, places notions of rights and responsibilities around consensual, rather than oppressive, relationships in both private and public spheres.

Care, generation and civil society

Attention to ideas of care, in dialogue with moral theories around rights and justice, is necessary to move beyond 'thin' concepts of citizenship. Tronto's (1993) importance on attentiveness is key here, as this compels citizens to take seriously the issue of interdependence. In our private and public lives we are dependent on others, and, rather than making judgements on self-interests, it is more fruitful to explore our interests amid the web of dependencies and responsibilities we have with all. When we look at it this way, deliberation is necessary in a broader range of the circumstances in which we find ourselves, be it in our families, in civil society or in politics. The zero-sum game of rights, entitlements and interests becomes eclipsed by 'real world' issues of responsibilities, love and feelings that impact on issues of justice. This also draws attention to the spaces in which relationships occur and the way power and representation infuse and shape these spaces. The spaces where we all associate, including children, are shaped by material matters, and the fairness of the distribution of resources becomes manifest. Thus, social aspects of citizenship remain an important check to inequalities. However, it is not just the material that is crucial; non-material issues such as respect and recognition are also central. This book has looked at how the dynamic and historical nature of social power relations has shaped the lives of children. Children today have their contributions and the children are rendered 'invisible' and are unrecognised as significant players. This is more so in the public world, and less so in the privacy of their families, where their agency counts for more.

The task for adults in general, and policymakers in particular, is to provide the conditions for children to feel able and comfortable engaging with wider society. As was noted in Chapter 8, children do make their mark in more public contexts, such as open spaces, shops, leisure and learning amenities, that Oldenburg (2007) has called 'Third Places'. It is just that their participation in these spaces is not recognised, or their presence there is considered a danger to themselves or others. It is important for there to be a toleration, even an encouragement, for children to claim such spaces, as it is their actions that will enable the newer generations to shape these in ways that are important to them. This may be through making spaces more 'playful', although it is necessary to note that children will recognise that sometimes this is not appropriate, such as in places of learning. This may also be less convenient for adults sharing those spaces, but they would usually become more vibrant and safer for all. Most importantly, children will taste the experience of participating, and hopefully being taken seriously and listened to. As children experiment with the movement from private to public spaces, a conducive environment where they can express themselves freely and learn to take responsibility will encourage them to continue with this in their adult lives. An empowered, confident and interested generation is surely in the interest of all.

Notes

1 Children and Citizenship in the Classical Period

1. The characterisation of positive and negative aspects of liberty is well discussed in Isaiah Berlin's (1959) classic essay *Two Concepts of Liberty*.

2 Renaissance: Prelude to Modern Political Theory

1. This was not necessarily a 'revolution' as the term was later used to describe the French, American and Industrial Revolutions. It was more a takeover of the Catholic Stuart throne by the Protestant William of Orange.

5 Children's Rights and their Limitations

1. http://www.unhchr.ch/huridocda/huridoca.nsf/%28symbol%29/a.conf.157. 23.en, accessed 26 June 2012.

8 Participatory Citizenship of Children

1. 'Estate children' is an undefined term but refers to those children living on local government housing estates and in other forms of social housing.
2. School Councils are groups of students who are elected to represent the views of their peers and to feed into improvements of the school.

References

Abbott, Pam, Wallace, Claire and Taylor, Melissa (2005) *An Introduction to Sociology: Feminist Perspectives*, 3rd edn, London: Routledge.

Abbott, Pamela and Wallace, Claire (1990) *The Sociology of the Caring Professions*, London: Falmer.

Adams, Paul (1972) *Children's Rights: Towards the Liberation of the Child*, London: Panther.

Adorno, Theodor (1998) 'Education after Auschwitz' in Theodo Adorno (ed.) *Critical Models: Interventions and Catchwords*, New York: Columbia University Press, pp. 196–197.

Alanen, Leena (1994) 'Gender and Generation: Feminism and the "Child Question" ' in Jens Qvortrup, et al. (eds) *Childhood Matters*, Brookfield, VT: Avebury, pp. 27–42.

Alanen, Leena (2001) 'Explorations in Generational Anaysis' in Leena Alanen and Berry Mayall (eds) *Conceptualizing Child–Adult Relations*, London: Routledge Falmer, pp. 11–22.

Alanen, Leena (2009) 'Generational Order' in Jens Qvortrup, William Corsaro and Michael-Sebastian Honig (eds) *The Palgrave Handbook of Childhood Studies*, Basingstoke: Palgrave Macmillan, pp. 159–174.

Alberici, Lisa and Harlow, Mary (2007) 'Age and Innocence: Female Transitions to Adulthood in Late Antiquity' in Ada Cohen and Jeremy Rutter (eds) *Constructions of Childhood in Ancient Greece and Italy*, Athens: The American School of Classical Studies, pp. 193–204.

Alderson, Priscilla (2008) 'When Does Citizenship Begin? Economics and Early Childhood' in Antonella Invernizzi and Jane Williams (eds) *Children and Citizenship*, London: Sage, pp. 108–120.

Alderson, Priscilla, Hawthorne, Joanna and Killen, Margaret (2005) 'Are Premature Babies Citizens with Rights? Provision Rights and the Edges of Citizenship' in Antonella Invernizzi and Brian Milne (eds) *Children's Citizenship: An Emergent Discourse on the Rights of the Child*, Delhi: Krepublishers, pp. 71–81.

Alen, Andre, Vande Lanotte, Johan, Verhellen, Eugene, Ang, Fiona, Berghmans, Eva and Verheyde, Mieke (2006) *A Commentary on the United Nations Convention on the Rights of Child*, Leiden: Martinus Nijhoff.

Alexander, Robin (2000) *Culture and Pedagogy: International Comparisons in Primary Education*, Oxfrod: Blackwell.

Als, Heidelise (1999) 'Reading the Premature Infant' in Edward Goldson (ed.) *Developmental Interventions in the Neonatal Intensive Care Nursery*, New York: Oxford University Press, pp. 18–85.

Anderson, Michael (1990) 'The Social Implications of Demographic Change' in F. M. L. Thompson (ed.) *The Cambridge Social History of Britain, 1750–1950*, Vol. 2, Cambridge: Cambridge University Press, pp. 1–70.

Ann-Marie Smith (2007) 'The Children of Loxicha, Mexico: Exploring Ideas of Childhood and Rules of Participation', *Children, Youth and Environments* 17(2): 35–55.

Archard, David (2003) *Children, Family and the State*, Aldershot: Ashgate.
Archard, David (2004) *Children: Rights and Childhood*, London: Routledge.
Arendt, Hannah (1958) *The Human Condition*, Chicago: University of Chicago Press.
Arendt, Hannah (1973) *One Revolution*, Harmondsworth: Penguin.
Ariés, Phillippe (1973) *Centuries of Childhood*, Harmondsworth: Penguin. (Orig. pub. 1960.)
Armstrong, David (1995) 'The Rise of Surveillance Medicine', *Sociology* 17: 393–404.
Back, Les (2005) ' "Home from Home": Youth, belonging and Place' in Claire Alexander and Caroline Knowles (eds) *Making Race Matter*, Basingstoke: Palgrave Macmillan.
Baier, Annette (1994) 'Trust and Its Vulnerabilities' in Annette Baier (ed.) *Moral Prejudices*, Cambridge, MA: Harvard University Press, pp. 130–151.
Bailey, Gavin and Jones, Kate (2006) *Our Kids, Our Community*, London: Community Development Foundation.
Baiocchi, Gianpailo (2003) 'Emergent Public Spheres', *American Sociological Review* 68(1): 52–75.
Baird, A. and Fugeslang, J. (2004) 'The Emergence of Consequential Thought: Evidence from Neuroscience', *Philosophical Transactions of the Royal Society of London, Series B* 359: 1804–1979.
Bakhtin, Mikhail (1981) *The Dialogical Imagination*, Austin, TX: University of Texas Press.
Baraldi, Claudio (2008) 'Promoting Self-Expression in Classroom Interactions', *Childhood*, 15(2): 239–257.
Barbalet, Jack (1988) *Citizenship*, Milton Keynes: Open University Press.
Barnardos (2006) *Hidden Lives: Unidentified Young Carers in the UK*, London: Barnardos.
Barnes, Jonathan (1982) *Aristotle*, Oxford: Oxford University Press.
Barratt, Michelle and MacIntosh, Mary (1991) *The Anti-Social Family*, London: Verso.
Barry, Andrew (2001) *Political Machines: Governing a Technological Society*, London: Athlone.
Bateson, Gregory (1972) *Steps to an Ecology of Mind*, Aylesbury: Intertext.
Bauman, Zygmunt (2002) 'Postscript: Cultural Variety or Variety of Cultures?', *Critical Studies* 20: 317–330.
Beaumont, Lesley (2000) 'The Social Status and Artistic Presentation of 'Adolescence' in Fifth Century Athens' in Joanna Sofaer Derevenski (ed.) *Children and Material Culture*, London: Routledge, pp. 39–50.
Beck, Lewis (1963) 'Introduction to Immanuel Kant's *On History*' in Lewis Beck (ed.) *On History*, Indianapolis: Bobbs-Merrill, pp. 2–40.
Beck, Ulrich (1992) *The Risk Society*, London: Sage.
Beck, Ulrich (1998) *Politics of Risk Society*, Cambridge: Polity, pp. 9–22.
Beck, Ulrich (2006) *The Cosmopolitan Vision*, Cambridge: Polity.
Behlmer, George (1982) *Child Abuse and Moral Reform in England, 1870–1908*, Stanford, CA: Stanford University Press.
Beigbeder, Yves (2007) 'Children' in Thomas Weiss and Sam Daws (eds) *The Oxford Handbook on the United Nations*, Oxford: Oxford University Press, pp. 511–524.
Bell, Susan and Offen, Karen (1983) *Women, the Family, and Freedom: 1880–1950*, Stanford, CA: Stanford University Press.

Bellamy, Richard (2006) 'Between Past and Future: The Democratic Limits of EU Citizenship' in Richard Bellamy, Dario Castiglione and Jo Shaw (eds) *Making European Citizens: Civic Inclusion in a Transnational Context*, Basingstoke: Palgrave MacMillan, pp. 238–265.

Bellamy, Richard (2008) *Citizenship: A Very Short Introduction*, Oxford: Oxford University Press.

Bellamy, Richard and Warleigh, Alex (2001) 'The Puzzle of EU Citizenship' in Richard Bellamy and Alex Warleigh (eds) *Citizenship and Governance in the European Union*, London: Continuum, pp. 3–18.

Benhabib, Seyla (1989) 'Autonomy, Modernity, and Community' in Axel Honneth (ed.) *Cultural-Political Interventions in the Unfinished Project of Enlightenment*, Cambridge, MA: The MIT Press, pp. 601–623.

Benhabib, Seyla (1998) 'Models of Public Space: Hannah Arendt, the Liberal Tradition and Jurgen Habermas' in J. B. Landes (ed.) *Feminism: The Public and the Private*, Oxford: Oxford University Press.

Benhabib, Seyla (2002) *The Claims of Culture: Equality and Diversity in the Global Era*, Princeton, NJ: Princeton University Press.

Benhabib, Seyla (2004) *The Rights of Others, Aliens, Residents and Citizens*, New York: Cambridge University Press.

Berlin, Isaiah (1959) *Four Essays on Liberty*, Oxford: Oxford University Press.

Bingham, Tom (2009) 'The Power of Pardon', *London Review of Books* 31(6): 25–28.

Blackburn, Helen (1902) *A Record of the Women's Suffrage Movement in the British Isles*, London: Williams and Longate.

Blatterer, Harry (2007) 'Contemporary Adulthood. Reconceptualisation an Uncontested Category', *Current Sociology* 55(6): 771–792.

Block, James (2012) *The Crucible of Consent: American Childrearing and the Forging of Liberal Society*, Cambridge, MA: Harvard University Press.

Bojer, Hilde (2000) 'Children and Theories of Social Justice', *Feminist Economics* 6(2): 11–22.

Bojer, Hilde (2005) 'Social Justice and the Rights of Children' in Jens Qvortrup (ed.) *Studies in Modern Childhood. Society, Agency and Culture*, Basingstoke: Palgrave Macmillan, pp. 221–230.

Bourdieu, Pierre (1992) *Invitation to a Reflexive Sociology*, Chicago: University of Chicago Press.

Bowles, Samuel and Gintis, Herbert (1977) *Schooling in Capitalist America*, London: Routledge and Kegan Paul.

Bowles, Samuel and Gintis, Herbert (1987) *Democracy and Capitalism: Property, Community and the Contradictions of Modern Social Thought*, New York: Basic Books.

Brannen, Julia and Moss, Peter (2003) 'Some Thoughts on Rethinking Children's Care' in Julia Brannen and Peter Moss (eds) *Rethinking Children's Care*, Buckingham: Open University Press, pp.198–209.

Brennan, S. and Noggle, R. (1997) 'The Moral Status of Children. Children's Rights, Parent's Rights and Family Justice', *Social Theory and Practice* 23(1): 1–26.

Brighouse, Harry and Swift, Adam (2006) 'Parents' Rights and the Value of the Family', *Ethics* 117(1): 80–108.

Brighouse, Harry and Swift, Adam (2008) 'Social Justice and the Family' in Gary Craig, Tania Burchardt and David Gordon (eds) *Social Justice and Public Policy: Seeking Fairness in Diverse Societies*, Bristol: Policy Press, pp. 139–156.

Brown Alyson and Barrett David (2002) *Knowledge of Evil*, Devon: Willan Publishing.

Brubaker, William Rogers (1992) *Citizenship and Nationhood in France and Germany*, Cambridge, MA: Cambridge University Press.

Bruegel, Irene (2006) *Social Capital, Diversity and Education Policy*, Unpublished paper from ESRC Families and Social Capital Research Group.

Buck, N. (2005) 'Social Cohesion in Cities' in N. Buck, I. Gordon, A. Harding and I. Turok (eds) *Changing Cities*, Basingstoke: Palgrave MacMillan.

Burke, Edmund (1790/1969) *Reflections on the Revolution in France*, Harmondsworth: Penguin.

Burman, Erica (1994) *Deconstructing Developmental Psychology*, London: Routledge.

Burman, Erica (2008) *Developments: Child, Image, Nation*, Abingdon: Routledge.

Butler, Udi Mandel (2008) 'Freedom, Revolt and Citizenship': Three Pillars of Identity for Youngsters Living on the Streets of Rio de Janeiro', *Childhood* 16(1): 11–29.

Castells, Manuel (1996) *The Information Age, Volume 1. The Rise of the Network Society*, Oxford: Blackwell.

Castells, Manuel (1998) *The Information Age, Volume 3. End of the Millenium*, Oxford: Blackwell.

Chalmel, Loïc (2003) 'Early Childhood Education' in Marianne Bloch, Kerstin Holmlund, Ingeborg Moqvist and Thomas Popkewitz (eds) *Governing Children, Families and Education: Restructuring the Welfare State*, Basingstoke: Palgrave Macmillan, pp. 131–147.

Chan, Phil (2006) 'No It Is Not Just a Phase: An Adolescent's Right to Sexual Minority Identity under the United Nations Convention on the Rights of the Child', *International Journal of Human Rights* 10(2): 161–176.

The Children Society (2007) *A Good Childhood?* London: The Children Society.

Chodorow, Nancy (1978) *The Reproduction of Mothering: Psychoanalysis and the Sociology of Gender*, Berkeley, CA: University of California Press.

Citizenship Advisory Group (1998) *Education for Citizenship and the Teaching of Democracy in Schools*, London: QCA.

Clark, Alison and Percy-Smith, Barry (2006) 'Beyond Consultation: Participatory Practices in Everyday Spaces', *Children, Youth and Environments* 16(2): 1–9.

Clark, Gillian (1994) 'The Fathers and the Children' in D. Wood (ed.) *The Church and Childhood*, Oxford: Basil Blackwell, pp. 1–27.

Clarke, Paul (1994) (ed.) *Citizenship: A Reader*, London: Pluto Press.

Cobbe, Frances Power (1878) 'Wife Torture in England', *The Contemporary Review, Volume 31* pp. 276–296.

Cobban, Alfred (1965) *History of Modern France, Volume 2, 1799–1871*, Harmondworth: Penguin.

Cobbe, Frances Power (1904) *The Life of Frances Power Cobbe as Told by Herself*, London: Swan Sonnenschein.

Cockburn, Tom (2005) 'Children and the Feminist Ethic of Care', *Childhood: A Global Journal of Child Research* 12(1): 71–89.

Cockburn, Tom (2010) 'Children, the Feminist Ethic of Care and Childhood Studies: Is This the Way to the Good Life?' in Sabine Andresen, Isabell Diehm, Uwe Sander and Holger Ziegler (eds) *Children and the Good Life: New Challenges for Research on Children*, Heidelberg: Springer, pp. 29–40.

Cockburn, Tom and Cleaver, Frances (2009) *How Children and Young People Win Friends and Influence People*, London: Carnegie.

Cohen, Ada (2007) 'Introduction: Between Past and Present' in Ada Cohen and Jeremy B. Rutter (eds) *Constructions of Childhood in Ancient Greece and Italy, Hesperia Supplement 41*, Princeton, NJ: The American School of Classical Studies at Athens, pp. 2–25.

Collins, Tara (2008) 'The Significance of Different Approaches to Human Rights Monitoring: A Case Study of Child Rights', *International Journal of Human Rights* 12(2): 159–187.

Connell, Rob (1987) *Gender and Power: Society, the Person and Sexual Politics*, Cambridge: Polity.

Coole, Diana (1993) *Women in Political Theory: From Ancient Misogyny to Contemporary Feminism*, London: Harvester-Wheatsheaf.

Cornides, Jakob (2008) 'Human Rights Pitted Against Man', *The International Journal of Human Rights* 12(1): 107–134.

Corsaro, William (1997) *The Sociology of Childhood*, California: Pine Forest.

Coveney, Peter (1968) *The Image of Childhood*, Harmondsworth: Penguin.

Cox, Pamela (2002) 'Race, Delinquency and Differences in Twentieth Century Britain' in Pamela Cox and Heather Shore (eds) *Becoming Delinquent: British and European Youth, 1650–1950*, Aldershot: Ashgate.

Crawford, Sally (1999) *Childhood in Anglo-Saxon England*, Stroud: Sutton.

Cruickshank, Marjorie (1981) *Children and Industry*, Manchester: Manchester University Press.

Cunningham, Hugh (1995) *Children and Childhood in Western Society since 1500*, London: Longman.

Dahlberg, Gunilla (2003) 'Pedagogy as a Loci of an Ethics Encounter' in Marianne Bloch, Kerstin Holmlund, Ingeborg Moqvist and Thomas Popkewitz (eds) *Governing Children, Families and Education: Restructuring the Welfare State*, Basingstoke: Palgrave Macmillan, pp. 261–286.

Daniel, Paul and Ivatts, John (1998) *Children and Social Policy*, Basingstoke: Macmillan.

Davidoff, Leonore and Hall, Catherine (1988) *Family Fortunes: Men and Women of the English Middle Class, 1780–1850*, London: Hutchinson.

Davies, Lynn et al. (2007) *Inspiring Schools: Impact and Outcomes*, Carnegie, UK: Esmée Fairbairn Foundation.

Davies, Norman (1997) *Europe: A History*, London: Pimlico.

Davis, Mike (1990) *City of Quartz*, London: Pimlico.

Dean, Hartley (2008) 'Social Policy and Human Rights: Re-thinking the Engagement', *Social Policy and Society* 7(1): 1–12.

Delanty, Gerard (2000) *Citizenship in a Global Age*, Buckingham: Open University Press.

Delanty, Gerard (2008) 'European Citizenship: A Critical Assessment' in Engin Isin, Peter Nyers and Bryan Turner (eds) *Citizenship between Past and Future*, London: Routledge, pp. 61–70.

Delver, A (pseud Alfred Alsop) (1870) *A Cry for Help From the Slums*, Manchester: John Heywood.

Dencik, Lars (1995) 'Modern Childhood in the Nordic Countries: "Dual Socialisation" and Its Implications' in L. Chisolm, P. Buchner, H-H. Kruger and M. du-Bois-Reymond (eds) *Growing up in Europe. Contemporary Horizons in Childhood and Youth Studies*, Berlin: Walter de Gruyter, pp. 105–309.

Denzin, Norman (1977) *Childhood Socialization*, San Francisco: Jossey-Bass.

Dewey, John (1916/1961) *Democracy and Education*, London: Macmillan.

Dewey, John (1938/1963) *Experience and Education*, New York: Collier.

Dickens, Charles (1949) *Hard Times*, London: Oxford University Press.

Diddle Uzzi, Jeannine (2007) 'The Power of Parenthood in Official Roman Art' in Ada Cohen and Jeremy B. Rutter (eds) *Constructions of Childhood in Ancient Greece and Italy, Hesperia Supplement 41*, Princeton, NJ: The American School of Classical Studies at Athens, pp. 61–81.

Directorate-General for Employment, Social Affairs and Equal Opportunities (2008) *Child Poverty and Well-Being in the EU Current Status and Way Forward*, Luxembourg: European Commission.

Dixon, Marjorie (2006) *Freedoms Orphans: Raising Youth in a Changing World*, London: IPPR.

Dixon, Suzanne (1992) *The Roman Family*, Baltimore, MA: John Hopkins University Press.

Donnelly, Jack (1985) *The Concept of Human Rights*, Basingstoke: Palgrave Macmillan.

Donnelly, Jack (2003) *Universal Human Rights in Theory and Practice*, Ithaca; London: Cornell University Press.

Donzelot, Jacques (1980) *The Policing of Families*, London: Hutchinson.

Doolittle, M. (2004) 'Sexuality, Parenthood and Population: Explaining Fertility Decline in Britain from the 1880s to 1920s' in J. Carbine (ed.) *Sexualities: Personal Lives and Social Policy*, Bristol: Policy Press.

Durkheim, Emile (1957) *Professional Ethics and Civil Morals*, London: Routledge.

Dworkin, Ronald (1977) *Taking Rights Seriously*, Cambridge, MA: Harvard University Press.

Dwyer, Peter (2004) *Understanding Social Citizenship: Themes and Perspectives for Policy and Practice*, Bristol: Policy Press.

Dyhouse, Carol (1981) *Girls Growing up in late Victorian and Edwardian England*, London: Routledge and Kegan Paul.

Edwards, Michael (2004) *Civil Society*, Cambridge: Polity.

Eisenstein, Hester (1984) *Contemporary Feminist Thought*, London: Unwin.

Elias, Norbert (1994) *The Civilizing Process*, Oxford: Blackwell.

Elseley, Susan (2004) 'Children's Experience of Public Space', *Children and Society Volume 18*, Chichester: Wiley, pp. 155–164.

Elshtain, Jean Bethke (1998) 'Political Theory and Moral Responsibility' in Richard Fox and Robert Westbrook (eds) *Moral Inquiry in American Scholarship*, New York: University Press of America, pp. 40–57.

Emsley, Clive (2011) *Crime and Society in Twentieth Century England*, Harlow: Longman.

Engels, Friedrich (1969) *The Condition of the English Working Class*, St Albans: Panther.

Ennew, Judith (2008) 'Children as "Citizens" of the United Nations (UN)' in Antonella Invernizzi and Jane Williams (eds) *Children and Citizenship*, London: Sage, pp. 66–78.

Eppstein, John (1929) *Ten Years of the League of Nations*, London: May Fair Press.

Esping-Anderson, G. (1990) *The Three Worlds of Welfare Capitalism*, Cambridge: Polity.

Esping-Anderson, G. (2002) 'A Child Centred Social Investment Strategy' in Gøsta Esping Anderson, Duncan Gallie, Anton Hemerijck and John Myles (eds) *Why We Need A Welfare State*, Oxford: Oxford University Press, pp. 26–67.

Ester, Peter and Vinken, Henk (2003) 'Debating Civil Society', *International Sociology* 18(4): 659–680.

Etzioni, Amitai (1995) *The Spirit of Community: Rights, Responsibilities and the Communitarian Agenda*, London: Fontana.

European Volunteer Centre (2004) *Voluntary Activities in the United Kingdom: Facts and Figures*, Brussels: CEV.

Evans, Ruth and Becker, Saul (2009) *Children Caring for Parents with HIV and AIDS: Global Issues and Policy Responses*, Bristol: The Policy Press.

Faist, Thomas (2001) 'Social Citizenship in the European Union: Nested Membership', *Journal of Common Market Studies* 39(1): 37–58.

Farson, Richard (1974) *Birthrights*, London: Macmillan.

Farthing, Rys (2010) 'The Politics of Youthful Antipolitics: Representing the "Issue" of Youth Participation in Politics', *Journal of Youth Studies* 13(2): 181–195.

Faulkner, Kathryn (2009) 'Presentation and Representation: Youth Participation in Ongoing Decision-making Projects', *Childhood* 16(1): 89–104.

Faulks, Keith (2000) *Citizenship*, London: Routledge.

Feinberg, Joel (1980) 'The Child's Right to an Open Future' in W. Aiken and H. LaFollette (eds) *Whose Child? Children's Rights, Parental Authority, and State Power*, Totowa, NJ: Littlefield, Adams, & Co, pp. 124–153.

Feinstein, Leon, Bynner, John and Duckworth, Ken (2006) 'Young People's Leisure Contexts and their Relation to Adult Outcomes', *Journal of Youth Studies* 9: 305–527.

Fielding, Michael (2008) 'Personalisation, Education and the Market', *Soundings* 38: 56–69.

Fielding, Michael and Moss, Peter (2011) *Radical Education and the Common School: A Democratic Alternative*, London: Routledge.

Finn, Dan (1987) *Training Without Jobs*, Basingstoke: Macmillan.

Foley, Pam (2001) 'The Development of Child Health and Welfare Services in England (1900–1948)' in Pam Foley, Jeremy Roche and Stanley Tucker (eds) *Children and Society: Contemporary Theory, Policy and Practice*, London: Palgrave, pp. 9–17.

Fortin, Jane (2008) 'Children as Rights Holders: Awareness and Scepticism' in Antonella Invernizzi and Jane Williams (eds) *Children and Citizenship*, London: Sage, pp. 55–65.

Foucault, Michel (1973) *Birth of the Clinic*, London: Routledge.

Foucault, Michel (1976/1998) *The History of Sexuality Vol. 1: The Will to Knowledge*, London: Penguin.

Fraleigh, Matthew (2011) 'Glittering Cities', *London Review of Books* 33(8): 25–26.

France, Alan (2007) *Understanding Youth in Late Modernity*, Maidenhead: Open University Press.

Fraser, Nancy and Honneth, Axel (2003) *Redistribution or Recognition: A Philosophical Exchange*, London and New York: Verso.

Fraser, Nancy and Linda Gordon (1997) 'A Genealogy of "Dependency": Tracing a Keyword of the U.S. Welfare state' in Nancy Fraser (ed.) *Justice Interruptus: Critical Reflections on the 'Postsocialist' Condition*, London: Routledge, pp. 121–151.

Freeden, Michael (1991) *Rights*, Milton Keynes: Open University Press.

Freeman, Michael (1992) *Children, Their Families and the Law*, Basingstoke: Macmillan.

Freeman, Michael (2002) *Human Rights: An Interdisciplinary Approach*, Cambridge: Polity.

Freeman, Michael (2007) *A Commentary on the Rights of the Child, Article 3: The Best Interests of the Child*, Lieden: Martinus Nijhoff.

Frow, Edmund and Frow, Ruth (1970) *A Survey of the Half Time System in Education*, Manchester: E J Morten.

Fukuyama, Francis (1992) *The End of History and the Last Man*, London: Hamilton.

Gagnon, Paul (1995) 'What Should Children Learn?', *Atlantic Monthly* 276: 65–78.

Gaiser, Wolfgang, De Rijke, Johann and Spannring, Reinhart (2010) 'Youth and Political Participation: Empirical Results for Germany within a European Context', *Young* 18(4): 427–450.

Galbraith, John Kenneth (1929/1973) *The Great Crash, 1929*, London: Hamilton.

Galston, William (1991) *Liberal Purposes*, Cambridge: Cambridge University Press.

Galtung, Johan (1977) *Is the Legal Perspective Structure-Blind?* Oslo: University of Oslo.

Galtung, Johan (1981) 'Social Cosmology and the Concept of Peace', *Journal of Peace Research* 18(2): 183–199.

Gearty, Conor (2010) 'Terms of Art', *London Review of Books* 32(5): 27–29.

Giddens, Anthony (1990) *The Consequences of Modernity*, Cambridge: Polity.

Giddens, Anthony (1992) *The Transformation of Intimacy, Sexuality, Love and Eroticism in Modern Societies*, Cambridge: Polity.

Giddens, Anthony (1994) *Beyond Left and Right: The Future of Radical Politics*, Cambridge: Polity.

Gildea, Robert (2008) *Children of the Revolution*, London: Allen Lane.

Gilligan, Carol (1982) *In a Different Voice: Psychological Theory and Women's Development*, London: Harvard University Press.

Glauser, Benno (1997) 'Street Children: Deconstructing a Construct' in Alison James and Alan Prout (eds) *Constructing and Reconstructing Childhood*, 2nd edn, Basingstoke: Falmer.

Goldson, Barry (2002a) 'New Labour, Social Justice and Children: Political Calculations and the Deserving/Undeserving Schism', *British Journal of Social Work*, 32: 683–695.

Goldson, Barry (2002b) *Vulnerable Inside: Children in Secure and Penal Settings*, London: The Children's Society.

Goodhart, Michael (2008) 'Neither Relative nor Universal: A Response to Donnelly', *Human Rights Quarterly* 30(1): 183–193.

Goody, Esther (1982) *Parenthood and Social Reproduction: Fostering and Occupational Roles in West Africa*, Cambridge: Cambridge University Press.

Gordon, David (2008) 'Children, Policy and Social Justice' in Gary Craig, Tania Burchardt and David Gordon (eds) *Social Justice and Public Policy: Seeking Fairness in Diverse Societies*, Bristol: Policy Press, pp. 157–179.

Gordon, Linda (2002) *The Moral Property of Women*, Champaign, IL: University of Illinois Press.

Gorham, Deborah (1978) 'The "Maiden Tribute to Modern Babylon" Re-examined', *Victorian Studies* 21: 353–379.

Gorham, Deborah (1982) *The Victorian Girl and the Feminine Ideal*, London: Croom Helm.

Graham, Anna and Fitzgerald, Robyn (2010) 'Progressing Children's Participation: Exploring the Potential of a Dialogical Turn', *Childhood* 17(3): 343–359.

Gramsci, Antonio (1971) *Selections from the Prison Notebooks of Antonio Gramsci*, edited and translated by Quinton Hoare and Geoffery Nowell Smith, London: Lawrence and Wishart.

Grazia, Victoria de (1991) 'Fascisme et Féminisme Latin: Italie 1922–1945,' *Genésis* 5: 107–131.

Green, Thomas Hill (1895) *Lectures on the Principles of Political Obligation*, London, New York: Longmans, Green and Co.

Grover, Sonja (2008) 'Child Soldiers as "Non-Combatants": The Inapplicability of the Refugee Convention Exclusion Clause', *International Journal of Human Rights* 12(1): 53–63.

Gutman, Amy (1980) 'Children, Paternalism and Education: A Liberal Argument', *Philosophy and Public Affairs* 9(2): 338–358.

Gutman, Amy (1987) *Democratic Education*, Princeton, NJ: Princeton University Press.

Habermas, Jürgen (1990) *Moral Consciousness and Communicative Action* [German Original 1983] translated by Christian Lenhardt and Shierry Weber Nicholsen, Cmbridge, MA: The MIT Press.

Habermas, Jürgen (1987) *The Theory of Communicative Action. Vol. 2. Lifeworld and System*, Cambridge: Polity.

Habermas, Jürgen (1994) 'Citizenship and National Identity' in B. Van Steenbergen (ed.) *The Condition of Citizenship*, London: Sage, pp. 20–35.

Hair, P. (1982) 'Children in Society 1850–1980' in Thoe Barker and Michael Drake (eds) *Population and Society in Britain 1850–1980*, London: Batsford.

Hall, Catherine (1994) 'Rethinking Imperial Histories: The Reform Act of 1867', *New Left Review* 208: 3–29.

Hallett, Christine, Murray, Cathy and Punch, Samantha (2003) "Young People and Welfare: Negotiating Pathways' in Christine Hallett and Alan Prout (eds) *Hearing the Voices of Children: Social Policy for a New Century*, London: Routledge Falmer, pp. 123–138.

Halsey, Albert Henry (2000) 'Further and Higher Education' in Albert Henry Halsey and Josephine Webb (eds) *Twentieth Century British Social Trends*, Basingstoke: Macmillan, pp. 221–253.

Halsey, Albert Henry, et al. (1961) *Education, Economy and Society*, London: Free Press.

Handelman, Don (1990) *Models and Mirrors: Towards an Anthropology of Public Events*, Cambridge: Cambridge University Press.

Hansard (1885) *Parliamentary Papers 1885*, London: HMSO.

Hanson, Karl and Vandaele, Arne (2003) 'Working Children and International Labour Law: A Critical Analysis', *The International Journal of Children's Rights* 11: 73–146.

Harding, Lorraine Fox (1997) *Perspectives in Child Care Policy*, London: Longman.

Harris, Anita (2009) *Young People, Politics and Citizenship*, London: Routledge.

Harris, Jose (2004) 'Nationality, Rights and Virtue: Some Approaches to Citizenship in Great Britain' in Richard Bellamy, Dario Castilglione and

Emilio Santoro (eds) *Lineages of European Citizenship*, Basingstoke: MacMillan, pp. 73–91.

Harris, Jose (2009) *'Social Evils' and 'Social Problems' in Britain, 1904–2008*, York: Joseph Rowntree Foundation.

Harrison, M. L. (1991) 'Citizenship, Consumption and Rights: A Comment on B. S. Turner's Theory of Citizenship', *Sociology* 25(2): 209–213.

Hart, Roger (1997) *Children's Participation: The Theory and Practice of Involving Young Citizens in Community Development and Environmental Care*, New York: UNICEF.

Haste, Helen and Hogan, Amy (2006) 'Beyond Conventional Civic Partipiation, Beyond the Moral–Political Divide: Young People and Contemporary Debates around Citizenship', *Journal of Moral Education* 35(4): 473–493.

Hayward, Bronmyn (2012) *Children, Citizenship and Environment*, London: Routledge.

Heater, Derek (1990) *Citizenship: The Civil Ideal in World History, Politics and Education*, Manchester: Manchester University Press.

Hegel, Georg Wilhelm (1942) *Hegel's Philosophy of Right*, translated by T. M. Knox, Oxford: Clarendon Press.

Held, David (2010) *Cosmopolitanism: Ideals and Realities*, London: Polity Press.

Held, Virginia (1995) *Justice and Care: Essential Readings in Feminist Ethics*, Boulder, CO: Westview Press.

Hendrick, Harry (1994) *Child Welfare: England 1872–1989*, London: Longman.

Hendrick, Harry (1997) "Constructions and Reconstructions of British Childhood: An Interpretative Survey, 1800 to the Present' in A. James and A. Prout (eds) *Constructing and Reconstructing Childhood: Contemporary Issues in the Sociological Study of Childhood*, 2nd edn, London: Falmer.

Hendrick, Harry (2005) *Child Welfare and Social Policy*, Bristol: Policy Press.

Hendrick, Harry (2011) 'Review of Andre Turmel a Historical Sociology of Childhood', *Childhood* 18(1): 142–143.

Hicks, William (1936) *Lady Barn House and the Work of W. H. Hertford*, Manchester: Manchester University Press.

Hirst, Paul and Thompson, Grahame (1996) *Globalisation in Question*, Cambridge: Cambridge University Press.

Hobbes, Thomas (1651/1968) *Leviathan*, London: Penguin.

Holford, J. and Van Der Veen, R. (2003) Lifelong Learning and Citizenship in Europe. Final Report of the ETGACE Project.

Holland, Sally and O'Neill, Sean (2006) 'We Had to be There to Make Sure It Was What We Wanted': Enabling Children's Participation in Family Decision-Making through the Family Group Conference', *Childhood* 13(1): 91–111.

Hollis, Patricia (1987) *Ladies Elect: Women in English Local Government, 1865–1914*.

Hollway, Wendy (2006) *The Capacity to Care: Gender and Ethical Subjectivity*, London: Routledge.

Holman, Bob (1995) *Children and Crime*, Oxford: Lion.

Holsdworth, W. (1936) *A History of English Law*, London: Methuen.

Holt, John (1974) *Escape from Childhood: The Needs and Rights of Children*, London: Penguin.

Home Office (2003) *Home Office Citizenship Survey, 2003*, London: HMSO.

Honneth, Axel (1995) *The Struggle for Recognition: The Moral Grammar of Social Conflicts*, Cambridge: Polity Press.

Howe, Robert and Covell, Katherine (2005) *Empowering Children: Children's Rights Education as a Pathway to Citizenship*, Toronto, ON: University of Toronto Press.

Hudson, Bob (2005) 'User Outcomes and Children's Services Reform: Ambiguity and Conflict in the Policy Implementation Process', *Journal of Social Policy* 5(2): 227–236.

Hudson, Bob (2006) 'User Outcomes and Children's Services Reforms: Ambiguity and Conflict in the Policy Implementation Process', *Social Policy and Society* 5(2): 227–236.

Huizinga, Johan (1949/1970) *Home Ludens: A Study of the Play Element in Culture*, London: Temple Smith.

Hunt, Margaret (2009) *Women in 18th Century Europe*, London: Longman.

Huntington, Clare (2006) 'Rights Myopia in Child Welfare', *UCLA Law Review* 53: 637–699.

Hurt, J. S. (1979) *Elementary Schooling and the Working Classes, 1860–1918*, London: Routledge and Kegan Paul.

Hutchby, Ian and Moran-Ellis, Jo (1998) 'Siting Children's Social Competence' in Ian Hutchby and Jo Moran-Ellis (eds) *Children and Social Competence: Arenas of action*, London: Falmer, pp. 1–25.

Hutchins, B. and Harrison, A. (1907) *A History of Factory Legislation*, London: P. S. King.

Illich, Ivan (1971) *Deschooling Society*, New York: Harper & Row.

Inglis, Fred (2009) *History Man: The Life of R.G. Collingwood*, Princeton, NJ: Princeton University Press.

Jacobs, Lawrence et al. (2004) *American Democracy in an Age of Rising Inequality*, Washington, DC: American Political Science Association.

James, Adrian and James, Allison (2004) *Constructing Childhood: Theory, Policy and Social Practice*, Basingstoke: Palgrave.

Jamieson, Lynn (1986) 'Limited Resources and Limiting Convention' in Jane Lewis (ed.) *Labour and Love*, Oxford: Basil Blackwell, pp. 49–69.

Jeffries, Sheila (1982) 'Free from All Uninvited Touch of Man: Women's Campaigns Around Sexuality, 1880–1914', *Women's Studies International Forum* 5: 629–645.

Jenks, Christopher (1996) *Childhood*, London: Routledge.

John, Angela (1984) *By The Sweat of Their Brow: Women Workers at Victorian Coal Mines*, London: Routledge and Kegan Paul.

Joppke, Christian (2008) 'Transformation of Citizenship: Status, Rights and Identity' in Engin Isin, Peter Nyers and Bryan Turner (eds) *Citizenship between Past and Future*, London: Routledge, pp. 36–47.

Joseph, Rita (2009) *Human Rights and the Unborn Child*, Leiden: Martinus Nijhoff.

Julie Wileman, Julie (2005) *Hide and Seek: The Archaeology of Childhood*, Stroud: Tempus.

Kabalo, Paula (2006) 'Constructing Civil Society: Civil Associations in Israel in the 1950s', *Nonprofit and Voluntary Sector Quarterly* 35(2): 161–182.

Kamur, Krishan (1978) *Prophecy and Progress*, Harmondsworth: Penguin.

Kant, Immanuel (1785/1998) *Groundwork to the Metaphysics of Morals*, Cambridge: Cambridge University Press.

Kant, Immanuel (1788/1967) *Critique of Practical Reason*, London: Longman.

Kant, Immanuel (1964) *On Pedagogy*, Ann Arbor, MI: University of Michigan Press.

Katz, Phyllis (2007) 'Educating Paula: A Proposed Curriculum for Raising a 4th Century Christian Infant' in Ada Cohen and Jeremy B. Rutter (eds) *Constructions of Childhood in Ancient Greece and Italy, Hesperia Supplement 41*, Princeton, NJ: The American School of Classical Studies at Athens.

Keeling, Frederic (1914) *Child Labour in the United Kingdom*, London: P. S. King.

Kilkelly, Ursula and Lundy, Laura (2006) 'Children's Rights in Action: Using the UN Convention on the Rights of the Child as an Auditing Tool', *Child and Family Law Quarterly* 18(3): 1–15.

Kimlicka, Will (1995) *Multicultural Citizenship: Inclusion and Democracy*, Oxford: Oxford University Press.

Kirby, Perpetua and Bryson, Sara (2002) *Measuring the Magic? Evaluating and Researching Young People's Participation in Public Decision-Making*, London: Carnegie.

Kirby, Perpetua et al. (2003) *Building a Culture of Participation: Involving children and young people in policy, service planning, delivery and evaluation*, handbook, London: Department for Education and Skills.

Kitchen, Sarah et al. (2006) *2005 Citizenship Survey: Cross-Cutting Themes*, London: Department for Communities and Local Government.

Kitzinger Jenny (1997) 'Who Are You Kidding? Children, Power and the Struggle against Sexual Abuse?' in Alison James and Alan Prout (eds) *Constructing and Reconstructing Childhood: Contemporary Issues in the Sociological Study of Childhood*, London: Falmer, pp. 165–189.

Kohli, Martin (2006) 'Aging and Justice' in Robert H. Binstock and Linda K. George (eds) *Handbook of Aging and the Social Sciences*, 6th edn, San Diego, CA: Academic Press, pp. 456–478.

Kufeldt, Kathleen and McKenzie, Brad (2003) *Child Welfare: Connecting Research, Policy, and Practice*, Waterloo: Wilfrid Laurier University Press.

Kymlicka, Will (1995) *Multicultural Citizenship: A Liberal Theory of Human Rights*, Oxford: Clarendon Press.

Kymlicka, Will (2002) *Contemporary Political Philosophy*, 2nd edn, Oxford: Oxford University Press.

Laborde, Cécile (2004) 'Republican Citizenship and the Crisis of Integration in France' in Richard Bellamy, Dario Castiglione and Emilio Santoro (eds) *Lineages of European Citizenship*, Basingstoke: MacMillan, pp. 46–72.

LaFolette, Hugh (1980) 'Licensing Parents', *Philosophy and Public Affairs* 9(2): 182–197.

Lansdown, Gerrison (2001) 'Children's Welfare and Children's Rights' in Pam Foley, Jeremy Roche and Stanley Tucker (eds) *Children in Society: Contemporary Theory, Policy and Practice*, Basingstoke: Palgrave, pp. 87–97.

Lansdown, Gerrison (2002) *Challenging Discrimination against Children in the European Union*, Brussels: EURONET.

Lansdown, Gerrison (2005) *The Evolving Capacities of the Child*, Geneva: UNICEF, Innocenti Research Centre.

Lappi-Seppala, Tapio (2006) 'Finland: A Model of Tolerance?' in John Muncie and Barry Goldson (eds) *Comparative Youth Justice*, London: Gage, pp. 177–195.

Larkin, Mary (2011) 'What about the Carers?' in Cathy Lloyd and Tom Heller (eds) *Long Term Conditions: Challenges to Heath and Social Care*, London: Sage, pp. 124–138.

Larsson, Bengt, Andersson, Magnus and Osbeck, Christina (2010) 'Bringing Environmentalism Home: Children's Influence on Family Consumption in the Nordic Countries and beyond', *Childhood* 17(1): 129–147.

Lasch, Christopher (1977) *Haven in a Heartless World*, London: Basic Books.

Laslett, Peter (1981) *The World We Have Lost*, London: Methuen.

Lawy, Robert and Biesta, Gert (2006) 'Citizenship-as-Practice: The Educational Implications of an Inclusive and Relational Understanding of Citizenship', *British Journal of Education Studies* 54(1): 34–50.

Layard, Richard and Dunn, Judy (2009) *A Good Childhood: Searching for Values in a Competitive Age*, London: Penguin.

Leach, Edmund (1968) *A Runaway World?* London: BBC.

Leonard, Madeleine (2007) 'Trapped in Space? Children's Accounts of Risky Environments', *Children and Society* 21: 432–445.

Levine, Philippa (1987) *Victorian Feminism 1850–1900*, London: Hutchinson.

Lewis, Jane (1980) *The Politics of Motherhood*, London: Croom Helm.

Lewis, Jane (1992) *Women in Britain Since 1945*, Oxford: Blackwell.

Leys Stepan, Nancy (1998) 'Race, Gender, Science and Citizenship', *Gender and History* 10(1): 26–52.

Liebel, Manfred (2003) 'Working Children as Social Subjects: The Contribution of Working Children's Organizations to Social Transformations', *Childhood* 10(3): 265–286.

Liebel, Manfred (2004) *A Will of Their Own: Cross-cultural Perspectives on Working Children*, London: Zed Books.

Liebel, Manfred (2012) *Children's Rights from Below: Cross-Cultural Perspectives*, Basingstoke: Palgrave Macmillan.

Lister, Michael and Pia, Emily (2008) *Citizenship in Contemporary Europe*, Edinburgh: Edinburgh University Press.

Lister, Ruth (1997) *Citizenship: Feminist Perspectives*, Basingstoke: Macmillan.

Lister, Ruth (2004) 'The Third Way's Social Investment State' in Jane Lewis and Rebbeca Surender (eds) *Welfare State Change: Towards a Third Way?* Oxford: Oxford University Press, pp. 157–181.

Lister, Ruth (2008) 'Unpacking Children's Citizenship' in Antonella Invernizzi and Jane Williams (eds) *Children and Citizenship*, London: Sage, pp. 9–19.

Lister, Ruth, Williams, Fiona, Anttonen, Anneli, Bussemaker, Jet, Gerhard, Ute Heinen, Jacqueline, Johansson, Stina, Leira, Arnlaug, Siim, Birte and Tobio, Constanza (2007) *Gendering Citizenship in Western Europe: New Challenges for Citizenship Research in a Cross-national Context*, Bristol: The Policy Press.

Livingstone, Sonia and Haddon, Leslie (eds) (2009) *Kids Online: Opportunities and Risks for Children*, Bristol: The Policy Press.

Locke, John (1690/1986) *Two Treatises of Government*, London: Everyman.

Lockyer, Andrew (2003) 'The Political Status of Children and Young People' in Andrew Lockyer et al. (eds) Education for Democratic Citizenship, Aldershot: Ashgate, pp. 120–138.

Lopes, Joana, Benton, Thomas and Cleaver, Elizabeth (2009) 'Young People's Intended Civic and Political Participation: Does Education Matter?', *Journal of Youth Studies* 12(1): 1–20.

Low Pay Commission (2011) *National Minimum Wage. Low Pay Commission Report 2011.* Cm 8023. March. London: The Stationery Office.

Lynch, Julia (2006) *Age in the Welfare State: The Origins of Social Spending on Pensioners, Workers, and Children*, Cambridge: Cambridge University Press.

Macedo, Stephen (1990) *Liberal Virtues: Citizenship, Virtue and Community in Liberal Constitutionalism*, Oxford: Oxford University Press.

Macfarlane, Alan (1978) *The Origins of English Individualism: The Family, Property and Social Transition*, Oxford: Basil Blackwell.

MacIntyre, Alisdair (1988) *Whose Justie? Which Rationality?* London: Duckworth.

Macnicol, John (1986) 'In Pursuit of the Underclass', *Journal of Social Policy* 16(3): 293–318.

Mann, Kirk (1992) *The Making of the English 'Underclass'*, Buckingham: Open University Press.

Mann, Michael (1987) 'Ruling Class Strategies and Citizenship', *Sociology* 21(3): 339–354.

Mannheim, Hermann (1940) *Social Aspects of Crime in England between the Wars*, London: Allen and Unwin.

Mannheim, Karl (1952) *Essays on the Sociology of Knowledge*, London: Routledge and Kegan Paul.

Marshall, T. H. (1950/1992) *Citizenship and Social Class*, London: Pluto.

Marx, Karl (1977) 'On the Jewish Question' in David McLellan (ed.) *Selected Writings*, Oxford: Oxford University Press, pp. 49–62.

Mayall, Berry (2002) *Towards a Sociology of Childhood*, Maidenhead: Open University Press.

Mayall, Berry (2008) 'Conversations with Children' in Pia Christensen and Alison James (eds) *Research with Children: Perspectives and Practices*, 2nd edn, Abington: Routledge, pp. 109–124.

Mayall, Berry (2009) 'Generational Relations at Family Level' in Jens Qvortrup, William Corsaro and Michael-Sebastian Honig (eds) *The Palgrave Handbook of Childhood Studies*, Basingstoke: Palgrave Macmillan, pp. 175–187.

Mayo, Marjorie and Rooke, Alison (2008) 'Active Learning for Citizenship: Participatory Approaches to Evaluating a Programme to Promote Citizen Participation in England', *Community Development Journal* 43(3): 371–381.

McGrellis, Sheena (2005) 'Pure and Bitter Spaces', *Gender and Education* 17(5): 515–529.

Melling, Joseph (1991) 'Industrial Capitalism and the Welfare of the State', *Sociology* 25(2): 219–239.

Meyer, Philippe (1977) *The Child and the State: The Intervention of the State in Family Life*, Cambridge: Cambridge University Press.

Middleton, Emily (2006) 'Youth Participation in the UK', *Children, Youth and Environments* 16(2): 180–190.

Mill, John Stuart (1975) *Three Essays: On Liberty; Representative Government; The Subjection of Women*, Oxford: Oxford University Press.

Miller, David (1995) *On Nationality*, Oxford: Oxford University Press.

Milne, Brian (2008) 'From Chattels to Citizens? Eighty Years of Eglantyne Jebb's Legacy to Children and Beyond' in Antonella Invernizzi and Jane Williams (eds) *Children and Citizenship*, London: Sage, pp. 44–54.

Minnow, Martha (1990) *Making All the Difference: Exclusion and American Law*, Ithaca: Cornell University Press.

Mizen, Phil (2004) *The Changing State of Youth*, Basingstoke: Palgrave Macmillan.

Moosa-Mitha, Mehmoona (2005) 'A Difference-centred Alternative to Theorization of Children's Citizenship Rights', *Citizenship Studies* 9(4): 369–388.

Morgan, K. (2002) 'Does Anyone Have a "Libre Choix"? Subversive Liberalism and the Politics of French Child Care Policies' in S. Michel and R. Mahon (eds) *Child Care Policy at the Crossroads: Gender and Welfare State Restructuring*, London: Routledge.

Morrow, Virginia (1999) 'Conceptualising Social Capital in Relation to the Well-being of Children and Young People', *The Sociological Review* 47(4): 58–77.

Morrow, Virginia (2004) 'Conceptualizing Social Capital in Relation to Children and Young People: Is it Different for Girls?' in B. O'Neill and E. Gidengil (eds) *Social Capital and Gender*, London: Routledge/Taylor & Francis, pp. 127–150.

Morrow, Virginia (2005) 'Social Capital, Community Involvement and Community Cohesion in England: A Space for Children and Young People', *Journal of Social Sciences Special Issue* 9: 57–69.

Morrow, Virginia (2009) 'Editorial: The Global Financial Crisis and Children's Happiness: A Time for Re-visioning?', *Childhood* 16(3): 293–298.

Mort, Frank (1987) *Dangerous Sexualities: Medico-moral Panics in England since 1830*, London: Routledge and Kegan Paul.

Mouffe, Chantal (1992) *Dimensions of Radical Democracy: Pluralism, Citizenship, Community*, London: Verso.

Muncie, John and Goldson, Barry (2006) 'Rethinking Youth Justice', *Youth Justice* 6(2): 91–106.

Murray, Thomas (1996) *The Worth of a Child*, Berkeley: University of California Press.

Musgrave, Peter (1968) *Society and Education in England since 1800*, London: Methuen.

Nardinelli, Clark (1990) *Child Labor and the Industrial Revolution*, London: John Wiley.

Nathans, Eli (2004) *The Politics of Citizenship in Germany*, Oxford: Berg.

National Statistics Office (2004) *Sport and Leisure: Results from the 2002 GHS*, London: The Statistics Office.

National Youth Agency (2005) 'A National Framework for Youth Action and Engagement', *Spotlight: Briefing Paper for the National Youth Agency*, Issue 26.

Newell, Peter (1989) *Children Are People Too: The Case against Physical Punishment*, London: Bedford Square Press.

Newman, Janet, Glendiniing, Caroline and Hughes, Michael (2008) 'Beyond Modernisation? Social Care and the Transformation of Welfare Governance', *Journal of Social Policy* 37(4): 531–557.

Nonnan, J. T. (1971) *The Morality of Abortion: Legal and Historical Perspectives*, Cambridge, MA: Cambridge University Press.

Norris, Pippa (2011) *Democratic Deficit: Critical Citizens Revisited*, Cambridge: Cambridge University Press.

Nozick, Robert (1974) *Anarchy, State and Utopia*, Oxford: Blackwell.

Nussbaum, Martha C. (2000) *Women and Human Development: The Capabilities Approach*, Cambridge: Cambridge University Press.

O'Brien, Mary (1981) *The Politics of Reproduction*, London: Routledge and Kegan Paul.

Office for National Statistics (2004) *Focus on Social Inequalities*, London: HMSO.

OFSTED (2007) *Building on the Best: Overview of Local Authority Youth Services 2005/6*, Crown Copyright.

Okin, Susan Moller (1980) *Women in Western Political Thought*, Princeton, Guildford: Princeton University Press.

Oldenburg, Ray (2007) 'The Character of Third Places' in Matthew Carmona and Steve, Tiesdell (eds) *Urban Design Reader*, Oxford: Architectural Place, pp. 163–169.

O'Leary, Siofra (1998) 'The Options for the Reform of the European Union Citizenship' in S. O'Leary and T. Tiilikainen (eds) *Citizenship and Nationality Status in the New Europe*, London: IPPR, pp. 81–116.

Oliver, Dawn and Heater, Derek (1994) *The Foundations of Citizenship*, London: Harvester and Wheatsheaf.

Olk, Thomas (2009) 'Children, Generational Relations and Intergenerational Relations' in Jens Qvortrup, William Corsaro and Michael-Sebastian Honig (eds) *The Palgrave Handbook of Childhood Studies*, Basingstoke: Palgrave Macmillan, pp. 188–201.

O'Neill, John (1994) *The Missing Child in Liberal Theory: Towards a Covenant Theory of Family, Community, Welfare and the Civic State*, Toronto, ON: University of Toronto Press.

O'Neill, Onora (1988) 'Children's Rights and Children's Lives', *Ethics* 98: 445–463.

Osgerby, Bill (1998) *Youth in Britain since 1945*, London: Blackwell.

Pajnik, Mojca (2006) 'Feminist Reflections on Habermas's Communicative Action: The Need for an Inclusive Political Theory', *European Journal of Social Theory*, 9(3): 385–404.

Panter-Brick, Catherine (2000) 'Nobody's Children? A Reconsideration of Child Abandonment' in Catherine Panter-Brick and Malcolm Smith (eds) *Abandoned Children*, Cambridge: Cambridge University Press, pp. 1–26.

Parry, Geraint (1991) 'Conclusion: Paths to Citizenship' in Ursula Vogel and Michael Moran (eds) *The Frontiers of Citizenship*, Basingstoke: Macmillan, pp. 177–183.

Parton, Nigel (1985) *The Politics of Child Abuse*, Basingstoke: Macmillan.

Pateman, Carole (1970) *Participation and Democratic Theory*, London: Cambridge University Press.

Pateman, Carole (1988) *The Sexual Contract*, Cambridge: Polity.

Pateman, Carole (1992) *Feminist Interpretations and Political Theory*, Cambridge: Polity Press.

Paterson, Chris (2011) *Parenting Matters: Early Years and Social Mobility*, London: Centre Forum.

Penovic, Tania (2011) 'Human Rights and the Unborn Child (Review)', *Human Rights Quarterly* 33(1): 229–243.

Percy-Smith, Barry and Thomas, Nigel (2010) *A Handbook of Children and Young People's Participation: Perspectives from Theory and Practice*, London: Routledge.

Pestalozzi, John Heinrich (1801) *den Müttern Anleitung zu geben*, Zurich: Heinrich Gessner.

Piaget, Jean (1929/1951) *The Child's Conception of the World*, London: Littlefield Adams.

Pinchbeck, Ivy and Hewitt, Margaret (1969) *Children in English Society, Vol 1*, London: Routledge and Kegan Paul.

Pinkney, Sharon (2006) 'Response to Nigel Thomas, Joy Moncrieffe and Michael Gallagher', Paper presented to Theorising Children's Participation:

International and Interdisciplinary Perspectives, University of Edinburgh, UK, 4th–6th September.

Pitts, John (2001) *The New Politics of Youth Crime: Discipline or Solidarity*, Basingstoke: Macmillan.

Plummer, Ken (2003) *Intimate Citizenship: Private Decisions and Public Dialogues*, Seattle: University of Washington Press.

Popkewitz, Thomas (2003) 'Governing the Child and Pedagogicalization of Parent' in Marianne Bloch, Kerstin Holmlund, Ingeborg Moqvist and Thomas Popkewitz (eds) *Governing Children, Families and Education: Restructuring the Welfare State*, Basingstoke: Palgrave Macmillan, pp. 35–61.

Popper, Karl (1966) *The Open Society and its Enemies*, London: Routeldge.

Porter, Elizabeth (1999) *Feminist Perspectives on Ethics*, London: Longman.

Pratt, Louise (2007) 'The Parental Ethos of the Iliad' in Ada Cohen and Jeremy B. Rutter (eds) *Constructions of Childhood in Ancient Greece and Italy, Hesperia Supplement 41*, Princeton, NJ: The American School of Classical Studies at Athens, pp. 26–40.

Prout, Alan and James, Alison (eds) *Constructing and Reconstructing Childhood: Contemporary Issues in the Sociological Study of Childhood*, London: Falmer.

Purvis, June (1991) *A History of Women's Education in England*, Milton Keynes: Open University Press.

Putnam, Robert (1993) *Making Democracy Work: Civic Traditions in Modern Italy*, Princeton, NJ: Princeton University Press.

Qvortrup, Jens (1987) 'The Sociology of Childhood. Introduction', *International Journal of Sociology* 17(3): 3–37.

Qvortrup, Jens (1994) *Childhood Matters: Social Theory, Practice and Politics*, Aldershot: Avebury.

Qvortrup, Jens (2005) *Studies in Modern Childhood*, Basingstoke: Palgrave.

Rawls, John (1972) *A Theory of Justice*, Oxford: Clarendon Press.

Rawls, John (1993) *Political Liberalism*, New York: Columbia University Press.

Rawson, Beryl (2003) *Children and Childhood in Roman Italy*, Oxford: Oxford University Press.

Reynaert, Didier, Bouverne-de-Bie, Maria and Vandevelde, Stijn (2009) 'A Review of Children's Rights Literature since the Adoption of the United Nations Convention on the Rights of the Child', *Childhood* 16: 518–534.

Roche, Jeremy (2005) 'Children, Citizenship and Human Rights' in Antonella Invernizzi and Brian Milne (eds) *Children's Citizenship: An Emergent Discourse on the Rights of the Child*, Delhi: Krepublishers, pp. 43–55.

Roker, Debi (2002) *A Longitudinal Study of Young People's Involvement in Social Action*, London: ESRC.

Roscoe, Henry (1889) *Transactions of the Manchester Statistical Society Session 1888–89*, Manchester: John Heywood.

Rose, Lionel (1991) *The Erosion of Childhood: Child Oppression in Britain 1860–1918*, London: Routledge.

Rose, Nikolas (1985) *The Psychological Complex: Psychology, Politics and Society in England, 1869–1939*, London: Routledge and Kegan Paul.

Rose, Nikolas (1996) *Inventing Our Selves: Psychology, Power and Personhood*, Cambridge: Cambridge University Press.

Rose, Nikolas (1999) *Governing the Soul: The Shaping of the Private Self*, London: Free Association Books.

Rosenblum, Nancy (1988) *Membership and Morals*, Princeton, NJ: Princeton University Press.

Rosenfeld, Sophia (2011) *Common Sense: A Political History*, Cambridge, MA: Harvard University Press.

Ross, Elaine (1993) *Love and Toil: Motherhood in Outcast London, 1870–1918*, Oxford: Oxford University Press.

Rowbotham, Sheila (1979) *Beyond the Fragments: Feminism and the Making of Socialism*, London: Islington Community Press.

Rowntree, Seebohm (1901/2000) *Poverty: A Study of Town Life*, Bristol: Polity.

Royal Commission on the Elementary Acts (1888) *Final Report*, London: HMSO.

Ruxton, Sandy (2005) *What About Us? Children's Rights in Europe*, Brussels: Euronet.

Sandel, Michael (1982) *Liberalism and the Limits of Justice*, Cambridge: Cambridge University Press.

Sandel, Michael (1984) 'The Procedural Republic and the Unencumbered Self', *Political Theory* 12(1): 81–96.

Sarri, Rosemary and Shook, Jeffrey (2005) 'Human Rights and Juvenile Justice in the United States: Challenges and Opportunities', Paper presented at the annual meeting of the American Society of Criminology, Royal York, Toronto.

Sassatelli, Monica (2002) 'Imagined Europe: The Shaping of a European Cultural Identity through EU Cultural Policy', *European Journal of Social Theory* 6(1): 25–45.

Schechter, Michael and Bochenek, Michael (2008) 'Working to Eliminate Human Rights Abuses of Children: A Cross-National Comparative Study', *Human Rights Quarterly* 30(3): 579–606.

Sen, Armatya (1992) *Inequalities Reexamined*, Oxford: Oxford University Press.

Sevenhuijsen, Selma (1998) *Citizenship and the Ethics of Care: Feminist Considerations on Justice, Morality and Politics*, London: Routledge.

Sevenhuijsen, Selma (2004) 'Trace: A Method for Normative Policy Analysis from the Ethic of Care' in S. Sevenhuijsen and A. Svab (eds) *The Heart of the Matter*, Ljubljana: Mirovni Institute, pp. 13–46.

Shahar, Shulamith (1990) *Childhood in the Middle Ages*, London: Routledge.

Shanley, Mary (1989) *Feminism, Marriage and the Law in Victorian England, 1850–1895*, London: I. B. Taurus.

Shaw, Jo (2007) *The Transformation of Citizenship in the European Union: Electoral Rights and the Restructuring of Political Space*, Cambridge: Cambridge University Press.

Skevik, Anne (2003) 'Children of the Welfare State: Individuals with Entitlements, of Hidden in the Family?', *Journal of Social Policy* 32(3): 423–440.

Smith, Amy (2007) 'Komos Growing up among Satyrs and Children' in Ada Cohen and Jeremy B. Rutter (eds) *Constructions of Childhood in Ancient Greece and Italy, Hesperia Supplement 41*, Princeton, NJ: The American School of Classical Studies at Athens, 153–171.

Smith, Emma (1954) *A Cornish Waif's Story: An Autobiography*, London: Odhams.

Smith, Roger (2010) *A Universal Child?*, Basingstoke: Palgrave Macmillan.

Smithers, Rebecaa (2011) 'Cost of Raising Child Breaks £200,000', *Guardian*, 23 February 2011.

Soothill, Keith and Walby, Sylvia (1991) *Sex, Crime in the News*, London: Routledge.

Soysal, Yasemin (1994) *Limits of Citizenship. Migrants and Postnational Membership in Europe*, Chicago: The University of Chicago Press.

Spender, Dale (1987) *The Education Papers: Women's Quest for Equality in Britain 1850 – 1912*, London: Routledge and Kegan Paul.

Sport England (2004) *The Framework for Sport in England*, London: Sport England.

Squires, Peter and Stephens, Dawn (2005) 'Rethinking ASBOs', *Critical Social Policy* 25(4): 517–528.

Stalford, Helen (2003) 'The Rights of the Child in International Family Proceedings – An EU Perspective', *International Family Law Journal* 68: 1–10.

Stalford, Helen (2008) 'The Relevance of European Union Citizenship to Children' in Antonella Invernizzi and Jane Williams (eds) *Chldren and Citizenship*, London: Sage, pp. 159–170.

Stalford, Helen and Drywood, Eleanor (2009) 'Coming of Age?: Children's Rights in the European Union', *Common Market Law Review* 46: 143–172.

Stedman Jones, Gareth (1984) *Outcast London: A Study in the Relationship between Classes in Victorian Society*, Harmondsworth: Penguin.

Steedman, Carolyn(1990) *Childhood, Culture and Class in Britain: Margaret MacMillan 1860–1931*, London: Virago.

Stone, Lawrence (1969) 'Literacy and Education in England, 1640–1900', *Past and Present* 42: 69–139.

Stone, Lawrence (1977) *The Family, Sex and Marriage in England, 1500–1800*, London: Weidenfeld and Nicolson.

Stone, Lawrence (1990) *The Road to Divorce England 1530–1987*, Oxford: Oxford University press.

Strachey, Ray (1931) *Millicent Garrett Fawcett*, London: John Murray.

Sünker, Heinz (1997) 'Heydorn's Bildungs Theory and Content as Social Analysis' in Russell Farnen and Heinz Sünker (eds) *The Politics, Sociology, and Economics of Education*, Basingstoke: Macmillan, pp. 113–128.

Sutton, Liz (2007) *A Child's-eye View of Social Difference*, York: Joseph Rowntree Foundation.

Taskforce on Active Citizenship (2006) *Report on Active Citizenship Consultation Process*, Dublin: Secretariat to the Taskforce on Active Citizenship.

Tawney, Richard Henry (1938) *Religion and the Rise of Capitalism: A Historical Study*, Harmondsworth: Penguin Books.

Taylor, Charles (1992) *Multiculturalism and "The Politics of Recognition"*, Princeton, NJ: Princeton University Press.

Thomas, Nigel (2007) 'Towards a Theory of Children's Participation', *International Journal of Children's Rights* 15: 199–218.

Thomas, Paul (1984) 'Alien Politics: A Marxian Perspective on Citizenship and Democracy' in T. Ball and J. Farr (eds) *After Marx*, Cambridge: Cambridge University Press, pp. 124–140.

Thompson, Flora (1954) *Lark Rise to Candleford*, Oxford: Oxford University press.

Thorne, Barrie (1987) 'Re-visioning Women: Where Are the Children?', *Gender and Society* 1(1): 85–109.

Thorpe, David, Smith, Dave, Green, Colin and Paley, John (1980) *Out of Care: Community Support of Juvenile Offenders*, London: George Allen and Unwin.

Tocqueville, Alexis de (1994/1838) *Democracy in America*, London: David Campbell.

Tomlinson, Sally (2001) *Education in Post-Welfare Society*, Buckingham: Open University Press.

Tomlinson, Sally (2005) 'Race, Ethnicity and Education under New Labour', *Oxford Review of Education* 31(1): 153–171.

Tong, Rosemary (1997) *Feminist Approaches to Bioethics*, Boulder, CO: Westview Press.

Townsend, Peter and Abel Smith, Brian (1965) *The Poor and the Poorest*, London: Bell.

Tronto, Joan (1993) *Moral Boundaries: A Political Argument for an Ethic of Care*, London: Routledge.

Turmel, Andre (2008) *A Historical Sociology of Childhood: Developmental Thinking, Categorization and Graphic Visualization*, Cambridge: Cambridge University Press.

Turner, Bryan (1990) 'Outline of a Theory of Citizenship', *Sociology* 24(2): 189–217.

Turner, Victor (1969) *The Ritual Process*, London: Routledge and Kegan Paul.

Twine, Fred (1994) *Citizenship and Social Rights: The Interdependence of Self and Society*, London: Sage.

Van Ginneken, Anique (2006) *Historical Dictionary of the League of Nations*, Lanham, MY: Scarecrow Press.

Van Goethem, Geert (2006) 'An International Experiment of Women Workers: The International Federation of Working Women, 1919–1924', *Belgisch Tijdschrift voor Filologie en Geschiedenis/Revue Belge de Philologie et d'Histoire* 84(4): 1025–1047.

Van Steenbergen, Bart (1994) 'Towards a Global Ecological Citizen' in B. Van Steenbergen (ed.) *The Condition of Citizenship*, London: Sage, pp. 141–152.

Verheyde, Mieke (2006) *A Commentary on the United Nations Convention on the Rights of the Child, Article 28: The Right to Education*, Leiden: Martinus Nijhoff.

Vincent, J. (1991) *Poor Citizens: The State and the Poor in the Twentieth Century*, London: Longman.

Vygotsky Lev (1978) *Mind in Society: The Development of Higher Psychological Processes*, London: Harvard University Press.

Walters, F. P. (1952) *A History of the League of Nations*, Oxford: Oxford University Press.

Walzer, Michael (1998) 'The Concept of Civil Society' in Michael Walzer (ed.) *Toward a Global Civil Society*, Oxford: Berghahn.

Wardle, David (1970) *English Popular Education, 1780–1975*, Cambridge: Cambridge University Press.

Wayper, Charles (1959) *Political Thought*, London: English Universities Press.

Weber, Max (1927/1992) *General Economic History*, New Brunswick: Transaction Books.

Weeks, Jeffrey (1977) *Coming Out: Homosexual Politics in Britain from the Nineteenth Century to the Present*, London: Quartet Books.

Weeks, Jeffrey (1998) 'The Sexual Citizen', *Theory, Culture and Society* 15(3): 35–52.

Weil, Patrick (2002) *Qu'est-ce qu'un Francaise?* Paris: Bernard Grasset.

Weller, Suzie (2009) 'Exploring the Spatiality of Participation: Teenagers' Experiences in an English Secondary School', *Youth and Policy* 101: 15–32.

Weller, Suzie (2010) 'Young People's Social Capital: Complex Identities, Dynamics, Networks', *Ethnic and Racial Studies* 33(5): 872–888.

Whiteley, Paul, Clarke, Harold, Sanders, Davis and Steward, Marianne (2010) *Polling and Forecasting the General Election of 2010*, Colchester: University of Essex.

Williams, Fiona (1999) 'Good Enough Principles of Welfare', *Journal of Social Policy* 28(4): 200–219.

Williams, Fiona (2003) 'Social Policy: Culture and Nationhood' in Peter Alcock, Angus Erskine and Margaret May (eds) *The Student's Companion to Social Policy*, 2nd edn, London: Blackwell.

Williams, Fiona (2004) *Rethinking Families*, London: Calouste Gulbernian.

Williams, Raymond (1988) *Keywords*, London: Fontana.

Wilson, Everett (1962) 'Introduction' in Emile Durkheim (ed.) *Moral Education*, New York: Free Press.

Wolff, Jonathan (2008) 'Social Justice and Public Policy: A View from Political Philosophy' in Gary Craig, Tania Burchardt and David Gordon (eds) *Social Justice and Public Policy: Seeking Fairness in Diverse Societies*, Bristol: Policy Press, pp. 17–31.

Wyness, Michael (2000) *Contesting Childhood*, London: Falmer.

Wyness, Micheal (2006) *Childhood and Society: An Introduction to the Sociology of Childhood*, Basingstoke: Palgrave Macmillan.

Wyness, Michael (2009) 'Children Representing Children: Participation and the Problem of Diversity in UK Youth Councils', *Childhood* 16(4): 535–552.

Yardley, Elizabeth (2009) 'Teenage Mothers' Experiences of Formal Support Services', *Journal of Social Policy* 38(2): 241–257.

Young, Iris Marion (1990) *Justice and the Politics of Difference*, Princeton, NJ: Princeton University Press.

Young, Iris Marion (2000) *Inclusion and Democracy*, Oxford: Oxford University Press.

Young, Iris Marion (2008) 'Structural Justice and the Politics of Difference' in Gary Craig, Tania Burchardt and David Gordon (eds) *Social Justice and Public Policy: Seeking Fairness in Diverse Societies*, Bristol: Policy Press, pp. 77–104.

Yuen, Felicity, Pedlar, Alison and Mannell, Roger (2005) 'Building Community and Social Capital through Children's Leisure in the Context if an International Camp', *Journal of Leisure Research* 37(4): 494–518.

Yuval-Davis, Nira (1997) *Gender and Nation*, London: Sage.

Zelizer, Viviana (1985) *Pricing the Priceless Child*, New York: Basic Books.

Index

Printed and bound in Great Britain by
CPI Antony Rowe, Chippenham and Eastbourne